The Wisdom of Being
Your Own
Psychotherapist
and other reflections

James R. Fisher, Jr., Ph.D.

For Billy G. Gunter, Emeritus Professor of Sociology

University of South Florida

ORDER OF APPEARANCE

FOREWORD

THE LAST WORD

You are so special to me, Jim. I know it's your ability to be honest and not sugar coat or make excuses for things over which you have no control that resonates with me. I always look forward to whatever endeavors you work towards. Life is short. It is a pleasure to know someone who sees life for what it is and does what his heart urges him to do. I imagine much of this comes from your mother – it something that mine gave to me also. Bless their hearts. Unfortunately, life was not as welcoming back then as most people could not pursue their dreams. Thankfully, they urged us to follow our own paths. Thank you for sharing your gifts and hard work.

Linda Casey, Clinton, Iowa artist, creative craftsman and friend

You Can't Go Home Again

Thomas Wolfe's 1929 novel, *"Look Homeward, Angel"* made the Asheville, North Carolina native famous while his *"You Can't Go Home Again,"* published posthumously in 1940, translated into art his personal anguish coming out of a small mountain community that failed to have a mind capable to understand him.

He would not make it to his 38th birthday in life (1900 – 1938) but would be remembered as a 6'6" giant of the American literature of his time. A graduate of the *University of North Carolina*, and *Harvard University's Graduate Program in the Humanities,* his mother thought him an embarrassment if not a humiliation to her and his birth community for never having a regular job. Consider this, from his novel *"You Can't Go Home Again"*:

"He had learned some of the things that every man must find out for himself, and he had found out about them as one has to find out--through error and through trial, through fantasy and illusion, through falsehood and his own damn foolishness, through being mistaken and wrong and an idiot and egotistical and aspiring and hopeful and believing and confused. Each thing he learned was so simple and obvious, once he grasped it, that he wondered why he had not always known it. And what had he learned? A philosopher would not think it much, perhaps, and yet in a simple human way it was a good deal. Just by living, by making the thousand little daily choices that his whole complex of heredity, environment, and conscious thought, and deep emotion had driven him to make, and by taking the consequences, he had learned that he could not eat his cake and have it, too. He had learned that in spite of his

strange body, so much off scale that it had often made him think himself a creature set apart, he was still the son and brother of all men living. He had learned that he could not devour the earth, that he must know and accept his limitations. He realized that much of his torment of the years past had been self-inflicted, and an inevitable part of growing up. And, most important of all for one who had taken so long to grow up, he thought he had learned not to be the slave of his emotions . . .

"Perhaps this is our strange and haunting paradox here in America -- that we are fixed and certain only when we are in movement. At any rate, that is how it seemed to young George Webber, who was never so assured of his purpose as when he was going somewhere on a train. And he never had the sense of home so much as when he felt that he was going there. It was only when he got there that his homelessness began."

*   *   *

Many faceted artist and novelist Romain Gary (1914 – 1980) had a different experience. His mother hovered over him like a Roman candle turning him into her idealized image as to what he should be. Romain Gary's telling autobiographical novel *"Promise at Dawn"* (1960) captures that tortured experience:

"I sat day after day in my little room, waiting for inspiration to visit me, trying to invent a pseudonym that would express, in a combination of noble and striking sounds, our dream of artistic achievement, a pen name grand enough to compensate for my own feeling of insecurity and helplessness at the idea of everything my mother expected from me."

Much accomplished, Gary was a celebrated French novelist, diplomat, film director, screen writer, WWII decorated aviator and winner of France's most prestigious literary prize, *The Prix Goncourt,* not once but twice, a prize that could only be won, once!

Gary managed this by penning the novel, *The Life Before Us* (1975) about a female *Holocaust survivor* under the name of a relative. It was voted the greatest French novel of the 20th century. Among other accomplishments, Gary was fluent in six languages as well as *French Ambassador to the United Nations*, yet he felt he never lived up to his mother's expectations, committing suicide in 1980 at the age of 66. Romain Gary's life was a novel as he was the quintessential fabulist of his time.

"Promise at Dawn" begins as the story of a mother's sacrifice. Alone and poor, she fights fiercely to give her son the very best. Gary chronicles his childhood with her in Russia, Poland, and on the French Riviera. And he recounts his adventurous life as a young man fighting for France in the *Second World War*. But above all, he tells the story of the love for his mother that was his very life, their secret and private planet, their wonderland. He writes:

"Born out of a mother's murmur into a child's ear, a promise whispered at dawn of future triumphs and greatness, of justice and love."

Then imagine beautiful and innocent Jean Seberg (1938 – 1979) from *Marshalltown, Iowa* entering such a world. Seberg became instantly famous when chosen by film director Otto Preminger as a teenager to play *"Saint Joan"* (of Arc) in that 1957 film, winning that role over 18,000 other hopefuls after a worldwide search.

Seberg would marry international swashbuckling Gary Romain in 1962 and spin off into that heady world of ubiquitous anxiety that was "light years" from her pastoral Iowa home, being constantly harassed by the paparazzi, criticized by the literary media for her lack of sophistication, while under constant surveillance by the FBI for her alleged communist/socialist leanings only to commit suicide in 1979 at the age of forty.

✻   ✻   ✻

Norman Vincent Peale (1898 – 1993) was pastor of the *Marble Collegiate Church in New York City* from 1932 until his death in 1993 with President Richard Nixon a personal friend, while Donald Trump with his family, regularly attended Sunday services in Peale's church. Pastor Peale became famous with the publication of *"The Power of Positive Thinking"* (1952) which became a runaway national bestseller although criticized by psychologists and other rationalists as being without depth advocating a form of hypnosis (autosuggestion) that played on the reader's weakness for grand solutions in an attempt to avoid self-mastery. Despite this, the book spawned scores of self-help imitators to our present day.

Peale writes in *"The Reader's Digest"* after becoming famous of making a rare visit to his hometown, Bowersville, Ohio, and running into a high school classmate. The classmate chirped, "I remember you in school. You were nothing special. That is for sure. How do you explain the life you have now?"

Momentarily, thrown by this comment, Peale responded not sure he remembered the classmate. "Explain it. I don't know what you mean." "What I mean," the classmate returned bluntly, "is that you weren't a big deal in school. As a matter of fact, I don't remember you distinguishing yourself in anything."

In a modest way, I could relate to a similar experience. The committee for my *50th High School Class Reunion*, asked me to give the keynote speech, being a published author with a national bestseller and another book nominated for a *Pulitzer Prize*. Marquis Childs (1903 – 1990), a native Clintonian, graduate of the University of Iowa, syndicated national correspondent, and winner of the *Pulitzer Prize*, gave the commencement address at my high school graduating class, the basis for nominating me to give that speech.

Ten years later, at the 60th class reunion in which my Beautiful Betty also attended, but who was noticeably absent for the 50th class reunion, knowing when I prepare for giving a speech that I'm not much fun to be around. For that 60th class reunion, however, I had no role other than that of an attendee.

The resourceful organizers of this reunion happened on the idea of having attendees collect "signatures" of other attendees as an icebreaker. BB raced around asking people if they had gotten Jim Fisher's signature, only to run into a dear high school friend of mine those many years ago to suffer a stunning rebuff, "Who the hell would want Jim Fisher's signature?" This stopped my BB in her tracks. Cheerful and sensitive to the extreme, she collected no more signatures.

Later this same person accosted me with the question, "What happened to you Jim Fisher?"

What happened to me? Indeed! Over the previous sixty years, I fathered four children, graduated from the University of Iowa, spent two years in the Mediterranean on the *Flagship of the US Sixth Fleet, USS Salem* (CA-139) been a R&D chemist for a chemical food processing company, then joined another chemical company as a chemical sales engineer, rising to an industrial division manager, and ultimately to an international executive for that chemical company working on four continents, and living in Johannesburg in South Africa to facilitate the formation of a new chemical conglomerate, retiring (the first time) at 35, taking a two year sabbatical to read extensively and write (one book), returning to the university to earn a M.A. and Ph.D. in a totally different discipline as a social and industrial psychologist, acting as an adjunct professor for several colleges and universities, then consulting public and private sector organizations across the continental United States, and finally taking a position with a hi-tech client first as a management & organizational development psychologist, eventually rising, once again, to international executive status for that hi-tech company, living in Brussels, Belgium then retiring (the second time to write full time) at the age of 58.

This person remembered me winning major letters in four high school sports and little more. She never had a single high school class with me, which was the four-year college prep program which included four years of math, four years of science, and four years of English literature and two years of Latin.

She knew me as she knew me, which is true of us all, not knowing that I graduated in the top 10 percent or our own high school graduating class, and was a scholar throughout my university career, earning academic keys for *Phi Eta Sigma* (freshman academic honorary), *Omicron Delta Kappa* (leadership academic honorary), and graduating from the university *Cum Laude, Phi Beta Kappa* (scholastic academic honorary). Years later as a mature student, I would earn a *Phi Kappa Phi* key in graduate school (academic honorary). *Awards as benchmarks are important to someone born so low in the pecking order.*

Nor did she know that "Jim Fisher" had a mother who took the pedestrian mind of her son who flunked kindergarten and willed energy and purpose into that mind that would sustain him over a lifetime. Equally troubling, it was rumored that a prominent Clinton doctor had put this "poor boy" through school. He did not. I never got a penny from anyone but worked five summers as a laborer in a local chemical corn processing company, earned merit scholarships in under graduate college, and had the G.I. Bill for graduate school which amounted to a significant sum when attending a land grant institution with a wife and four children as dependents.

Origin of the Fisher Drive:
Devlin, A Psychological Novel

Seamus Devlin wondered if people gave much thought to the things that changed them. We change by degrees, but do we only change in one direction? Or are we like a thermometer going hot and cold, up and down, back and forth? He didn't think so. Once we changed, we stayed changed for better or worse, or at least it seemed that way to him. Much as he would like it to be otherwise, he was finding innocence not a permanent state.

Writers see change as watershed moments, but how can they be so certain when changes are imperceptible? By the time watersheds have been perceived they are long past the moment of influence. We're always playing catch up explaining what is already past. Seamus was distrustful of what others said was true through constant repetition. Life was made up as you went along, not only for him but for everyone. Those paid to tell us how we think were no better informed. He could see how you spiral into a whole other dimension without assistance or knowing.

This was the case when his parents rented a tiny house at 1931 Roosevelt Street, and enrolled him in kindergarten at East Elementary School a short distance from his new home in Lyons. One day near the end of the school years he found himself standing before the principal, his teacher and his parents. They loomed like giants before him right out of the newspaper comics. The principal was explaining to his parents that it was of the "Utmost importance for the future of your son that he should repeat kindergarten."

My da acted as if a knife had been driven through his heart. "What the hell for? Are you saying my son is slow, or just stupid? Goddamn it, lady, this is kindergarten, not high school."

"You don't have to swear, Mr. Devlin. We don't know the answers to either of those questions," the principal looked to his teacher who nodded in agreement, "we only know he is not here. Since he is not here he is not teachable. I'm sorry."

"I don't have any goddamn time for this, sorry," my da said, "and I certainly don't understand your saying he is not here. Goddamn it, lady, he's standing right in front of us." He shook his head. "I suppose I'm not here."

The teacher looked at him with pity. "Mr. Devlin, we're not saying that at all. We're simply saying he is inattentive." The principal realizing language set the father off, added, "We're saying he doesn't listen or do what he is told. He just sits there. Now, is that because he doesn't understand, or for some other reason? We're not at all sure. What we do know is that he will have trouble doing the work in first grade as matters now stand." His teacher worked her head up and down in agreement.

His mother remained composed. When the principal ended her explanation, she smiled at the educators, rose, picked up her purse from the adjoining empty chair, and said. "We're taking Seamus out of East School, and enrolling him on Monday in a parochial school." Then looking daggers at her husband, "Meaning no offense, but we're Irish Roman Catholics, and he should be in a Catholic school."

The principal seemingly relieved, said, "No offense taken, Mrs. Devlin."

His teacher echoed the same sentiments, "Perhaps that is for the best," she said, pausing, "For everyone concerned."

Those words drove a chilling dagger into my da's heart shown by the glaring hatred and violence in his eyes. He shook as he took a cigarette out of his suit coat pocket, then realizing where he was, put it back.

For his mother, it had quite a different effect. "I am not faulting either of you for not recognizing genius." With that she took her husband's arm and his hand and marched them out of the room with her head held high.

What was the problem? His mother read his report card to his da once out of the building. It said he lacked social skills, preferred being by himself, wouldn't participate in class projects, and preferred to color with crayons anything including books from the school's library to the school's distress.

Moreover, it appeared that he could not talk, or preferred not to, did not know his numbers, had no idea what the alphabet was, while already towering over his classmates like a blond cherubic angel. He overheard his teacher whisper to the principal one-day when they were going out for recess. "My Seamus gives new meaning to the expression dumb blond." They both laughed. This puzzled him. He wondered what his da would think, but he told only his mother. She was armed with this when they had this conference, promising never to tell his father. Her hand shaking as she smoked a cigarette, "God only knows what that man would do."

They were a new family, only having been together since July when his mother came home from hospital and his da rented a house in the north end, their first real home. He was again with his little sister, Darcy, who was more precious to him than any puppy.

His da never got over his flunking kindergarten. It dogged him the rest of his short life. His mother accepted it as a workable problem and dedicated herself to redress these fault lines in his construction. She taught him the alphabet, his numbers, how to read, and then went a step further planting the seeds of a compulsive reader in him like herself stimulating his curiosity never to take anything at face value, or to value anyone's mind superior to his own. "Seamus," she would say with that little chuckle, "no one knows about the quiet fire in your belly, but your mother. You will be a work in progress for the rest of my life."

It was that day at East School, she told him years later, that she decided to make him a scholar and make the world take notice. Scholarship became a new temple of church, and Catholicism a new school of that temple.

With this rigorous programming, it seemed he was headed for the priesthood. His mother was a romantic, seeing him going from the black cassock of the priest to the red lined cape of the monsignor then to the red cassock of the bishop, and one-day resplendent in the red robes of a Doctor of the Church, as an American Catholic Cardinal.

His da wanted him to be a medical doctor, least of all a man of the cloth. It looked as if he was going to get his wish as he was good in science, tried medicine, but became bored with it almost from the beginning realizing the best doctors who came from the working class poor were sons and daughters of plumbers, not dreamers and wordsmiths like he was, people who adapted mechanical aptitude to medical requirements when he was devoid of either that propensity or

*drive.   He would learn that he would suffer the consequences if the
context of his motivation lacked the complement of its subtext.*

*His preference was to be a professional baseball player, but he knew he
lacked the Major League tools of the trade and was destined at best to be
a journeyman catcher in the minors.*

*Do choices make watershed moments or do watershed moments create
choices?   That was the puzzle.   You would think that terrible start
Seamus made as a student would have evaporated his misgivings, but
in a way it was a needle in his side that never allowed him to relax;
forever discontented with whom he was or what he had accomplished.
He always had to be more, do more, not to have more; no, not that at
all; but never to waste time; never to be content; to keep pushing, ever
harder, faster, more determined; never to be afraid to jump from one
fire into another.*

*It was why labels didn't fit him.   People were only comfortable with
people who fit comfortably into labels.   To the credit of that first school,
it had identified his true nature without realizing it had.   He was
imperceptibly outside of labels, but that was his genius not his
weakness, as he was not meant to fit in or be understood.   Did his
mother make him that way, or did God?   The point was moot.*

*Like his mother, he was enchanted with Irish Roman Catholicism, the
weirdest of the many branches of Roman Catholicism with its talismans,
superstitions, mysticism, violence, vengeance, righteous belligerence,
and Celtic taste for freedom of expression.*

*Now, in his room at the YMCA, knowing he had blundered into the most
momentous watershed moment of his life, he sat on the edge of the bed,
rested his arms on his knees and bent his head in exhaustion, and thought
of the Stations of the Cross.   He looked around the room at the bare walls,
the peeling paint, the rusted steam heater, the cracked linoleum floor, and
the door to his room, alerting the residence in big red letters: You must
vacate the room by noon, register for the next day, or be charged the full
price of the room.   He thought of the First Station of the Cross: Jesus is
condemned to death.   He whispered, Lord Jesus, crucified, have mercy
on me!   He fell back into the bed with his legs still touching the floor, and
fell asleep.*

∗   ∗   ∗

At the *Veterans Administration Affairs Office* where I went to sign up for the *G.I.
Bill*, I told the VA officer that I planned to change fields and earn a Ph.D. in this new
field at my advanced age of 37.   He said to me, "If you do, Fisher, you'll be the
exception.   Most vets I see milk the system doing as little as possible to get the
benefits.   How do you expect to do this?"   I answered, "Going to school full time."

He countered, "For how long?" I reflected. "I have to take undergraduate courses in this new field, earn an M.A. and write a thesis before doing Ph.D. level work, then I have to write a dissertation. My academic advisor at the university believes that this should take four to six years." The VA officer smiled, "Good luck with that!" He was right. It was a grind, and it did take six years, but I stuck it out. I planned to go back and show the VA officer my Ph.D. degree, but never did.

Persistence is perhaps as critical as natural ability. Most people don't lack ability; they lack commitment. This cannot be taught. It simply exists or it doesn't. We have an inclination to freeze frame a person as remembered on limited information in the best of instances.

The obsessive flaw of our culture is "comparing & competing," the measuring of ourselves in terms of others. With this mindset, we are easily distracted from our self-discovery journey into self-knowing, veering off on a series of tangents that are not our own.

My mother once said, *"We all end up half-finished which can become worrisome; not because we are not diligent. No, not that at all, but because we are not focused. We fail to use ourselves as best we can. You have good looks, a decent enough brain, and an ungodly drive that I didn't give you. My role was simply to release it, the rest was up to you. That doesn't make you a big deal. It means you have promise and purpose. Few will remember you for this when you are gone. If that seems cruel, think again. That is life. You either have control of your life or everyone else does. Don't worry about being understood; try to be understanding."*

So, all I said to this former high school friend is, "Diane, I got old."

Promise at Dawn

Early in my life before I could read or write, there are patches of awareness that if I had been more self-aware I might have been less disturbed; might have appreciated and embraced a more involved and spontaneous exterior life. Romain Gary's words come to mind:

"Others thought I suffered from lack of exterior, when I suffered from an excess of interior."

Early childhood trauma is water off a duck's back for some, but for others, trauma defines them. When that is the case, life becomes a constant interior dialogue. It made Gary the artist and warrior that he was, never quenching the ambers of his raging consciousness.

My early life was less dramatic as I'm no Romain Gary nor do I purport to be. It does explain, however, many things that I can now write about eight decades later.

As matters once stood for me as a five-year-old, I lived almost solely in my imagination, collapsing exterior visual images into interior dialogue with neither the language nor the knack to comfort my soul.

My earliest memory is when I was three and my sister Patsy Ann was one and we lived with "Aunt Saddie," who was not our real aunt, on North Roosevelt Street in Lyons, the north end of Clinton, Iowa. We lived in the loft of a house that when it rained, we could hear the gentle pitter patter on the roof and its easements which was quietly calming.

My sister was spirited, happy and adventuresome and my entertainment. She delighted me in everything she did, until she ran into the street one day to retrieve a ball she was playing with. A car nearly hit her driving instead into a tree, crushing the car's front fenders, the driver clearly relieved that he had not hit the little girl.

Hours later a man came by who said he was our da, scolding me for not watching out for my little sister, causing me to cry, as I also blamed myself. The next day, Patsy Ann was gone, and another car came to take me to my great Aunt Annie and Uncle Martin Dean's tenement house on Second Street off Sixth Avenue North just a stone's throw from *The Clinton County Courthouse*. I would not see my sister again until I was five.

Aunt Annie and Uncle Mart lived in the front apartment of this two story apartment building with commercial tenants on the first floor and renters in the back four apartments on the second floor. Often children of the sons and daughters of the Dean's stayed with them when their parents were between divorces.

My nights were spent on the floor at the feet of Aunt Annie and Uncle Mart, coloring the cartoons of *The Clinton Herald*, my favorite being Brick Bradford who conquered mechanical and other monsters in distant galaxies.

My days were spent on the back roof of the building that stretched nearly to the alley. Here I listened with fascination to the chiming of the giant green clock at the top of *The Clinton County Courthouse*, tolling every fifteen minutes and then chiming on the hour to tell the world in *"the shadow of the courthouse"* the time of the day or night. I would imagine Brick Bradford controlling this giant and marching it off to save the world. Once I told Aunt Annie what I imagined. She tapped my towhead with a smile, "That's best kept to yourself, Jimmy Ray."

The alcove of the second-floor apartment extended over the sidewalk below with a wraparound window in which I could see my da coming to take me for a walk of a

Friday. If he was late, as often he was, I would stand rigid looking down South Second Street with tears welling up in my eyes. Annie Dean once told my da, "Your Jimmy Ray must have the cleanest eyeballs in the county as he cries every Friday until you arrive."

My da would walk with that cocky walk of his with one hand holding mine and the other his cigarette. He was a giant to me, and I thrilled every time we had these walks greeting everyone along the way with a happy face and cheerful banter. This was during *The Great Depression*. I always looked with anticipation as we approached the railroad station at South Second Street before the railroad bridge that separated Clinton proper from "South Clinton," the origin of my family, which was known as a "working class neighborhood." Near the railroad station was a soup kitchen offering anyone coming by a giant bowl of chili and fresh saltine crackers, for free! How I loved that chili! In all these years, I've never had a bowl of chili to match what I had at that soup kitchen.

Then one Friday, after walking not even two blocks, we crossed the street, and entered a house with my da saying, "This is your new home." Then out of the kitchen came a very pretty blond woman with a baby in her arms and Patsy Ann at her side. I rushed to hug my sister, and she smiled with delight in seeing me. I was so full of emotions I thought I would pass out, while my little sister was calm and composed, and almost stoic in comparison. Hadn't she missed me the way I missed her?

"This is your mother, and this is your little brother, Jackie." I looked at her and at the baby in her arms and came crashing to the floor. It was too much. My mother put the baby down and rushed to see that I was all right. I was. I could not remember my mother, although I was going on two when she went back into hospital, and I never knew I had a little brother. The pretty lady who was my mother smiled a lot and smoked a cigarette, something I had never seen a woman do before.

The next thing I knew I was being marched down a half block on Fourth Avenue North to St. Patrick Elementary Catholic School where I saw, for the first time, the *Sisters of St. Francis* in their black habits, their faces framed in a close-fitting white cap that held their headdresses in place with a white piece that covered their necks and cheeks, while the dome of the headdress was black and covered their hair while they were dressed in a flowing black gown accentuated with a large Crucifix on the front of their habits. Rather than being frightened, I was intrigued to the point of experiencing an incredible calm. With their cherubic faces, they seemed as if they rose out of my *Clinton Herald* cartoons as agents of good.

Finally, we are a family: Patsy Ann, 3, Jimmy Ray, 5, Jackie, 1.

"This is your mother, and this is your little brother, Jackie." I looked at her and at the baby in her arms and came crashing to the floor. It was too much. My mother put the baby down and rushed to see that I was all right. I was. I could not remember my mother, although I was going on two when she went back into hospital, and I never knew I had a little brother. The pretty lady who was my mother smiled a lot and smoked a cigarette, something I had never seen a woman do before.

The next thing I knew I was being marched down a half block on Fourth Avenue North to St. Patrick Elementary Catholic School where I saw, for the first time, the

Sisters of St. Francis in their black habits, their faces framed in a close-fitting white cap that held their headdresses in place with a white piece that covered their necks and cheeks, while the dome of the headdress was black and covered their hair while they were dressed in a flowing black gown accentuated with a large Crucifix on the front of their habits. Rather than being frightened, I was intrigued to the point of experiencing an incredible calm. With their cherubic faces, they seemed as if they rose out of my *Clinton Herald* cartoons as agents of good.

Although at St. Patrick's only briefly, I would walk back to my home, and have to have my mother bring me back to school. I did this so often that Sister Mary Julianne watched me like a hawk at recess.

Years later my mother told me that this troubled her greatly. *"You didn't make any ruckus. You simply didn't want to be there, so you left. Why, I could never figure out, but it would become a pattern of your young life. You don't stay where you don't want to be."*

Only five, my mother along with Helen Dean, Freddie Dean's wife, the son of Uncle Mart and Aunt Annie, would take me to the movies every Friday at the *Strand Theatre* on Second Street and Fourth Avenue South. It was called "bank night" and the films were westerns of Gene Autry, Tom Mix, and Hopalong Cassidy with comedies of Buster Keaton, Laurel and Hardy, or serials of Flash Gordon. It was exciting.

That idyllic situation changed when my da came home, from wherever he had been, as he had no job, and always seemed a little tense. "Freddie's kid, Francis Martin, can tell time, and he's like Jimmy, only five-years-old." "So?" my mother answered distractedly, as she was making dinner.

My da disappeared and came back with a clock with the glass face removed. "Does your kid know how to tell time?" My mother smiled, "No, he doesn't, Ray, but I suppose you're going to teach him." "You goddamn right I am," he thundered." I had never heard him yell like that before but I would get used to it over the years.

So, he sat me down, and moved the long hand and short hand of the clock, and barked out what time it was. He did this for several settings moving his hand across the clock's surface. "Now, Jimmy, you tell me what I have done; tell me what the long hand and short hand mean; tell me what time those hands are pointing at now." I not only didn't tell him; I didn't respond at all. This only made him angry. "Goddamit, Jimmy, say something!"

"Ray, you're frightening Jimmy."

"I'm frightening Jimmy? I'm frightening your goddam kid? Is that what you're saying I'm doing? Or are you saying he's an idiot like his father, who has no job, never went to high school like you did, doesn't know his ass from a hole in the ground, and can't support his family? Is that what you're saying?"

"What I'm saying, Ray," she paused as she lit a self-made cigarette, "you let Freddie Dean get to you like you know he can, who has his parents' roofing business to support him or he wouldn't have a job, simpleton that he is."

With that Jimmy jumped a foot as the clock crashed against the wall with tears rolling down his eyes. Rather than say anything, his mother nestled him against her knowing that her husband wouldn't be back to normal until his rage had simmered and died. "Let's get you ready for bed," she said with some finality, when he had had no dinner, but knew she would bring him something later.

In a strange way, this episode would stay with me all my life, finding me although high strung myself, becoming amazingly calm in crisis with everything seemingly to slow down. It happened in the navy when a destroyer's gun mount "hang fired" during military maneuvers in the Mediterranean with a dozen badly burned sailors being brought aboard my ship as we were nearby and had a complete medical hospital. I worked with the doctors on these badly burned sailors for 36 hours without sleep, one dying in my arms. As a consultant with 550 sworn police officers threatening to mutiny in Raleigh, North Carolina, I uncovered the cause before the turmoil exploded into crisis, thus preventing a major community embarrassment. As a young father, when my three-year-old son could not breathe, and had turned blue, I rushed him into our little bathroom, turned the shower on to maximum heat, put him over my knee, slapping his little backside until he threw up a thick ball of mucous, his breathing returning to normal as well as his color.

Fast Forward

It has often occurred to me over my long life how important treatment by our parents, teachers, priests and nuns can be; or likewise, how damaging. Today, given the insular way I behaved when quite young, I suspect I would be diagnosed as autistic, indeed, to be suffering from some neurological malady that perhaps might seal my fate; and of course, this would have been wrong; likewise, the chances of me writing these words. My wonder is how often misdiagnoses occur. Obviously, psycho-neurological conditions exist, requiring special treatment, but if wrong, can they not kill the spirit of that child?

After East Elementary in Lyons, I went to school a mile north of this school at *St. Boniface School* on North Pershing Boulevard. Sister Mary Martini, a missionary nun from Ireland, taught kindergarten through sixth grade in a single first floor room.

She was my teacher for the balance of kindergarten, first, second and third grade, transferring to St. Patrick's school for fourth through eighth grade when my parents bought a house in the *Shadow of the Courthouse,* also the title of a book I would write on the subject.

Sister Martini was a no-nonsense disciplinarian who reminded me in a way of my da, extremely gentle and loving one moment and seemingly out of control the next. For some reason, Sister Martini was always gentle with me. Perhaps that was because I gave her no trouble, was quiet and attentive as a mouse, and would pound out the chalk erasers to the blackboard at lunchtime, as one of her minions.

My little brother, Jackie, was a different story. Little for his age, even for a kindergartener, mischievous and something of a cut-up, he was popular with his classmates and older students.

One day, Sister Martini left the room to go upstairs to talk to the seventh and eighth grade nun. Before she left, she advised us that no one should talk or get up from their desks. Of course, everyone talked and moved about.

When she returned, she asked if anyone had talked. My little brother, from his desk in the middle row in front of Sister's desk, raised his hand with an innocent grin; no one else did. She motioned him to stand up and come forward, which he did. "Let this be a lesson to you all," Sister said as she backed handed my little brother across the face sending him flying over his desk. There followed a diabolical silence across the classroom. "When I say 'don't talk' I mean it!"

Little Arnold John, Jackie's given name, didn't cry as we walked home from school, but my sister Patsy Ann asked me accusingly, "Jimmy, why didn't you do something? You're our big brother."

Why didn't I do something? That hurt. My little brother had been treated brutally by Sister Mary Martini for which there was no excuse, penetrating my imprisoning cocoon in which I had been forever trapped. How could she be so nice to me and so wretched to my little brother? That puzzle would cling to me into my advanced years surfacing with some clarity with German American philosopher Hannah Arendt's "banality of evil."

"We can't tell daddy," my little sister declared, "or he will take us out of school, and I like my friends here." I said nothing but agreed with her, as I walked home holding my little brother's hand. Whatever was going on in his little mind, he would come to resent nuns, priests and Roman Catholicism with extreme prejudice. Secretive by nature, implicitly cynical, this would define his life moving forward. Adults in authority have no idea the permanent damage they can cause to a young awakening mind.

My sister and I, now in our eighties, still talk by phone every week, she from Iowa and me from Florida, as we have for years, while we have been estranged from our little brother who is also in his eighties. Our baby sister died two years ago after a long illness. She was a casualty of my da's yelling which apparently got much worse once we three left the homestead.

Yelling was his safety valve. Today, his behavior would be called, "verbal abuse." That said, he never hit any of us, but the sting of his raised voice was nonetheless devastating. For instance, our sister Janice as wife and mother would quickly retreat to the sanctuary of her clothes closet should her husband raise his voice. The rest of us treated his constant roaring as if background music with no more danger to us than the blue heron might expect prancing through a crowded Florida neighborhood.

My salvation growing up was books and conversations with my mother when my da was on the road in his job as a *Brakeman* on the *Chicago & Northwestern Railroad,* a run between Clinton and Boone, Iowa of 202 miles.

Then there was the respite of playing baseball over at the courthouse, basketball at St. Patrick's, and football, basketball, track and baseball later at Clinton High School. Irish Roman Catholicism gave me form, the Sisters of St. Francis gave me confidence, academics gave me a language and a platform for my thoughts and ideas, and athletics gave me discipline.

My family was working class poor but in a two-parent family where it was clear there was love between our parents, and for their children. It never occurred to me until I had children and grandchildren how important living and playing in a neighborhood could be. My children and grandchildren have lived almost exclusively in tiny self-contained islands with neighbors at a distance. Now these islands are even more isolated as most contact is electronically through social media.

American sociologist Peter Berger writes of modern consciousness as being a *"homeless mind,"* the mind that has been the focus of my writing for the past forty years in terms of work, the worker and the corporate organization. How so?

Work now is mostly for money devoid of pride of performance; management is about power and control devoid of purpose; family has lost its status and is devoid of function; religion has been reduced to survival and self-preservation devoid of mission; government is about international clout and dominance devoid of integrity; and personal life has devolved to narcissism and self-indulgence devoid of community.

The mind of the time has lost its moral compass and its way. I've said about all I have to say on that subject from an empirical and scholastic point of view to clearly the point of redundancy.

James Burke and Robert Ornstein write perceptively about "what was" and "what has been lost" in terms of what they call our "cut & control" fixation. They show in *"The Axemaker's Gift"* how runaway technology has captured and controlled our minds and culture to the point of self-estrangement. This finds us, paradoxically, on the brink of no longer being especially relevant as a species.

Lee Dembart of the *New York Times* captures the essence of *The Axemaker's Gift* in his review suggesting that modern civilization has made a Faustian bargain:

"We have made a pact with the devil in exchange for the knowledge we have and the comforts we enjoy."

Having written more than a score of books in this and related genres, it is time to move on. So, this collection of essays and excerpts of my books is "The Last Word" in that connection. That said, should God give me the stamina to write in the future, I hope to explore the more subtle realities of life that fiction provides perhaps with a pseudonym. Until then, be always well.

James R. Fisher, Jr.

A BRIEF INTRODUCTION

*All of the ideas in this diverse collection of provocative essays were first introduced either via my blog, **theperipateticphilosopher.blogspot.com**, or contained in one of my books. I wish to emphasize that many of the concepts presented here relate directly to **The Fisher Paradigm of Organizational Development (OD)**, a paradigm that evolved over my many working years. The 'Fisher Paradigm' has never been publicly promoted; yet it has been an indispensable tool in my work. To whet your appetite, I'll say only that it once literally saved my life and then launched my career as an organizational consultant and global executive. It's all explained in these essays. Not surprisingly, the 'Fisher Paradigm' has positively influenced my writing.*

The deep insights I've gleaned from my hands-on work eventually led to my initial bestseller 'Confident Selling'. Later, it contributed to my Pulitzer Prize nominated 'Confident Selling for the 90's', to 'Work Without Managers', to 'The Worker, Alone', to 'Six Silent Killers' and to 'Corporate Sin'. (The complete list of my books is on page 358)

As a social psychologist, I am passionate about my ideas, principally because they address those dilemmas that directly impact our everyday working lives. My inclination is to delve into matters of common distress; things that tend to throw people off stride, disrupting their lives hurtling them into chaos. It's for that reason I am especially proud of this collection with it's potential to guide hard-working people through the straits of chaos that inevitably confront us all in our endeavors, especially where we work, that place we spend so much of our lives with such high hopes.

IS SOCIETY MENTALLY ILL

OR IS IT JUST ME?

James R. Fisher, Jr., Ph.D.
© November 14, 2015

The following is an excerpt from *"Time Out for Sanity:
Blueprint for Dealing with an Anxious Age"*

It's an intriguing question. Three generations ago Sigmund Freud posed the same question:

"May we not be justified in reaching the diagnosis that, under the influence of cultural urges, some civilizations, or some epochs of civilizations – possibly the whole of mankind – have become 'neurotic'? We may expect that one day someone will venture to embark upon a pathology of cultural communities."

Nearly three quarters of a century later, sociologist Ernest Becker speaking of mental illness, wrote:

"The great breakthrough in the contemporary theory of mental illness is that it represents a kind of stupidity, a limitation or obtuseness of perception, a failure to see the world as it is. It

is not a disease in the medical sense, but a failure to assign correct priorities to the real world."

The suggestion, implicit in these remarks, is that society is indeed sick, being simply a matter of definition. Psychiatrist Thomas Szasz asserted that mental illness, per se, is a myth that has been gaining momentum since the nineteenth century. He writes about this with reference to psychiatry:

"A person might feel sad or elated, insignificant or grandiose, suicidal or homicidal, and so forth; he is, however, not likely to categorize himself as mentally ill or insane; that he is, is more likely to be suggested by someone else. This, then, is why bodily diseases are characteristically treated with the consent of the patient, while mental diseases are characteristically treated without his consent. In short, while medical diagnoses are the names of genuine diseases, psychiatric diagnoses are stigmatizing labels."

Psychologist Bernie Zilbergeld sees the trend towards "shrinking" of our grasp of reality as a rush to consult psychologists, psychoanalysts, psychotherapists and psychiatrists, believing therapy is the painless solution to the most pressing problems of modern life as we have no intentions whatsoever to pay a personal price for changing our behavior.

When therapy falters, we turn to self-help books, or seek the counsel of gurus with their instant cures. When the guru disappoints, as they invariably do, we retreat into one of an assortment of obsessions or addictions, a shield from the uncomfortable reality we mean to avoid.

If experts agree on anything, it is that this is an anxious age. Since we cannot retreat from ourselves, and since we clearly have no intentions of changing our ways, American moralist Christopher Lasch insists we have become self-absorbed and have instead retreated into conspicuous consumption to deal with our anxiety.

Obedience Blind and Blind Obedience

What keeps a person from dealing head on with his personal demons? C. B. Chisholm writes:

"It almost always happened that among all the people in the world only our own parents, and perhaps a few people they selected, were right about

everything. We could refuse to accept their rightness only at the price of a load of guilt and fear, and peril to our immortal souls. This training has been practically universal in the human race. Variations in content have had almost no importance. The fruit is poisonous no matter how it is prepared or disguised."

We are taught at an early age not to think, just to obey and submit to the regimented programming of society. The same message is articulated at home, then reinforced at school, in church and dutifully reinforced by various media.

The incessant barrage of acceptable "points of view" and expected behaviors for every situation smother our natural curiosity. Consequently, the most unlikely person we are inclined to consult, much less trust is ourselves.

Yet, the authority we ought most to heed according to Indian mystic philosopher Krishnamurti is our own person. He writes:

"There is no intermediary between you and reality; and if there is one, he is a perverter, a mischief maker, it does not matter who he is, whether the highest savior or your latest guru or teacher."

It may seem an over-simplification, but if society is sick, mentally ill in fact, it must be from the interplay, the conflict actually, between *self-demands* and *role demands*. It does not occur to us that the life roles we try to play were designed for another time; a time long past. While various therapists go to great lengths to expose the underlying motives for our behavior and to reveal the root causes of our unhappiness and dysfunction, this effort may be entirely unnecessary.

Personal dysfunction may be simply a matter of faulty life role identity.

Fortunately, it may be enough simply to examine the life role a person has assumed, and assess how satisfying, how suitable, or esteeming that may or may not be.

People often pursue professions and career paths that their families urge them to follow. It is important, we are told, that we don't become misfits, thereby embarrassing our family. This striving to please others can result in personal tension, internal conflict, a battle between external *role demands* and internal *self-demands*.

On the other hand, if we occupy a role that is energizing, representing norms and goals consistent with our better lights, our actions will be faithfully guided by how we see ourselves, how we see the situation and how we relate to others.

The *ego state of the adult*, our "real self," will be evident and the situation will be defined in terms of reality, and the *role demands* of the job at hand. This will guide us, unscathed, against formidable obstacles. In other words, we will be in a healthy state of self-realization and thus, self-satisfaction.

However, if the role we try to play is punishing and unsatisfying, then the *superego state* of the righteous parent in our personality will surface. This draws out our "ideal self," the self we pretend to be or think we ought to be. The situation becomes sub-optimal, and *self-demands* take precedence over the job or *role demands*. This is a self-defeating, chaotic state, where confusion will lead possibly to aggressive and disruptive behavior.

Walking the Cat Back

There is a parallel between early 21st century America and the decade of the 1970s.

Young people in the 1970s were being forced to participate in an unpopular war; political upheaval was in the air; ruthless leadership was subverting democratic processes (President Nixon); while the country was gridlocked in partisan politics (Watergate Scandal). Traditional morality was on trial which saw young people escaping to Canada to avoid the draft or moving to the West Coast of the United States to form communes and live in a permanent state of a psychedelic high (Haight-Ashbury culture).

Fisher Model of Conflict and Stress Resolution

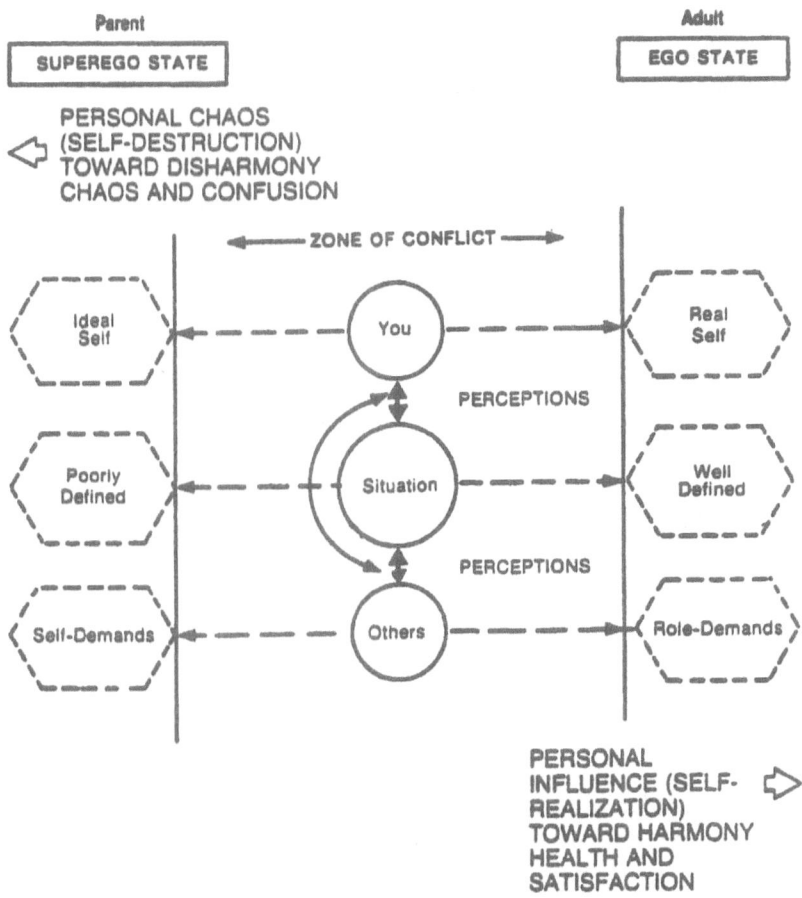

New forms of bigotry and hatred were hatching as the *"American Century"* was ending a little early, while GM and GE and other American industrial giants appeared mystified by their dwindling economic dominance in the marketplace.

At this most inauspicious moment, the "energy crisis" hit American motorists. An OPEC oil embargo rocked our national confidence while a beleaguered president hunkered down and became a law unto himself. The U.S. Congress missed its cues, failed to provide leadership, and stayed the same, refused to face its challenges, which left the future up for grabs.

This pattern of crisis now sounds familiar. We have come full circle in the early 21st century with the social and political landscape clearly resembling the 1970s.

It is as if we in this new century are battling the same crises, unable to free ourselves from their unyielding grip. If society is not mentally ill, it fails to diminish the fact that conventional practices no longer fit or serve our needs.

"Time out for Sanity" attempts to demonstrate that we are living in a continuation of the '70's, not a repeat. We're stuck, as it were. Becoming unstuck suggests an unavoidable fight against our natural state of denial and complacency.

The key is to understand that whole societies behave much like their collective individuals.

At the outset, one becomes stuck in intolerable situations because of resisting rather than embracing them. The dreaded state we resist ends up controlling us. We feel we cannot "let go," we cannot trust ourselves because we believe what threatens us will destroy us. But if we loosen the screws one turn, then another turn, and so on, eventually the hold unravels of its own accord finding us having solved the dilemma by embracing its mythic hold on us.

Only in crisis, and then only gradually, do we realize that our coping measures, our habits, our values and beliefs, our sacrosanct ideals, alas, our controlling measures are themselves inexorably destroying us, devices we ourselves have invented. Only in desperation do we then "let go," and re-experience freedom.

Reaching a state of awareness at a level of maturity, we "let go," let flow, and only then do we discern the shape of the enemy, which is ourselves. This vague and compromising threat was something that simply had to be faced. There was no other alternative. Little did we know before that we were the architect of our own failings. But as we "let go," control flows into the void for we are no longer in the way.

Individually and collectively as a society, we unconsciously push ourselves to the brink of despair, to the edge of the precipice, when our more effective option would be to yield, to trust ourselves.

We need to "walk the cat back," to retrace our steps to find that first wrong step that led to our current peril. You may recognize this expression from espionage novels. It fits our purposes here for in the process we discover the source of our angst.

The Manufacture of Madness

Time Out for Sanity argues that the more sophisticated our electronic devices the more childishly we behave. We think we have conquered time, but time always has the last laugh. We notice the abbreviated attention span of our children and are told these embarrassing states are syndromes of "disorders."

Attention Deficit Disorder (ADD) and Attention Deficit Hyperactivity Disorder (ADHD), among others, have conveniently transformed our stuckness into acronyms of behavioral diseases. Trauma is the new narrative and it dominates the discourse.

The influential *Diagnostic and Statistical Manual of Mental Disorders* (DSM-IV) is published by the *American Psychiatric Association* in collaboration with nine other officially sanctioned organizations, including the *American Academy of Pediatrics* and the *American Medical Association.*

DSM-IV criteria serve as virtual medical gospel for millions of professionals worldwide. It suggests an ADD or ADHD diagnosis for someone who has trouble keeping attention on tasks or play activities, does not follow instructions or complete school work, and so on.

These children reflect 'stuckness,' more as "coping habits" than mental disorders. Take away too much sugar in their diet, too much television, too much time playing electronic games, and much more family involvement and, "voila," these "diseases" disappear.

DSM-IV has elevated a cornucopia of behaviors to disease status, resulting on society being stuck on trauma. Alcoholism, alone, has hundreds of ailments treated as diseases: *alcohol-induced anxiety disorder*; *alcohol-induced persisting amnestic disorder*; *alcohol-induced mood disorder*; *alcohol-*

induced persisting dementia; *alcohol-induced psychotic disorder*; *alcohol-induced sexual dysfunction*; or *alcohol-induced sleep disorder*, to name a few.

Behavior is the culprit with the perpetrator of that behavior the innocent victim. Name a behavior, say gambling or promiscuity, and you have the same litany of disorders. Addiction and dependency have been rescued from self-responsibility for our actions.

Astutely, Thomas Szasz has called this *"the manufacture of madness."* It has of course generated a whole new industry, one supported by a cast of gurus, professionals and courtesans, who claim "cures" through occasional conversations, or magically, with prescriptions of mind-altering chemicals.

What so many doctors and gurus call *mental illness*, Szasz maintains, are inner human conflicts manifested outwardly in a way society can't condone. As a consequence, addiction is the fastest growing social psychological construct with medical pharmacology becoming a major growth industry.

Intrepid psychiatrist Dr. Szasz maintains that science must stand on the side of the people, of and for whom it studies, rather than being aligned with social engineers, medical professionals, pharmaceutical companies and allied advertisers who have a vested interest in perpetuating what could only be construed as a sick society dependent upon their respective services.

Of course, there are always legions of champions for these manufactured pathologies ranging from professionals in medicine, psychiatry, psychology, sociology, as well as the media, the government and corporate enterprises. They all have a vested interest in society stuck in trauma, as mental illness and dysfunctional processes provide the narrative to their legitimacy.

Irish dramatist George Barnard Shaw famously said, *"Every profession is a conspiracy against the public."* Nowhere has this been illustrated more compellingly than in the 1970s as a mirror reflection of our current times.

Yet, the more our society becomes focused on information technology and electronic entertainment, the more it devolves into swirling addictive fantasies likely to be elevated to disease status. Media guru Marshall McLuhan envisioned the space between reality and virtual reality vanishing, driving a wedge between people as persons, and the arms of despair.

Official Maladies, Official Cures

Time Out for Sanity asks the simple question: has the world changed and have we changed with it, and if not, why not?

The book argues that mental illness is only one of several myths into which we have retreated. We have many more choices than we had a mere forty years ago, but we still show a propensity for entering and staying in a very narrow comfort zone to avoid dealing with the mounting complexities of these new realities.

To put it another way, the chronic problems of forty years ago seem remarkably similar while not the same as those we face today.

As a society we continue to repeat the troublesome patterns of the immediate past. Given this premise, *Time Out for Sanity* is the equivalent of "walking back the cat" to the 1970s to show how we continue to ride the treadmill for fear of losing control, when our plight indicates it has already happened.

An indication of how life follows art rather than the other way around was the television series *The Time Tunnel*. The machine was meant for people to go back to the past or leap into the future at will. Some tried it and got stuck in the past and couldn't get out. The program was very disturbing to viewers and lasted only one season. Unlike the characters of this TV series, figuratively speaking, we willingly book flights into the past, get stuck in that nostalgia, and then seek professional help to lift the burden of this "illness" from us.

Dr. Thomas Szasz in 1973, speaking of psychiatry, though he could have been addressing the claims of infallibility of several other professions, said:

"There are fundamental similarities between persecution of heretics and witches in former days and the persecution of madmen and mental patients in ours. Just as a theological state is characterized by the preoccupation of the people with religion and religious matters, and especially with the religious deviance called heresy, so a therapeutic state is characterized by preoccupation of the people with medicine and medical matters, and especially with the medical deviance called illness."

The aim of a therapeutic state is not to provide favorable conditions for the pursuit of life, liberty, and happiness, but to repair the defective mental health of the client-patient as if a machine. The therapeutic state gives meaning to countless bureaucrats, physicians, and mental health workers while robbing patients of the meaning of their own lives independent of these care givers.

We thus persecute millions as drug addicts, homosexuals, suicide risks and so forth, all the while congratulating ourselves that we are great healers curing the sick of their mental illnesses. We have managed to repackage *The Inquisition* selling pharmaceuticals and psychotherapy as a new scientific cure-all.

Time Out for Sanity attempts to penetrate this cool façade, exposing the trite and ubiquitous rhetoric that masks chronic problems with semantics, while refusing to address them directly.

The silent ninety percent lingered on the sidelines in the 1970's, waiting for the ten percent in *big science* and *big government* to deliver it from itself. But, people forget, *big science* and *big government* are not immune to the social currents or aimless forward inertia of their time. In fact, they prefer matters as they are.

That said, I urge that we stop obsessing about the future, and instead open our minds to find fulfillment and involvement in the present. Krishnamurti writes:

In oneself lies the whole world, and if you know how to look and learn, then the door is there, and the key is in your hand. Nobody on earth can give you either that key or the door to open, except yourself.

WHO IS IN CHARGE?

James R. Fisher, Jr., Ph.D.
April 29, 2000

You want to be happy, to forget yourself, and yet the more you try to forget yourself, the more you remember the self you want to forget. You want to escape pain, but the more you struggle to escape pain, the more you inflame the agony. You are afraid and want to be brave, but the effort to be brave is fearing trying to run away from itself. You want peace of mind, but the attempt to pacify it is like trying to calm the waves with a flat iron.

We know that worry is futile, but we go on doing it because calling it futile does not stop it. We worry because we feel unsafe and want to be safe. What we need to discover is that there is no safety, that seeking it is painful, and that when we imagine we have found it, we don't like it.

There is no safety or security. One of the worst vicious circles is the problem of the alcoholic. In very many cases, he knows quite clearly that he is destroying himself, that for him liquor is poison, that he actually hates being drunk, and even dislikes the taste of liquor. It gives him the "horrors," for he stands face to face with the unveiled, basic insecurity of the world.

Alan W. Watts, *The Wisdom of Insecurity: A Message for an Age of Anxiety* (1951)

We all know the nursery rhyme of Humpty Dumpty sitting on, and falling off the wall, *"and all the king's horses and all the king's men couldn't put Humpty Dumpty together again."*

Whether we admit it or not, we are all broken, split apart in some fashion with our head separated from our body, while being driven by fear, and in the cage of memory. The contemporary mind has been haunted by the feeling that in some mysterious way the one struggling for security is nearer to hell than heaven, that the mazes of self-deception and self-mockery hide behind the masks that we assume.

St. Augustine has something to say about this split-mindedness:

The past is not dead, it is not even past . . . we cannot properly say that the future or the past exists, or that there are three times, past, present, and future. Perhaps we can say that there are three tenses, but that they are the present of the past, the present of the present, and the present of the future. This would correspond, in some sense, with a triad I find in the soul and nowhere else, where the past is present to memory, the present is present to observation, and the future is present to anticipation.

NO ONE PROMISED YOU A LIVING! NO ONE OWES YOU A JOB!

In an uncertain world, where job security is vital to our self-interests, we often do all the wrong things to put ourselves back together again. Instead of taking calm inventory of our situation, we panic or become traumatized when made redundant; when our place of work closes; when the skills we have that once were in demand no longer exist; when we are asked to take a 10 percent cut in wages and benefits for the company's survival; and are barely making ends meet as matters now stand. How could this happen when we've done nothing wrong? Turns out we've done a lot wrong, starting with waiting for someone to rescue us from our predicament and ourselves.

Author Alan W. Watts sees such circumstances consumed with anxiety looking at nature backwards:

When we try to stay on the surface of the water, we sink; but when we try to sink, we float; likewise, when we try desperately to save our job, we lose it.

Insecurity, he maintains, is the result of trying to be secure in a topsy-turvy world in which the normal order of things seems completely out of order. Everything is turned inside out and upside down. Suddenly, circumstances force us to be in charge of our lives and no one has prepared us for that ordeal, leastwise ourselves.

We think we live in a time of unusual insecurity. This is not the case at all. In the past hundred years, or throughout the past twentieth century, long established traditions have broken down continuously: the traditional family, social life, government, economic order, religious beliefs, values, ethics, and most notable of all, our morality.

We have seen society stagger out of the *Industrial Age* only to be caught in a breathless dance in the *Information Age*, as manufacture assembly lines have become a shadow of that former benchmark. The assembly line was the early watershed moment of the twentieth century. It created mindless jobs requiring little or no skills, while giving birth to the working middle class.

For the first time in history, working men and women in mass could afford to purchase homes and company automobiles at a discount and live in comfortable circumstances, conditions working people had never before dreamed of experiencing.

Then in the late twentieth century information technology spirited the working middle class away from the comfortable status of *Machine Age Thinking*. This found robotics increasingly present, replacing assembly line workers, while most jobs now required quick minds and agile fingers to master computer keyboards as work was in the process of being transformed from brawn to brains, obliterating the blue-collar working class.

There is no longer any certainty if certainty ever existed. Yet, certainty remains a myth perpetuated by a society deep in denial. Academic, political, religious and commercial institutions have denied this reality by failing to pay attention. Workers denied it by failing to learn new skills. Companies denied it by failing to press for change as the workforce was being transformed from 80 percent blue-collar to 80 percent college trained white collar.

Elementary and secondary schools as well as universities continued to teach curriculums locked in 1945 nostalgia. Private and public workplaces continued to be managed as if the color of the workers' collars had not changed. If blame is the game, there is more than enough to go around, but that doesn't get us off the dime.

That said, for far too long the majority were willing to put up with lives largely doing jobs that were boring, content to seek relief from that tedium with periodic respites of drinking and partying or going on expensive shopping sprees with reckless abandon. Saving for a rainy day was not in the specs.

People were drunk with optimism seeing the weather ahead full of sunshine and promise with no dark clouds. To suggest otherwise would be to be branded a pessimist or "negative thinker." As a consequence, neither workers nor employers were looking ahead. It wasn't anybody's job!

We often refer to assembly line blue-collar workers' jobs as boring. Nothing can compare to the boredom of managers' and administrators' jobs. They spend 50 to 75 percent of their working day in inconsequential meetings. These meetings take away from meaningful work, and consistently have no purpose other than to fulfill the routinely scheduled meetings. The mantra "meeting for meeting's sake" is a corporate disease that has been institutionalized to produce a report that few are likely to read.

A survey of a monthly sales report went out to affiliates and manufacturing facilities in 13 countries involving some 14,000 employees. When asked, first, if they were aware of the report, second, if they had read it, and third, if it was useful, most confessed that they didn't even know the report existed. Yet, several people spent a good deal of time each month preparing this report. Further inquiries found that the report was redundant as all the information was accessible electronically.

Speaking of redundancy, consider the *performance appraisal process*. This process is designed to bring managers and workers together to assess performance criteria and create a developmental roadmap for workers to build on their assets and manage their liabilities. Any organization has 15 percent *hard chargers*, who manage themselves, 70 percent *followers* who are management dependent, and 15 percent who are *foot draggers*, or essentially beyond salvation.

In this one instance, a facility of some 4,000 professional workers and 350 managers dedicated several hundred hours to the performance appraisal process. Six workers were found to be declining in rating, and four were designated to need improvement. All others received automatic merit increases.

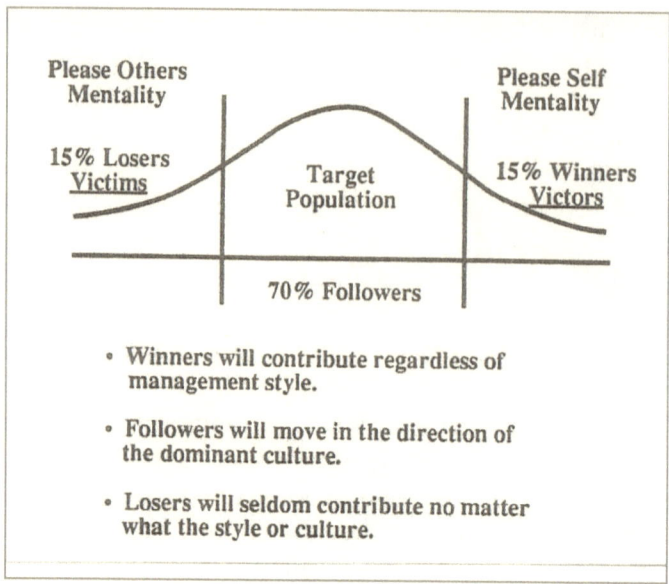

Given the normal bell curve breakdown of the working population, at least some 600, or 15 percent of the workforce should have been considered possible poor performers and treated accordingly. This is another indication of the company lock stepping to a routine that is counterproductive with the company taking two steps backward for every step forward.[1]

Performance appraisal did these workers no favors. That company is only a shadow of its former self today. Hundreds of these workers, once well paid and comfortably employed in what were supposed to be lifetime employment jobs, have many now on the street and out of work. Unfortunately, this is a promise no company can guarantee or should. At best, what a company can do is pay a worker what he is contracted to do.

In an ideal world, these workers – engineers, administrators and managers – would have acknowledged this and taken charge of the situation. Unfortunately, they had no incentive to do so. Poor as they might perform, they had job security and their income was not in jeopardy. *In many cases, 20 percent of the workforce was doing 80 percent of the productive work, yet there were no protests from these contributors.* Nobody wants to make waves when the tsunami has not yet hit the shore.

Alas, we don't live in an ideal world. Workers have come to be dependent on the company to do for them what they best do for themselves. When the company fails, workers derive satisfaction accusing the company of failing in its function, unwilling to see their tacit complicity in the act.

When a company is struggling and needs the full support and cooperation of its workers, often management keeps this fact from the workers, or the workers choose to misread management's reluctance to share this information, become moody, call in sick, or go on strike on the job by engaging in counterproductive passive behaviors, cutting off the hand that literally feeds them.2

In the 1950s, after World War II, General Motors' blue-collar workers earned as much as many practicing physicians in the medical field. I was often a guest in their Detroit homes, and played baseball with their kids during my summer visits.

In many households, both parents worked for GM, Ford or Chrysler, and spent as much as they made. It was evident in their fine brick homes and new automobiles in their driveways. Their children expected to follow their parents working for the "Big Three" right out of high school with no break in the continuum.

Then came the late 1960s. *The Rising Sun of Japan* entered the automotive market and cut deeply into these automakers' customer base and profits, producing better, cheaper, smaller, and gas efficient automobiles. Tom Brokaw delivered an NBC television "white paper" on June 24, 1980 with the resounding lament, *"Japan Can! Why Can't We?"*

Japan was using American technology that American manufacturers scoffed at as being too costly, too time consuming, and not necessary.3 What was the technology? It was *statistical quality control*, involving production workers in decision-making teams, where they were asked to identify and solve chronic work-related problems.

Fifty years later, Detroit's automotive hemorrhaging has still not stopped despite now using these statistical quality control tools. The auto industry's workers and managers could not escape the controlling mindset of 1945 when corporate America could do nothing wrong. In 2008 with the near total collapse of the United States economy, and with it much of the Western world, GM and Chrysler had to be "bailed out" by the federal government with the rationale "they were too big to fail." It is now 2019 and there is little evidence that much has been learned from this meltdown.

Brett Farve, former NFL quarterback for the *Green Bay Packers*, has it about right: *"We get paid for practicing all week, playing on Sunday should be for free."*

Yet, one of the main complaints of professional athletes is the reverse of this: they hate practice, don't think they need it, and believe they get paid for Sunday's performance only. Many workers in other professions display this same attitude. They acquire a quality degree that they think speaks for itself: "Why do we have to take orders from someone less qualified than we are?"

They don't want a job; they want a position with an automatic pass to a satisfying career. After all, they reason, why else would they dedicate four, six or eight years to a university education? The reality is that is the wrong question.

A CASE IN POINT!

A survey was conducted of 1,000 engineers in a high-tech company. The demographic profile revealed staggering results. Of the engineering population: 72 percent were over 35; 50 percent over 45; and 15 percent over 55. Fully 60 percent were working on technology developed long after they had left university. Despite this technical gap, they were doing little if anything to upgrade their skills.

Complicating the picture, it was evident that job performance decreased precipitously as job complexity increased for veteran engineers. Yet, their salaries continued to increase. At age 45, salaries for veterans peaked reaching a plateau with no noticeable decline for the balance of their careers. This represented, in some cases, a $20,000 differential with neophyte engineers, many of whom had advanced engineering degrees with state-of-the-art technical acumen.

Concomitantly, engineers ages 21 to 39 represented a spiraling upward linear curve of increasing job performance and job complexity, but modest salaries compared to veterans. In an environment dedicated to the gospel "pay for performance," they clearly weren't.

What did they do about it? They complained among themselves or retreated into the *"six silent killers"* of passive behaviors.[4] In a word, they took no initiative or action to redress the issue. They were being paid a dollar more an hour than they felt they could afford to rock the boat or quit.

- Engineers choose an engineering education because they have talent for and an interest in solving technical problems.

- Research indicates that this gives engineers only a 3 to 5 year window of competence before their technical talent starts to erode if they are not exposed to a significant continuing education program.

- The burden in the past has rested on engineers for continuing engineering education, which is another way of saying it is not likely to have been initiated.

- Engineers who have become key contributors to long-term programs are often protected from more diverse experience and therefore suffer greatly when programs reach completion or assume the next iteration in sophistication. They are likely ill prepared to take on new engineering assignments.

- Engineers, who cannot contribute meaningfully, may become anxious, frustrated, angry, hostile, passive, and eventually alienated from work and their associates, exhibiting the tendency to coast and drift into apathy.

- Engineers, once realizing they can't keep up, may also show initiative by going back to school, asking for specialized training, attempting to find on-the-job mentors, or going to another company. This is more the exception than the rule.

Confrontation, managing conflict, indeed, interpersonal relations are not high on the list of preferred activities of engineers. The social content of the job is the least appealing to many engineers.

By creating an assessment center process, and then sharing the results with management, it was possible to convince management of this specific need, which resulted in the inauguration of a comprehensive *Continuing Technical Education Program.*

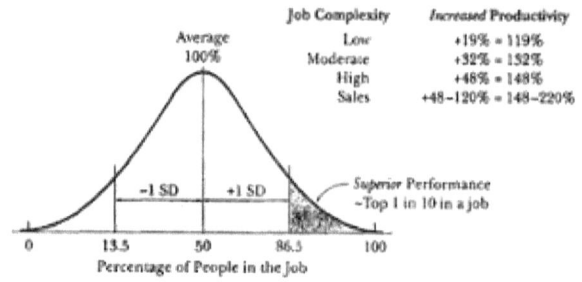

Source: Data from Hunter, Schmidt, & Judiesch (1990).

Management initially pledged $1 million for this program, which has grown in sophistication to where technicians can now earn their engineering degree in cooperation with the *University of South Florida's School of Engineering,* while attending engineering classes and laboratories at work. This is feasible because many engineers have advanced engineering degrees.

Meanwhile, veteran engineers continue to upgrade their skills concurrent with new technologies. Once the seed was planted, engineers took control of the technical education program with a rotating *Engineering Chair* providing its continuity and enhancement. This was accomplished with no interference from management. Engineers now owned the program and the process.5

THE NEW REALITY: *Self-Confidence is Self-Directed!*

A job is a sacred trust between employee and employer. It is a contract, a bond. We have moved into a climate where workers must exercise more control over the process than ever before. For far too long employment in most cases has been to be other directed, or reactive to management's instruction; depending on the company to take care of you as your second home. As a result, workers have devolved into *learned helplessness* dependent on management and counter dependent on the company for their total well-being. This has suspended most workers in terminal adolescence, a luxury no company can any longer afford.

Opportunities are limited only by our perceptions of their horizons.

Prudent workers in this new climate of self-dependency will make the appropriate assessments of where they are, who they are, what they do well (strengths) and where they need help (weaknesses) and seek to exploit their strengths and to assess what they need to do to minimize their weaknesses.

Self-directed individuals will create their own career roadmap, not wait for management to create one for them. Likewise, they will seek out mentors and exploit the opportunities available. They won't wait for opportunities to present themselves but will create them by taking the initiative. They will study their jobs as owners, not renters, and assume the role of leader of their function.

They won't waste energy or time campaigning for the next position at the expense of what they are being paid to do. Nor will they spend countless hours chatting on the Internet or cell phones, texting or tweeting, entertaining themselves when they should be working. They won't bad mouth colleagues or the company as they are too busy bringing new life into their function.

They won't look for fantasy jobs beyond their recognized limits. Fantasy jobs are positions in which they have no stomach for the pain, frustration, commitment, sacrifice, or risks involved to realize the return. Boring as their present job may be, they find ways to make it stimulating, as they are learners, not tellers; listeners, not tellers; students of what they do, not complainers.

In this new reality, some see others less able prospering because they are less afraid to venture outside the box and embrace the unknown. They are not only students of what they do but find ways to complement the skills of associates so that they might be equally successful. They look for opportunities to make the company stronger without fanfare.

They are not on the make but on the making. They are systemic thinkers consistent with Russell Ackoff observations:

If you take a system apart to identify its components, and then operate those components in such a way that every component behaves as well as it possibly can, there is one thing of which you can be sure. The system as a whole will not behave as well as it can. Now that is counterintuitive to Machine Age thinking, but it is absolutely essential to system thinking. The corollary to this is that if you have a system that is behaving as well as it can, none of its parts will be.[5]

If this describes you, and your approach to work, there is no reason to worry. Should the company be forced to downsize or relocate, it would find a place for you; if not with that company certainly with another. You are poised to look at opportunities in your industry because the misfortune of one is likely to lead to the good fortune of another.

This new reality forces many companies to make hard choices. Some workers critical of the company's relocating plans refuse to admit they wouldn't move under any circumstances. They insist on the company providing security for them when the company is in a survival mode teetering on bankruptcy. Not to worry, these workers expect to be treated from birth to death by the company as surrogate parent to meet their economic and emotional requirements at any cost, reality be damned!

This is not to make light of the fact that many lives have been disrupted if not destroyed by plant closings. By the accident of their birth, workers today have come of age in a transitional and transforming period when the definition of work itself is in a state of change; when a place of employment is no longer an assumed fixed place; when brains are much more in demand than brawn; when the role of worker and manager are in flux; when working hard has been replaced by working smart; when a manufacturing based economy has been eclipsed by a service based economy; when information technology disrupts provincial stability with global fluidity.

It was bound to happen. It just happened during your working years. Now, you must deal with it, or it will deal with you.

Much criticism has been directed at companies such as Walmart and others who have forced their suppliers to manufacture their finished products in China and India. The downside is that it takes away jobs in the United States. The upside is that it produces cheap consumer goods that the less fortunate can afford to purchase. It is an old cliché, but the world is in fact getting smaller and more interdependent. In time, as the standard of living of third world countries improve, somewhere down the road equilibrium will be reached. Then cheap labor will not be the bargaining chip that it is today.

That trend has started and is gaining momentum. The dominance of the West is now being challenged by the emerging economic powers of the East. The days of the fictive belief in the economic and political dominance of one nation over others seems to be in the twilight. The combination of technology and population growth is forcing yet another reality on workers. The onus is on them to be contract consultants and their own agents in a most competitive, but opportunistic marketplace, where it will be necessary to hone workers' skills and match them to the demands of that marketplace. Here is one story.

NOT FOR EVERYONE!

When he was a boy, he discovered he was dyslexic. School was difficult for him, and he had to work harder than most to earn average grades. The problem wasn't any less difficult in high school, as schoolwork remained a challenge. He met it with every ounce of energy he could muster without complaint. Some thought college was too high a hill for him to climb, but he persisted, and graduated with a B.S. degree in *Criminal Justice* from *Michigan State University.*

His first job out of school was as a police officer in *Tampa, Florida.* That soon appeared a dead end as he could see seniority controlled his destiny. So, he went back to school at the *University of South Florida* and earned an MS degree in *Criminal Justice.* He continued to be a police officer, gradually separating himself from it to become an assistant professor in Criminal Justice at the university.

As a professor, he met a number of rising legal minds in the community. This sparked his interest in the law. He took to studying law at night school. Reading was always a challenge, now it was the main requirement as law school meant reading scores of books. Undaunted, he persevered and graduated with a law degree, and promptly committed himself to taking the bar examination. He studied so hard that he lost weight, but it paid off, as he passed it on his first try.

Everything changed. He became a junior lawyer of a law firm in which much of the work was pro bono or handling cases others took a pass on. By nature, kind and generous, unassuming and even humble, he noticed that in his new work environment that there was a distinct pecking order, which included preferred billing hours, client exploitation, and amoral arrogance. He remained stoic, as unhappy as he was, and refused to complain. Instead, he studied diligently for his *Doctor's in Jurisprudence*, which he again passed on his first try. At this point, he changed law firms.

The new law firm was more of the same. Only here the partners were treated like royalty, or as "crown princes." They talked about him behind his back because he didn't spend as many hours billing as they did. What's more, to their chagrin, he didn't seem to feel guilty about it. He couldn't see billing clients excessively because you could, feeling this was as good as fraud. So, he moved on again, this time opening his own law firm.

He invited more than one hundred lawyers and former clients and friends to celebrate the new opening but only a handful showed up. It had to hurt, but he said nothing, going about his business working as hard as ever to make a go of it. The firm prospered.

Fortunately, years earlier, he had purchased five acres of prime real estate on Lake Thonotosassa in Hillsborough County, Florida, which had a large house, and a smaller one on the property. He moved into the larger one and rented out the smaller one.

The economy changed and with it his law firm's fortunes. Business deteriorated and then things got so desperate that he had to split his property down the middle and sell half. He also sold the little house on his side of the five-acre split. This kept him solvent, but barely so. Not dissuaded, he was still not through pushing the envelope.

He decided to create an entertainment center in Ybor City, Tampa, Florida, a Cuban community of historic significance modeled after the *French Quarters in New Orleans*. Never a timid spender on projects, he brought in a cadre of entertainers and investors from St. Louis. They seemed interested until it was clear there were no guarantees. He scuttled that project and looked about for another. None were on the horizon so instead he bought an office building, renovated it, and then rented a good share of it out to small businesses, while keeping his law practice afloat.

Some twenty years ago, he married a model and now has a family of two children, a boy and a girl, both are now in college. A family is what he always wanted, as his parents and brother had died, and only a sister was left.

It was during this period that he met a number of entrepreneurs who were restless for a project but lacked the capital to seed it. He had the capital. Starting on a small scale, paying his partners and his small staff out of his own pocket, he operated the business like this for several months, nearly to the point of going broke again.

Then, with his partners, he created a website and the business took off. It grew every week. More people were brought on staff. Additional expertise was needed, so he sold part of his interest, bringing in another partner, still remaining the majority stockholder. His generosity continued. Operations were opened in other locations, and they took off as well. But again, his generosity and over optimism came crashing down on him as the economy changed and so did regulations.

During his affluent days, he designed an estate on his property of eye-catching delight. He had sold his little house, and now had to buy it back at twice what he paid for it and did this without complaint or regret. The new estate was in the Miami style with a two story white alabaster house with twenty foot windows overlooking the lake with a French stucco patio, an entertainment center, a gymnasium, and bar, a winding marble staircase, the floors a combination of marble and carpeting, a large contemporary kitchen, ornate fireplace, and enough original artwork to fill a gallery, gated with a quarter mile landscaped serpentine driveway with fountains and dolphin sculptures snaking along the way, a tennis court and swimming pool, three car attached garage, and a separate four car garage for his automobile collection, which included an auto workshop. He had a pier built on the lake with a covered boat hangar for his boat, and two wave runners, and other toys of a man with the disposable income to recapture his youth at age fifty.

He is now sixty-five and was set back again even prior to the 2007 – 2008 economic meltdown as were many others and has never regained his momentum. But his optimism has not faded. Nor has his fondness for taking risks or looking for new opportunities. He opened a new business in 2014, and with the same enthusiasm and élan that is part of his DNA.

He could be described as a visualizing investment capitalist for he has been doing what many only dream of doing, but never find the courage. It could also be said that given his propensity to design his own estate without the expertise to do it right indicates more of a capacity to do it on the cheap with a kind of arrogance that he has the knowhow when clearly, he doesn't. Moreover, his capacity to absorb failure and defeat philosophically and move on, while seemingly admirable in one sense seems quite the contrary in another sense.

Self-Confidence is displayed in having a moral center and an internal guidance system that when violated by others in any demonstrable way results in a counter reaction as indicative of that person's dignity.

Two questions come to the fore: who are you; what are you? The estate of this man's own design has aged as he has aged with the visual weariness of his optimistic perspective. While seemingly being self-directed, he has clearly been neither self-aware nor self-accepting, holding to dreams other people might envy. This is like building sand castles in the air, an odyssey where there is no real sense of what he would really like to do, or who he would like to be as his actions indicate more of a need to please others than to please himself.

Envy may be defined as wanting what other people have; jealousy fearing what you already have but fear of losing. In a peculiar way, this man seems to be driven by both.

Contrast his bumpy ride through life with other people who never metaphorically ever get out of bed. He is a handsome powerfully built man, seldom if ever shows anger, a man more generous than anyone you have ever met, and a man who frustrates his family with his misplaced generosity as if he feels compelled to buy loyalty and support from others. This is characteristically unhealthy and never sustainable.

Conflicting with this sense of generosity is the fact that he is a notoriously poor tipper to waiters in restaurants, people who count on customer generosity for their livelihood. Now, why do you believe this is so?

He is a family man in the truest sense of the word, has a beautiful wife and two adoring children. But he frustrates them because he is not into work as work is defined; is not into security as it is defined; and certainly not into a consistent rational approach to earning a living.

My sense is that he was burned out on work early in life, working at his father's automobile dealership after school and of a Saturday for hours washing and polishing cars, leaving little time to play sports or just hang out with friends.
Parents can stimulate or kill our appetites for life in many different ways.

I suspect this was what killed his work ethic as we know work. Again, he is a man who would never utter a negative word about his parents, or the ordeal he has suffered at their hands. It is not his nature. Yet, it is important to understand what motivates us in everyday life. Our parents were not saints, and in their struggles, developed their own scars, scars that their children often absorb as if their own.

This is not meant to denigrate parents, but simply to point out that self-confidence is impossible without some understanding of why we behave as we do.

Should you see this man on the street, chances are he'll be in a polyester warm-up suit, or an open polo shirt and stone-colored Timber Creek Wranglers and loafers or sandals. He seldom is seen in a coat and tie, although when forced to wear a suit he does so reluctantly for it is clear that such attire is uncomfortable.

He once belonged to a fashionable country club but didn't play golf where he was known to swim a hundred laps at the club's Olympic sized pool for warm-up to a workout with his body builder physique without the necessity of steroids.

One day he overheard someone say to another: "Why doesn't he work like the rest of us? It's not fair." He heard this but said nothing. It would have been uncharacteristic for him to say anything. In any case, it wouldn't have made any difference.

How do you explain someone who has overcome such mountains of difficulty, only to create new mountains more challenging, seemingly in a never-ending drive, to what no one knows?

Few of us have the courage or the appetite much less the energy for a life on the edge. Most of us prefer playing it safe and dreaming of winning the Lotto. The thought never crosses our minds to create our own wealth, or heaven forbid, to put our existence in jeopardy as this man has constantly put his.

The irony is he demonstrates a quest for money when money is not important to him. What he wants, apparently achieved, then lost again and again, is to be master of his own time. When he was enjoying a seven-figure income, he could have invested, but didn't. He is a man of modest appetites but a profligate spender seemingly clueless as to his motivation. Could the reason for not investing in the stock market be he doesn't want to think constantly about his investments? Whatever the reason, he is often broke and nearly always deeply in debt but doesn't seem to lose a step or any sleep over the fact. He is the antithesis of self-confidence because he is not charge of his life or himself, yet I suspect many who read this might envy him.

THE WISDOM OF INSECURITY

Alan W. Watts explains insecurity as a given that we best accept. Once we do, he insists, we miraculously overcome insecurity anxiety. We are able to act and do, to be and take the initiative, to take control. Insecurity, Watts discovered, is a mania for control of things we cannot control at the expense of the things we can, but don't.

Control all starts with recognizing the only person, we can change, if we but find the will to do so, is ourselves. No other. None. Nada.

Many of us are waiting for the boss to change; to be promoted; or to retire. We think others are the problem. Absent our nemesis, we believe our anxiety will vanish. The waiting never ends because we cannot allow ourselves to imagine that "we" are the problem.

We escape through denial or pleasure only to find it kills what we love. We delight in the rhythm and flow of music but are upset by a discordant cord, yet such notes are part of the rhythm and atonality of life.

We want certainty when life is full of dissonant uncertainty. Our anxiety is not new. Read *"The Confession of St. Augustine"* (397 A.D.), the Bishop of Hippo, a man who straddled the fourth and fifth centuries, and you hear your own mind spinning while you straddle the 20th and 21st century:

I am toppled back to earth, weighted with heavy burdens, plunged into compelled ways, netted, wailing strongly but strongly netted still. So great is compulsion's heavy baggage. Here I can abide but do not wish to; there, I wish to abide but cannot – miserable either way.[6]

How many of us have been in this state of mind when our careers have gone awry; when an expected raise or promotion did not occur; when out of the blue we were made redundant, or shockingly surprised to be fired; when we thought our job was secure, and our contribution appreciated and were instead given a pink slip; when our world crashed and burned and we thought we had finally realized security?

Those experiencing the greatest difficulty adjusting to new circumstances live in the illusory world of false expectations, not the reality of the times.

This is most troubling for workers who live only to make money. They are forever worrying about losing their jobs, and frequently do. Instead of earning a living, they are living an earning, and thus when the time comes to relax, they are unable to do so. They are likely to be bored and miserable when they retire, because all they know is work and making money. They think nothing of returning to work and taking a position away from a younger person. Their whole identity is work. Their essence is tied to making money.

The sad irony is that many have more money than they could ever spend the rest of their lives. Money isn't the point, they say, but they have made it so. They are a machine that has no other function than to make money when they no longer need to make a living. There is no one to master or to be mastered, no one to rule or to surrender to.

The purpose of life is what we do.

When what we value is only money, we are bound to live in misery when money no longer has a purpose. Watts sees such people caught in their own honey:

It is as if we were divided into two parts. On the one hand there is the conscious "I," at once intrigued and baffled, the creature who is caught in the trap. On the other hand, there is "me," and "me" is a part of nature, the wayward flesh with all its concurrently beautiful and frustrating limitations. "I" fancies itself as a reasonable fellow and is forever criticizing "me" for its perversity – for having passions, which get "I" into trouble, for being so easily subject to painful and irritating diseases, for having organs that wear out, and for having appetites, which can never be satisfied.[7]

The wisdom of insecurity is that truth, life, change, movement, and beauty are many names for the same thing. The rhythm of life in all its uncertainty produces its own music and makes all things lovable.

Life and death, career and retirement, security and insecurity are all simply ways of looking at the same thing through different eyes. We are at once all builders and destroyers, growing and dying, reaching high and low notes, all in the rhythm of life. I could not write these words if I had not known pain and loneliness, love and wonder, failure and success, pride and humiliation, science and religion.

It is difficult to realize job security when we compartmentalize work from life, and life from work; when we drive a wedge between the head and the heart; between thinking and feeling; between pain and pleasure, which are on a collision course instead of being treated as normal fare; between science, which covers the empirical realm of what is (fact) and why things work as they do (theory) and religion, which questions the ultimate meaning of why we are here.

It may sound absurd, but the highest pleasure is to be unconscious of one's own existence, to be absorbed in interesting sights, sounds, places, and people; to be lost in life. In that mindset, there are no thoughts of what's in it for me, no concerns about carrying other people's burden, and no worry about getting credit for this or for that.

On the other hand, one of the greatest pains is to be self-conscious, to be constantly worried about what other people think of us, and thus to be totally oblivious to the richness of life found through self-involvement in the greater community.

If we are obsessed with security, traumatized with the possibility of losing our job, then we are back to Humpty Dumpty, suffering split-mindedness between "me" (*self-demands*) and "I" (*role demands*); between the job at hand and anxiety concerning that function.

If I am afraid of losing my job, my efforts to feel and act bravely in the face of that possibility are moved by fear, for I am afraid of fear. This shows that my efforts to escape from my insecurity only drives me deeper into it, moving me into the vicious circle of collapsing possibilities, compressing my perspective, shrinking my options, and giving me a blinding headache. I know because I've been there. Unless we break this cycle, it can surely become a self-fulfilling prophecy.

CREATING JOB SECURITY IN AN UNCERTAIN WORLD

You can no longer expect to place your faith in a company. Companies are struggling against the most competitive odds to stay afloat in a shrinking world. You must rouse yourself from this fixation and take charge of your work, which is the only way to take charge of your life.

You can do this by creating your own job security by taking small steps. These are some that might be considered:

- *Embrace the reality of your situation.*

It no longer is enough to do your job, to put in your time and let management worry about the health of the company. *You are the company!* Without you, there is no company. Managers and workers are the arms and legs, brains and backbone of the same body. Nothing of sustaining value happens unless this body works together and moves in the same direction. There is no point in complaining. Ask yourself: why am I frustrated? What can I do about it? Needy people need not apply.

- *Pay attention to what is going on beyond the rhetoric and the rah rah!*

Long before a company is in crisis, there are indicators that something is awry. New competitors are on the horizon, orders fall off, quotas aren't met, and schedules are late. It suddenly gets very quiet. Some of the hard chargers resign.

The rumor mill goes into high gear. Workers who pay attention know when the workplace culture gets a cold. It is not enough to generate feedback, but to take personal action. You don't wait for management to resurrect a survival strategy, or for the workplace to develop pneumonia. You create innovations in your own function. Once this momentum starts on a personal level, it flows out in concentric rings touching all operations, and then miracles do sometimes occur. But it starts with attention and proceeds directly to action on a personal basis.

- *Organize your work and work your organization.*

Transparency is "in," as the vertical organization collapses into horizontal teams, where managers and workers are on the same page. Transparency is also in as the boundaries between disciplines blur and specialists promote user-friendly tools for all.

At the same time, and this is new, workers and managers have more discretionary control of what they do than ever before. The problem is not that this power suddenly exists. The problem is that it has always been there, but few have taken advantage of this fact, first by using it, and second, by using it effectively. Functions and disciplines have complementary relationships, but to benefit from them requires creative initiative. Put another way, it means asking for help when it is required.

- *Promote the mature adult in your personality and take action.*

The purpose of a company is what it does. The function of your job is what you do. The company's mission and your function must be clear, understood and mutually supportive. If they are not, it is your responsibility to make your case politely and as often as necessary, instead of infrequently and violently.

The company is a human group made up of conflicting, contradictory and sometimes colliding issues, all of which can be resolved with mature adult dialogue. *Managed conflict* is actually the glue that holds the company to its task, not harmony. A company that works hard to create the myth of harmony is a company in trouble. Confusion is bound to occur periodically; failure is parent to success; and sustained success is endemic to a *Culture of Contribution* where problems are never denied but worked through and out.[8]

Shakespeare has Macbeth saying: *And you all know, security is mortals' chiefest enemy.*

It continues to be so, but need not, especially in work if we recognize the wisdom of insecurity and embrace its possibilities. All problems contain their own solutions, and the highest happiness is found in awareness that impermanence and insecurity are inescapable and inseparable from life and work.

There is a new movement afoot. Maturity is gripping the workforce despite all the uncertainties of the times, perhaps because of them. Workers are remaining resolutely committed to the job, rolling with the punches. These workers, which are only a small contingent, are massing to become a large army as they show the way to go forward with the basic requirement of taking charge, leaving the cage of being taken care of behind.

NOTES

1. Dr. James R. Fisher, Jr., *Six Silent Killers: Management's Greatest Challenge*, St. Lucie Press, 1998, Chapter 6, The Culture of Contribution, Chapter 9.
2. Ibid, Chapter 5, *Echoing Footsteps.*
3. Ibid. *The Mad Monarchs of the Madhouse*
4. James R. Fisher, Jr., Ph.D., *"Combating Technical Obsolescence: The Genesis of a Technical Education Program."* Presented at the *World Conference of Continuing Engineering Education* in Orlando, Florida, May 7, 1986.
5. Russell L. Ackoff and Fred E. Emery, *On Purposeful Systems*, Intersystem Publications, Seaside, California, 1972, p.1.
6. Garry Wills, *Saint Augustine's Memory*, Viking, 2002, pp. 7-8.
7. Alan W. Watts, *The Wisdom of Insecurity*, Vintage Books, 1951, p. 39.
8. Op. Cit., Dr. Fisher, *Culture of Contribution.*

A CONVERSATION
WITH A READER
ABOUT SUBTEXT!

James R. Fisher, Jr., Ph.D.
© March 19, 2016

A READER WRITES:

So...am I correct that you are saying that the subtext we all carry with us will impact how we view the content and context of our current life/affairs?

It seems to me that the subtext, if that is correct, is the background of our lives and will be different depending on the time and place of our development. Consequently, though you and I are both from small town Midwest up-bringing, your subtext as someone whose formative years were during the late depression and WWII, will be different from mine which results from growing up in the 1950s. As one psychologist put it years ago – "who we are depends on where we were when..." If that is all even close to what you mean by subtext, let me know.

DR. FISHER RESPONDS:

That is precisely what I mean by subtext.

But subtext is more than many faceted. Subtext applies equally to race, religion, nationality and culture, indeed, civilization, as they are all protean to its construction.

Subtext relates to us individually and collectively and is marinated with our distinct histories. We bring our subtext in greetings to those with whom we interact and relate, and ultimately assimilate without conscious awareness of how the aspects of that exposure finds its way into our own subtext.

In the end, we are always richer for the exposure and attention although that may not seem so at first.

Humanity is one body. Subtext may differ but it rises from that same source. Philosopher Isaiah Berlin writes that no subtext is superior to another, but all can be identified through events.

The late paleontologist Stephen Jay Gould and etymologist E. O. Wilson developed the theory of "sociobiology," claiming that our subtext remains with those who follow. It surfaces quite dramatically and sometimes radically when continuity leads to discontinuity to disruption to catastrophe, or simply to mock catastrophe in comedic relief. The point is that subtext is not usually apparent.

The stock market crash of 1929 and 1987, and again in 2008 was evidence of the subtext surfacing and going awry in mass hysteria. Ironically, people who had no money to lose talked as if they did. It was an opportunity for subtext to be on display.

On the other hand, the current divisiveness in the *Republican Party* is playing out as dramaturgic relief as The Donald (Trump) exposes the hypocrisy in subtext. His popular bombast reveals an uptight nation comfortable and complacent in its denial.

Everything is subtext to behavior, but most people do not understand that.

Occasionally, over the years, I've published *"Fragments of a Philosophy."* It was quoted in a missive on my blog (peripateticphilosophr.blogspot.com) August 30, 2009, titled *"The Subtext of Life and Its Meaning."* It remains one of the most popular pieces I have ever posted:

There is general denial of the subtext of life. It is contained in a kind of culture that exists apart from the kind transmitted by schools and universities, a kind of culture that once flourished in typical neighborhoods across the country but is gone now. It helped to stem lawlessness, greed, corruption and other social diseases. It was a kind of social resistance that is lacking today, something upheld not only by average citizens, but by people in authority as well. There was a subtext of restrain undefined, unwritten, unspoken, but nonetheless felt, practiced and experienced.

Today, the gap between people's dreams and experience is too large. People have resorted to living life on the edge, running without thinking, and on automatic pilot in the rhythm of the content and context of things without a sense of restrain or penalty.

We see this in general apathy as people react to the lead stories on television nightly news and in the headlines of morning newspapers regarding murder, mayhem, rape, fraud, and malfeasance with irritation but little more. It is the ghost in the room.

The mind is homeless. It lacks roots. Most people aren't from where they are now residing. A kind of isolation from a sense of place and space breaks the continuity of people's character.

Easily forgotten is that shameful acts are committed by people, wounded human beings. There is an under dialogue to conversation, not spoken but subconsciously felt, suppressing conflict, anger, competition, pride, or a repressed desire to upstage the show off. Indeed, there is a cavalcade of implicit thoughts, ideas and emotions that have become toxic through social psychological repression.

Once restrain and shame were prominent in subtext. That world has been corrupted to place the emphasis on the "self" at the expense or concern for or about others.

The subtext world now is about how a person feels, about that person's unspoken thoughts and motives as a manifestation of a self-centered character; in other words, what a person really thinks about another person.

Moreover, it is often a surprise when a person steps out of character and exhibits shocking behavior. This behavior may emanate from the subtext and be as much a surprise to the person so inclined as to others observing.

If we pay attention, we may recognize subtext as it is inserted into social and political dialogue, used by politicians, crusaders, television pundits and commentators to subtly appeal to the subtext side of our nature, a side we would prefer to think does not exist.

The novels we read and the poems and music lyrics that we memorize use this device to exploit our subtext that some have called "the cords of our soul."

Once upon a time, we were all children, running down the street at the start of school with our backpacks bouncing in cadence with our happy feet. We were on our way to school and on our way out into life.

One wonders watching this parade now if there goes a thief, a wife beater, an addict, a drug dealer, a murderer, a rapist, an embezzler, a gang member, a prostitute, a pimp, a wastrel or some other drag of society, someone on the fringe who will garner those lead stories in the media that we essentially ignore.

Is this behavior predetermined? Quite the opposite. But only if people use their intelligence and good will to get beyond surface issues of class and race, status and wealth, education and profession, immigration and ethnicity, religion and ideology, language and culture to consider the subtext of life to uncover what destroys social restrain and how to prepare the damage.

The world gets better or worse one person at a time. Apathy or psychopathology occur because people are not acquainted with the subtext of their own thinking and lives, and therefore enslaved to surface issues.

It was the same a hundred years ago and is likely to be so a hundred years hence."

James R. Fisher, Jr., *"Fragments of a Philosophy"*

THE READER:

What is happening in the world is that at any given time the current content and context are what cultivates the subtext that will be the life background baggage for those who are at that time in their formative years.

DR. FISHER:

The subtext can include baggage, but it is not background. Oh, no! It is always there working its ways to the fore but just not always apparent. In any case, acknowledged or not, it influences events.

The subtext is what is. It is what drives events.

The source of subtext is the subconscious (of individual or the collective) from which the content and context of behaviors are displayed and ultimately managed or mismanaged.

You could liken subtext to values if you like or collective history but only as a gauge. The subtext is there, fully operational, but not apparent. By that I mean that during periods of order, surface consistency gives the mocking sense that all is well when it never is.

Great disruptions, personal or societal, bring the subtext to prominence and to the confusion of those in charge, who are so schooled in denial that "what is" does not get much attention. We have seen this in love and war, politics and religion, especially in politics and religion.

It is during these periods of disruption, such as our current *"Age of Technology,"* that subtext is neither acknowledged nor challenged. It is avoided by more wondrous technology.

To be fair, there has been more change in the past 30 years than the previous 300. So, rather than acknowledge subtext, and deal with its root attributes, we call this the *"Age of Anxiety"* and develop drugs to treat the condition, or write books to describe it, and on and on.

We valiantly avoid doing anything constructive about it, which would start by addressing the nature and function of subtext relative to the current age.

THE READER:

Hitler had not attacked the US and yet we declared war on Germany and in less than 4 years the US alone killed at least 2 million Germans. In the 1940s, there was no question in our collective American mind that Germans were bad people and in need of killing. Hence it was a short war.

DR. FISHER:

Oh, dear! That great justification, attrition! I fear your subtext is showing.

The use of the expression of content (numbers) and context (dead Nazis) was also used in Vietnam to suggest that the United States was winning that war when it was clearly losing it. Little if any attention was given to the subtext of the Vietnamese people which was Vietnam's history. I will have more to say about WWII shortly.

The US military routinely published its daily successes in Vietnam in terms of "body count" (Vietnamese killed) on the three major networks televised nightly news, as if a war of attrition was the answer to a war without a purpose.

This attention indicated a total ignorance of subtext, and yet no one in public life at the time seemed to see the absurdity.

The French ruled Vietnam for more than a century, the subtext of a colonial power. When France fell to Germany in WWII in 1940, this colonial power base was disrupted. Finally, in 1954, France lost the *First French Indo-China War*, and Vietnam received its independence, being divided into North and South Vietnam as if you could separate a common people without disruption.

Not surprisingly, that solution aggravated the problem of subtext as Vietnam as a common people had a passion for total independence from foreign influence.

President Kennedy stepped into the South Vietnam quagmire in support of a corrupt South Vietnam regime sending American advisers and trainers to shore up its fragile control.

From that point forward it became a descent into the subtext of hell with more than 55,000 Americans in the U.S. military losing their lives in a cause that history hasn't treated kindly. A generation of young Americans who protested against the war and refused to join in the fight were consumed in subtext and eventually stopped its advance.

The subtext has a very long pull from the collective historical subconscious of a people. The book I'm now writing, NOWHERE MAN IN NOWHERE LAND, is an attempt to give subtext to the American madness that currently dominates the content and context of our times, which is optimism in the face the reality of a pessimistic future.

To give you a closer sense of how pervasive subtext can be in history, consider WWII. It all started long before WWI.

Up until WWI, the aristocracy controlled every aspect of life of the European Western world. The pull of Queen Victoria of Great Britain, alone, is impressive. Kaiser Wilhelm II of Germany was a grandchild. Other grandchildren included queens of Greece, Norway, Romania, Spain and Sweden and the Tsarina Alexandra of Russia.

WWI broke up this comfy aristocratic status but not its aristocratic subtext. We are still feeling it to this day.

"O.K., you love me. What's the subtext?"

By the end of WWI, the high aristocracy collapsed. The tsar, a relative of King George V of Great Britain, was overthrown and he and his royal family murdered by the Bolsheviks. The great disruption didn't end there.

In the 1920s, the royal families across Europe had to find new ways to make a living as the aristocracy was in a state of collapse. Take Germany's aristocracy as palpable evidence. By 1938, nearly a fifth of the senior ranks of Heinrich Himmler's SS Gestapo were filled by holders of titles of nobility. The subtext goes even deeper.

The Third Reich of Hitler's Germany had a cozy relationship with King George and Queen Mary, current Queen Elizabeth's parents. Her father even taught her the Nazi salute as a child.

Many of the English aristocracy were fond of Hitler's Germany and believed he had restored political and social order to the continent. They also saw him as a perfect foil to communism. That was the content and context of the times with many with royal ties advocating an Anglo-German alliance.

Great Britain's Prime Minister, Neville Chamberlain, gave an appeasement speech (*Munich Agreement*) in 1938 essentially conceding the *Czech Republic* to Hitler while ceremoniously declaring, "We have peace in our time."

This speech was given one year to the month before Hitler invaded Poland on September 1, 1939, launching WWII.

Appeasement was but a mask to the prevailing subtext of those in power in the British government. Many prominent Brits were willing to make huge concessions to Hitler to avoid war. One man understood the subtext of events and their implicit meaning. He saved the day for the West.

Were it not for Winston Churchill being elected Prime Minister, it is difficult to imagine Great Britain not capitulating to the will of Adolf Hitler. Chamberlain resigned eight months after the start of WWII, the war going badly at the time, with Churchill taking office on May 10, 1940, and having to resist Nazi sympathizers in Great Britain from the first.

THE READER:

In the new century, based on a changing subtext, we have a very different context and content. We accept Islam as the religion of peace and are careful to sort out the bad Muslims who hi-jacked the religion, from the good ones. The present "war on terror," for that reason, is more a nuanced than a killing war or a war of attrition. That is not business as usual for us – that is progress.

DR. FISHER:

If I read you correctly, you are inferring that the subtext of history is changing. Subtext, unfortunately, is not that malleable.

The People of Islam are victims of a long history of abuse as were the Japanese. Demagogues throughout their histories adulterated the subtext of these people to twist the content and context of abuses to their advantage.

There is always a kernel of justification for revolution and that kernel never exists in the content and context of events, but always in subtext.

The subtext of a people's history can be ripped from the bowels of their beliefs to present ugly aspects of that subtext. No history is without this occasional momentum, not even ours.

The al-Qaeda terrorists have presented themselves as fighting a holy war, a jihad. To justify this war, they exploited the subtext of the people of Islam appealing to their pride, honor, identity, and nostalgia for a once glorious history. They were using religion the way Roman Catholicism justified the *Spanish Inquisition*, forcing Jews and Moors to become Christians, and the list goes on. No people or history is without an ugly side of subtext.

Seldom apparent in terms of content and context hides the true nature of the subtext of a situation.

[*In 711 Islamic Moors crossed the Strait of Gibraltar and onto the Iberian Peninsula, conquered Visigoth Christians and established Islam culture in Hispania. The Moors brought science, mathematics, architecture, literature, art and their religion to Spain, which to this day emanates through the subtext of Spanish history. Nearly 800 years later (1478), the Spanish Catholic Church desiring to reestablish its culture and dominants introduced The Inquisition, a manifestation of subtext.*]

Interestingly, your last word is "progress," seeing tolerance for Islam and Muslims a sign of progress. I see it as a common sign of decency for differences.

Everyone thinks progress is good, at least most Americans. General Electric once boasted *"Progress is our most important product."* Progress is as deceptive a word as is Islam or Christianity. African Americans understand what I mean by this.

Everyone influenced by such words thinks they understand and are simply dealing with the content and context of matters when it is subtext that is ruling the day, and not necessarily wisely.

Spain wouldn't be as Spain is today without the invasion of the Moors from North Africa in the eighth century. Nor would Europe be Europe without the Moors who would dominate well into the sixteenth century. The Moors brought with them to Europe art, literature, architecture, mathematics, science and culture, a culture of black men who taught discipline, military knowhow and tolerance.

Shakespeare would capture something of this with his "Othello" in the sixteenth century.

My views about the Moors were influenced by a Catholic nun, Sister Mary Cecile. She was my seventh and eighth grade teacher at St. Patrick's School, introducing me to the Moors and the influence of the Moor culture on Spain and other Europeans. It has never left me.

No, I have no love for terrorists of any stripe, but I have no fear of a new mosque going up in my neighborhood, or of a family of Muslims moving in next door.

Thank you and keep thinking and reflecting.

THE SUBTEXT OF LIFE

&

ITS MEANING

James R. Fisher, Jr., Ph.D.
© August 30, 2009

It's always been a subtext of our secular optimism that you solve the economic problem, and all other things sort of take care of themselves. Well, we seem to be doing well on the economic side – we are doing very well – and the other things are not solving – they're compounding.

Senator Daniel Patrick Moynihan

THE PRICE OF A CELEBRITY CULTURE – AN AVERSION TO SUBTEXT

Great talent wastes its gifts when it loses contact with its subtext. Richard Burton was the greatest Shakespearean actor of his generation but sold out to Hollywood. Norman Mailer saw himself as heir apparent to Ernest Hemingway and sold out to the false bravado and high jinx of that writer, and thus became a caricature of himself.

Albert Einstein was the exception. He had similar celebrity pressures although his most productive years were before he was thirty, and he lived into his seventies. He ignored this pull of celebrity because he was well acquainted with his subtext. This was not false modesty as he truly believed he had been lucky in his discoveries. He was lucky because he got beyond the content and context of Newtonian physics to explore the subtext that was not readily apparent, a subtext that physicists for more than two hundred years had not visited because they thought the work of physics had been completed.

Talented people ultimately sell themselves out to the celebrity culture when they are adored for all the wrong reasons. The herd mentality wants the talented to appreciate it for appreciating them. Thus, the talented form a symbiotic connection with the herd in a mock embrace.

The quest for celebrity allows critics that can't write, personalities that can't act, people with little more than good looks to be television journalists, and novelists with one idea captured in scores of books. The chiaroscuro of content and context pulsates with monotonous consistency. Gore Vidal is a good writer who has never been able to rise above his angst. Hundreds have copied him.

It is a different problem for John Updike. Critic Grandville Hicks of *The Saturday Review of Literature* said of him that he wrote like an angel but had nothing to say. Updike mastered content and context with his beautiful lyrical style but was less attentive to subtext of the lives he created. He seemed satisfied to create thematic caricatures such as "Couples" and his "Rabbit" series.

Updike, a favorite of *The New Yorker*, approached the sex revolution, and the feminine and civil rights movements on a tactile level without getting caught up in the tangled web and contradictory subtext of American lives. This found many Americans, especially children of baby boomers, abandoning the traditional value system of the "common good" for the more self-centered indulgence of "personhood."

SHIFTING AMERICAN VALUES

	Common Good	Personhood
Authority	Position Power	Popularity/knowledge
Loyalty	To the organization	To self/peers
Discipline	Reward/punishment	Caring/respect
Motivation	Fear	Challenge/contribution

Updike first wanted to be a graphic artist, a cartoonist, where linearity of content and context is featured. He gravitated from that to studying as a painter, mastering the techniques of texture and graphic composition, but unable to grasp the subtext that makes a Picasso a Picasso, taking up his pen to write novels, short stories, and criticism of art with the fluidity of the New England Puritan that he was.

Kurt Vonnegut, Jr., born in the middle of the United States, had a different problem. He lived in the subtext and tried desperately to reach an audience in content and context. The strain became the perplexity of his life. This frustration shows in his last book "Armageddon in Retrospect" (2008). There he challenged the Mona Lisa being a perfect painting. "Listen," Vonnegut writes, "her nose is tilted to the right, OK? That means the right side of her face is a receding plane, going away from us, OK? But there is no foreshortening of her features on that side, giving the effect of three dimensions. And Leonardo could so easily have done that foreshortening. He was simply too lazy to do it."

Da Vinci may have been lazy as he lived in an exceedingly casual subtext of life. That is how he came to envision the airplane, human anatomy, the submarine, automation and other devices that rose from his subtext to break through the world of content and context. It was enough to surface such issues and let posterity finish the process.

"No wonder she (Mona Lisa) has such a cockeyed smile," Vonnegut adds. But that is precisely it. She is meant to be enigmatic. The smile reflects what is going on beyond the surface. It is the mystery of her that haunts us to this day. Were the painting as Vonnegut proposed, it is doubtful it would be a masterpiece.

There is a reason why the Bronte sisters, Jane Austen, Shakespeare, Dostoyevsky, Tolstoy and Joyce are still read. They dealt with the subtext of their stories while telling the surface story on the popular level of content and context. Hemingway escaped all his bravado, while dealing primarily with subtext in "The Old Man and the Sea," and won the *Nobel Prize for Literature* for the gamble.

Over the last sixty years, I have seen a tectonic shift from subtext to content and context as the issues, which drive behavior and are endemic to our culture, are pushed aside for the superfluous. With the lack of restrain, without the tension to sublimate, creatively has fallen into a niche.

We have failed to produce great writers, composers, painters, and architects. Noise has become music; exhibitionism has become art; glass buildings have become architecture; and the shockingly bizarre has become popular entertainment. We have become a surface disposable culture with a damaged affect.

The reader may argue, what about the great electronic breakthroughs? What about them? Alas, what could be a better example of the charge!

Computers have been around for sixty years but have been perfected and made available to support people's lives at the content and context level as never before. We have innovation, not invention; replication, not creation; fads and fantasies, not transcendence.

Jobs and Wozniak were making electronic games when Jobs happened on the personal computer at Xerox, which management refused to fund, and so Jobs stole it. Bill Gates won the software contract with IBM by default when the wife and partner of a husband-wife company wanted more assurances. Gates wanted none because he basically had nothing but his boldness to sell. He quickly acquired the software from another fledgling company for peanuts and was off to the races, two decades later the richest man in the world has created his wealth on the foundation of other people's ideas.

DOUBLE-EDGED "CUT & CONTROL" HISTORY OF HUMAN CULTURE

We have just experienced a global economic meltdown that terrified advanced societies from one end of the globe to the other, a meltdown that to this moment is viewed in terms of content and context with hardly a glance at the subtext of the calamity. True, mention is made of our inclination to live high now and pay for it later. That is hardly profound.

Economics has proven a faulty profession, as has management. I wrote this in *"Work Without Managers"* (1991):

"We desperately need minds with a natural affinity for culture in the boardrooms across America, as well as in every other walk of professional life. We need poetry in commerce, government and industry. Engineers, economists, and political scientists have done about all the damage we can stand, perhaps more than we can absorb.

"Economists, for one, readily admit they are operating in a fog. From former Chairman of the Federal Reserve, Arthur Burns ("The rules of economics are not working quite the way they used to.") to Milton Friedman ("I believe that we economists in recent years have done vast harm by claiming more than we

can deliver."); from former Secretary of Treasury Michael Blumenthal ("I
*really think the economic profession is close to bankruptcy in understanding
the situation, before or after the fact.") to Juanita Kreps, former Secretary of
Commerce, when asked if she would go back to Duke University upon leaving
government ("I wouldn't know what to teach.").* (WWMs pp. 253 – 254)

Economists have always been enamored of algorithms and mathematical
models, analysis at the content and context level, while management has
treated people as things to be managed. Now they all have egg on their faces.

Geopolitics has also proven a faulty profession. Little time has been devoted
to the subtext of why the *Twin Towers of New York City* were destroyed.
Instead, there has been a visceral response at the content and context level of
military preemptive war. This response has put the United States and its future
in economic and political jeopardy without yielding cost benefit equal to the
investment in life and capital.

Much talk is about the recession being behind us, but what is ahead? Inflation?
The world sits on the precipice of inflation and a repeat recession/depression.
This is a matter of subtext.

We glory in instant communication where everyone has a cell phone,
BlackBerry, computer, or laptop busying themselves with the nonsense of
white noise. Electronics have become a form of addiction in this *Information
Age.* No longer is drunk driving the only major cause of deaths on our
highways and byways, but people tweeting on their electronic contraptions.

No one seems to be looking at the downside of this paradigm shift, which has
elevated content and context to the status of a new religion. We have cut
existence away from the way it was into a new sense of reality, a reality that
gained something desired – instant access and communication with others –
but at the expense of something lost – personal intimacy and rational stability.

It has been a "cut and control" journey throughout man's history. During the
hunting and gathering period 12,000 years ago, matriarchal society ruled and
there were no boundaries.

Agriculture followed under a patriarchal society where property and
boundaries were defined and defended.

This led to an industrial society where owners ruled, and cities grew. This broke up the cohesive harmony and domestic culture of life on the farm as young families flocked to the cities to work. They found themselves living in cramped unsanitary tenement houses imprisoned in squalor and crushing poverty, slaves to inanimate machines.

The gap between "haves and have nots" grew, as society moved swiftly through the modern management class to and through the postmodern era of capitalists, as managers first replaced owners, and then these managers were replaced by indifferent stockholders who valued profits above people.

This elevated finance, an industry that produces nothing but exchange rates, to become the ultimate power broker in the persons of investment bankers and venture capitalists. As significant differentiators, power shifted from people to property to products to floating capital.

This all came down as a crushing nightmare in 2008 when the wonder of electronic transfer of complex derivatives sped out of control as capital was leveraged thousands of times greater than its capacity to honor its debt as the "cut & control" journey of 12,000 years found the subtext of life once more breaking through the content and context of existence. Man keeps pushing forward blindly and incomprehensively, and then wonders what he has done wrong.

ALL TOO HUMAN

As a person who has worked about the globe, and who has thought about such things, I have concluded the subtext of life is the controller. This is not the life presented to the public or to friends, but the life that is the puppet master of us all, speaking either of the nature of enterprise or of our individual fates.

Imagine a rubber band with certain elasticity. We know a new rubber band has much more elasticity than a much-often used one. In the human psyche we don't look at elasticity, or flexibility in terms of use or age. We think we have the moxie, whatever the circumstances, to find our way out of our indiscretions. We don't believe we have nine lives like a cat but ninety-nine lives, and of course that is where the fallacy lies.

Think of people caught in embarrassing or shameful acts. Now think of all the people who lie for them, feel sorry for them, buy into their cheap excuses for shameful behavior, behavior that is repeated with little evidence of learning, and you have the making of a psychological crippled culture and society.

That person cold in the morgue killed by a hit and run driver has no sense of social justice and goes to his maker without anyone taking responsibility for his early demise.

I once knew a young man who went to the bachelor party of a friend. He didn't drink and when the party got ruckus he chose to leave and walk the two miles home. It was eleven o'clock.

He worked his job religiously, didn't make much money, lived alone in a modest apartment, read books, and that is how I got to know him. He read mine. He would discuss them intelligently and critically and I grew to respect him. Then one day, 42-years-of-age, he was no more.

It is assumed some drunken fool hit him, knocked him a hundred feet leaving him to die, his shoes left at the point of impact. There is a chance the person was so intoxicated that he didn't know he hit the man. The shoes however were fifteen feet off the road. His death is a cold case now ten years old, which is unlikely to ever be reopened.

I have no sympathy for drunks, no sympathy for people who smoke themselves to death, no sympathy for drug addicts because I have no sympathy for people who are unaware of the subtext of their lives, while friends and family don't have the courage to remind them of this fact. There is complicity here. We don't go haywire, alone.

It is in the subtext that the health of the elasticity of life is discovered. Nor will I accept that alcoholism and drug addiction are diseases. They are choices. They are people who choose to ignore their reduced elasticity, which is apparent in the subtext of life. Through artificial stimulation they promote the illusion they have much greater flexibility and elasticity than they have. The subtext of life reminds us we are dying a little every day and therefore should make the most of our days, not hide from them.

The subtext of life will not allow us to fool ourselves. The embezzler knows he is committing a crime but deludes himself that he will never get caught, justifying the behavior in rationalizations: his wife is dying of cancer, his sons need money for prep school, and he has the right to a better lifestyle given the many years of service in which he has been taken for granted and shown little respect.

Rationalization is the product of content and context but never the subtext of the matter, which is the fear that life in sum total amounts to nothing. The embezzler's elasticity is gone, and so he says, "Why not!"

I have no sympathy for Bernard Madoff who bilked investors and companies of billions of dollars while denying the subtext of his life. He is not a bad man but a little man with an obsessive need to please and feel important, but why? The answer is in his subtext.

Then there are people who have buried terrible deeds of their past in their subconscious. Now, having resurrected themselves as religious fanatics, they believe everyone suffers the same demons as they do.

Incredibly, they often are successful in convincing people that they have the same guilt. Sin becomes the boilerplate and validation of the proselytizer's message of salvation. A flock is formed as the evangelist exploits his own subtext as that of his cult. No one seems to see the folly in this.

The flock is badgered to repent or be damned! By whom? By God, of course, because the proselytizer is the self-anointed messenger of God. The individual caught up in this charade may forget he has a right to question the messenger's legitimacy.

What we cannot question is our own decreasing elasticity, which limits what we can and cannot do.

Speaking personally, I have refused to carry my own children once they had left the home.

To attempt to do for others what they best do for themselves is to weaken their resolve and diminish them as persons. The same holds true of ourselves.

The irony is that my second child, a daughter, has attempted to carry her other siblings well into their adulthood forgiving them for their improprieties, which has stunted their growth resulting in none of them becoming truly adults.

Now, when she has come into a hard patch in her own life, her siblings are not there for her. They are callous, insensitive and unsympathetic to her ordeal, angry that she has little time to listen to them, no longer an available ear to listen to their self-imposed miseries.

"You got my text...but did you get my *subtext?*"

Nickel, Scott Nickel. Cartoon Stock snin259

Has this made her bitter? No. Has this made her vindictive? No. Has this found her angry? No. It has made her resilient. The subtext of her life has proven to have much greater elasticity than one would expect. It came about when she stopped denying its existence and finally said, "Hey! That is where my strength lies. Hey, that is why I am so understanding of my siblings. Hey, that is why I can tolerate my parents. Hey! That is why I am me!"

With this resilience, she discovered she could refocus and reenergize her efforts to go forward accepting life's bumps in the road. That is what she is now doing. She finds she is a learner not a knower, a doer not a thinker, a problem solver but in the subtext of intuition not cognitive analysis. It is working for her.

She has two beautiful children who are a projection of herself. She married a person like her siblings. She is the best thing that has happened to him. He gets into one economic strafe after another. Will he ever grow up? I don't think so. Will he ever examine the subtext of his life? Not on a bet. Will he continue to repeat the same errors? Undoubtedly. Am I being cruel and unsympathetic? After more than fifteen years of observations, I don't think so.

In my subtext, there is a very strong moral authority that has little room for waste or variance from effective utilization of one's inherent ability. With regard to this moral authority, I have failed many times, but only I know, and I have to live with that. I also know that my elasticity is practically gone. The little bit that I still possess I deposit into words, ideas, philosophies and projections of what I've learned and what I know, and what might prove helpful to others before I pass on.

Do I think I am an especially kind person? No, but I'm not a malicious person either. I don't get any satisfaction seeing other people suffer or fail. Is it important for me to be liked? No, but it is important for me to be respected.

SUBTEXT UP CLOSE AND PERSONAL

The content and context of my life would suggest that I'm mainly an intuitive person because that is what I project. But my subtext suggests that I am analytical, critical, and conceptual. The fact that the subtext has come to the surface in the evening of my years is representative of another quality, the need to leave something of value behind.

My life has been one of being very structured, disciplined and demanding of myself with little give to my elasticity on display. The irony of my subtext suggests I am most in control in chaos and confusion.

ITEM:

I was only a junior corpsman in the medical division of the flagship USS Salem CA-139. We were having military exercises in the Mediterranean with more than one hundred American ships and some 50,000 men. The gun mount in a destroyer escort "hang fired." The blast of the explosion torched the gun crew of thirteen men, badly burning several. They were brought to the Salem and treated in our hospital. Three of them died while we were attending them.

Doctors from other ships were brought on board. It was general chaos. None of these doctors had experience with badly burned trauma cases nor did any of the corpsmen. Some could not deal with the carnage. By default, I had to assume a senior role to fill the void and received an accommodation for it. I was twenty-three-years-old and learned something about myself that day that I didn't know before. Highly emotional on the surface, there is a calm in my subtext that surfaced in that crisis. It has repeatedly surfaced throughout life.

Everything seems to slow down in my mind when everything on the surface seems to be speeding up.

I am painfully aware of our limited elasticity. I know we all have a breaking point. Our elasticity can go from resilient to brittle to snapping in an instant if we are not paying attention. It may be "emotional exhaustion," "hypertension" or "mental breakdown." Psychiatry has many labels to describe our mental state: schizophrenia, a bipolar disorder, or some other mental illness.

Dr. Thomas S. Szasz, author of "The Manufacture of Madness" (1970) and "The Myth of Mental Illness" (1974), among other books, himself a psychiatrist, sees modern psychiatry using its ideology and insanity plea as a convenience to avoid confrontation with the hard, moral conflicts and social problems of the day. Clear speech, what he calls the "second sin" is missing in the prognosis. Broadly speaking, Szasz is addressing subtext.

Of course, we all talk to ourselves; of course, we all have dreams of loss, confusion and betrayal. That is part of the subtext that is the driver of behavior.

Some people are made uncomfortable because they think you can read their minds. You can't. But you can read their behavior. It speaks volumes for anyone paying attention.

You don't do this with eye contact, which is supposed to indicate sincerity, for eyes can lie. We have all become very good liars. Some people can even control their emotions to the point of passing polygraph tests with ease.

You can tell from the rhythm of what people say whether they are sincere or disingenuous. You can see from nonverbal cues in their gestures, in the care of their nails, the texture of their skin whether they are or aren't what they wish to project. Our faces are roadmaps of self-indulgence. The subtext of our lives oozes up to confirm and deny the content and context on display. We all become eventually what we are.

There are palpable warning signs before a person commits suicide; before a person takes that first dollar out of the till that doesn't belong to him. There is no such thing as an innocent cup of coffee between a man and a woman married to other people. All indicators are there and all of them are rejections of the subtext of life.

When the subtext is ignored or rejected, life becomes a lie. There is no possibility for understanding the authentic self.

My nickname is "Rube," which is commonly translated to mean a farmer, or a rustic and unsophisticated person. In other words, it is meant as a derogatory identity.

At a dinner in New York City, someone once confronted me. "I understand your nickname is 'Rube.' Is that true?"

"Yes."

"Are you comfortable with that?"

"Quite so, why do you ask?"

"You're not offended?"

"No."

"Then you're a country bumpkin?"

"If you like."

"That doesn't offend you?"

"No, why should it?"

"Do you like being called 'Rube'?"

"I love being called 'Rube'!"

"Why is that?"

"Because it's a name associated with the most wonderful time in my life growing up in the middle of the country in the middle of the century when I was catching baseball for the *Courthouse Tigers* as a kid. There was no actively I loved more. I took pride in that. I would watch catchers in *The Men's Industrial Baseball League* with a dreamy like concentration as current Hollywood director Quentin Tarantino is alleged to obsessively watch films.

"I loved putting on the 'tools of ignorance' (catcher's equipment) knowing I was the best catcher around for my age. I am Rube. Rube gave me my first taste of excellence and how to achieve it."

The irony is that I come from a farm state and have never been on a farm. My people in Ireland as well as America have always been city dwellers. My da was born in Chicago as were his parents, but his mother died in childbirth delivering him and his father took off never to be seen again. He was reared in Clinton, Iowa, a small industrial city on the Mississippi River by his grandmother. My children gravitated to metropolitan areas, no farmers in our family tree.

The subtext of the connection, however, is real. I have the down-to-earth values of farmers, a love of the seasons of the year, of the planting, fertilizing and growing of ideas, the earthy norms that identify a person with a particular place and space, the sense that a man's word is his bond, the humility that Nature knows best, and that we are all connected, stuck with our subtext as we carry our geography wherever we go.

SELF CONFIDENCE

THAT ILLUSIVE KEY

Self-Confidence: That Illusive Key to Health, Wealth & Happiness

We all have our own idea of what confidence is. Confidence is often defined in terms of believing in something or trusting someone else. For example, "We had every confidence in the staff." That is not how it is defined in these essays.

Confidence here is defined as belief and trust in oneself. It is being comfortable in one's own skin and therefore equal to the tasks at hand. Confidence has nothing to do with feeling certain.

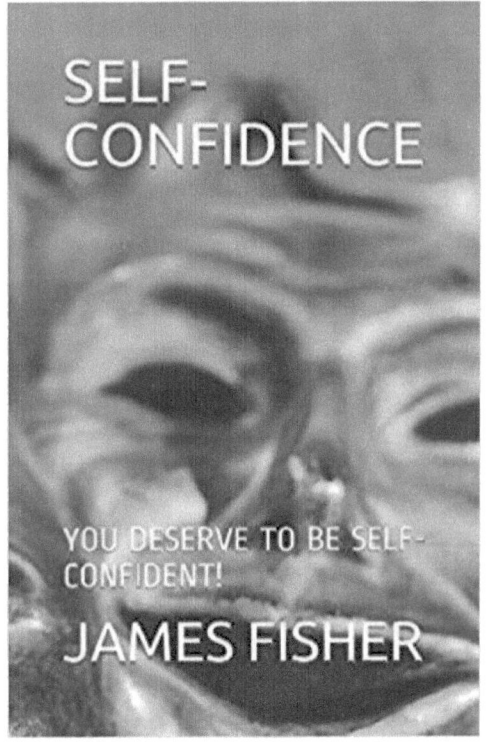

Nor does a confident person display superiority or preeminence in any way. On the contrary, the confident person recognizes his limitations, but is resolute in developing himself within those parameters. He knows that he may sometimes falter, prove less than equal to the task, but he will not get down on himself. Instead, he will learn from the situation and add it to the bank of his experience in moving forward.

Confidence is not something learned in a book, taking a course, attending a seminar, or following a set of rules. Confidence is a mindset, a state of mind.

Norman Vincent Peale published *"The Power of Positive Thinking"* (1952) after WWII, which was a collection of inspirational essays. It captured the mind of the time looking for a simple formula to regroup and go forward after the terrible trauma and sacrifice of that Great War.

Dr. Peale advised his readers in this self-help book that confidence can be attained by *positive thinking* through practice, training, and knowledge by talking to people. It was a rote agenda that fit the natural American inclination to optimistic thinking.

This rationale has survived despite a retinue of seemingly constant anxious and depressing issues. It is all right to see the glass half full, but it is equally all right to wonder about how to fill the other half of the glass. The confident person is dedicated to that quest.

Confidence cannot be taught. It can only be experienced. Confidence is the accumulative effect of learned experience. In chemistry, the valence of the atom determines the vigor with which atoms combine with other atoms of the opposite charge. The higher the valence the greater the activity.

Confidence mirrors this physical chemical phenomenon. To state it another way, the confident person embraces his anxieties rather than retreating from them. I learned this first hand as a chemical sales engineer making cold calls to prospects in the field. At first, I didn't want to make the calls. My hands would sweat, my temples would ache, and I was afraid I would stutter, embarrassing myself and looking stupid. But I had no choice. I had a young family to feed and I was a long way from my home roots. So, you could say I was motivated.

Once I broke the ice, once I made that first call, and then the next, and the next after that, I learned an important lesson about confidence. My contacts were at first as nervous as I was, apprehensive that I was there to take advantage of them. We worked through this awkward stage by talking and listening, developing common ground, and getting to know each other. *In the process, we found we were not buyer and seller adversaries, but partners attempting to solve a problem.*

It is natural for us to put up a shield of resistance as self-protection when we encounter a stranger no matter what the circumstances. Time and good intentions reduce the icy distance but not before encountering some combative resistance.

Remember others must break through their own wall of distrust. The irony is that it becomes easier for us once we break through our own self-distrust. Once we establish self-trust, it is catching. Without a word, it leads to dissolving the distrust of others.

Once I had that insight, I was on my way to self-confidence.

Confidence comes from feelings of well-being, a product of self-awareness and self-acceptance, not self-absorption. The mind, body, and spirit are focused on giving, not getting. This is learned behavior through experience. It is where the unknown and unpredictable are encountered, where criticism and disappointment are endured, and where surprise and failure become the ingredient of success.

Experience can build to confidence if we are willing to learn from every nuance of that involvement.

By nature, I am shy, introverted, reclusive and introspective. In the field, I found this not to be a handicap but an asset because I had a natural inclination to read people and the situation. Also, I was more comfortable listening than talking. I didn't understand it, at the time, but listening eases the discomfort of others by putting them in control giving them power over the situation.

By asking questions and directing the conversation to your purpose, you put yourself in control by not controlling the conversation. The traditional belief is that the extrovert makes the best salesperson, executive, public speaker, and leader. That has not been my experience.

Those happiest in the quiet of thought are apt to get inside words spoken, gestures made, and protests expressed because they are listeners, not talkers; learners, not tellers. Perhaps that is why I started out to be a chemist. Soon after, I realized I did not think like a bench chemist and lacked the mechanical dexterity to set up experiments but did have a conceptual sense.

The first challenge of self-confidence is self-discovery, that is, the personal struggle within. Confidence must first be felt before it can be leveraged to advantage. Since confidence is not a static measure, our confidence may fluctuate in the performance of our tasks or in our role relationships with others from day to day, but the intuitive experience that gave you that self-confident edge through self-discovery is always there. Like anything else, it has to be nurtured.

THE FISHER PARADIGM®©™ & CONFIDENCE

This realization led to the *Fisher Paradigm©™®* which is an intuitive diagnostic tool based on a simple formula: *the definition of a noun, which is of a person, place or thing.*

It can serve in any situation, but especially where there is a degree of uneasiness or tension. It is the prehensile reptilian brain being engaged. The heart is racing, the mind close to panic. Our reptilian brain comes to the fore. It is a survival mechanism man has relied on throughout human history. It gives us instant insight into the situation with an ability to calibrate the discomfort and even the danger. Yes, our whole body and mind feels the situation. It involves thinking with our whole body, not just our mind. This means allowing ourselves to feel the situation instantly with that evaluating signaling how we should act.

This paradigm is divided into three separate dimensions:

- *The Personality Profile.*

Personality is our acquired self.

It is the learned behavior that sets us off from other people so that others can say, "Oh, that is Jim Fisher," because that is how they see me acting. *Personality* is subject to change as circumstances change, and a person is apt to act differently in private than in public as we all wear masks, and these masks are part of our personality.

Personality involves the constant changing of these masks that we all wear. Moreover, our personality in private may differ again in public as the circumstances change or as our emotional state changes. The point is that personality is not static, and our intuitive senses can detect fluctuations in ourselves and in others so that we may deal with them accordingly.

- *Geographic Profile*

A sense of Place takes on a territorial imperative in terms of our familiarity with a place and our comfort level.

We carry a sense of place with us wherever we go. In popular parlance, we are apt to say we can move from New York City to Tampa, Florida but we carry our psychic baggage with us. That baggage, of course, is our personality.

If we are in a place of ease, our self-confidence, caring and carefreeness come to the fore. Conversely, if the place is not familiar and our ease level deserts us, our awareness is heightened, and our reptilian brain comes into play. It calibrates the unease and danger level of the situation or simply our discomfort with the unfamiliar.

We know some people are comfortable wherever they go, never seeming to meet a stranger, then there are others who are uncomfortable wherever they are. This in a peculiar way is an index of our self-awareness and self-acceptance or lack of the same which is the necessary precursors to self-confidence. We will always have difficulty with self-confidence if we cannot find it within ourselves to be our own best friend.

Some people are never comfortable in their own skin no matter where they are or with whom they find themselves. *Place* is designated as the *Geographic Profile*.

In other words, our personal baggage accompanies our geography. Our baggage includes our belief system along with our values, interests, and biases. *Place* is obvious in our speech patterns, syntax, semantics, use of words and comfort level with ideas. It is also apparent nonverbally expressed in our countenance, demeanor, and our carriage. *Geographic Profile* is an index of our cultural DNA.

- Our *Demographic Profile*

This relates to our essence. Essence is our real self, or our inherited gene pool.

Essence cannot be changed or modified. Essence simply is. Essence determines whether we are short or tall, light or dark skinned, intelligent or not. It is our genetic DNA.

We can change our personality, but we cannot change our essence. We can deny it, mask it, or fabricate it, but we cannot change it. It is for this reason that it is our *Demographic Profile.* It is what we are but not necessarily who we are.

As permanent and fixed as our essence is, this can be misread especially by a strong and convincing personality. For example, we may assume someone is intelligent because he reads books, can quote authors impressively, and carries the patina of brilliance. Politicians use this device, so do academics, as do gurus and experts of every ilk.

One of the most intuitive lessons to learn about the *Demographic Profile* is that intelligence is not an I.Q. score. *Intelligence is what it does.* Measure the *Demographic Profile* in terms of the person's actual history, experience, and character and how he handles adversity and disappointment as well as success. The *Demographic Profile* is the report card we receive every day of our existence.

"It wasn't quick thinking; it was everything else!"

To give a quick glance of how the mind, body and soul reacts to a sense of danger, consider this example. I was making an organization development (OD) intervention in the Fairfax County Police Department, Fairfax, Virginia. A riot had broken out in Herndon in the African American section of that community after a white police officer shot and killed an unarmed black youth in a 7-Eleven convenient store after an altercation.

When I interviewed plain clothed detectives about that incident, and asked sensitive questions, they would invariably adjust their shoulder holsters through their suit coats.

Later, I was invited by an Iowa government official to dinner and a play, who was in the Nation's capital on Iowa State business. He had earlier attended a seminar I had given in Kansas City and extended the invitation after learning that I was an Iowa native.

My hotel in Fairfax City was twelve miles from Washington, D.C. A Fairfax County police officer provided my transportation. After the play, the police officer said he would pick me up about 1 a.m. I said, "No problem," as I am a walker.

Walking down Pennsylvania Avenue of the Nation's capital at this early hour, I thought of a U.S. Senator from Mississippi who had been stabbed and robbed in this area and nearly died. Three youths walking parallel to me on the other side of the street, several lanes comfortably separating us, brought this memory to the fore, but not yet with noticeable apprehension.

Two blocks later these youth raced ahead and crossed the street to my side and were jiving and kibitzing as I closed the distance between us. My prehensile antennae went up as my mind said, *this can't be happening!*

Somehow, I reacted intuitively and continued to walk jauntily towards them. When I was two yards from them, I adjusted my mock shoulder holster, as I had seen those plain clothes detectives do in my interviews, and said, "Little late, isn't it boys? Going to be hard to get up for school."

The three faces froze, looked nervously at each other, then they allowed me to pass. When I was five yards past them, they said in unison, "There goes the fuzz," and laughed nervously.

When I told the Fairfax County police officer what had happened, he said simply, "I'll tell you one thing. You're one lucky bastard. That quick thinking may have saved your life."

It wasn't quick thinking. It was the *Fisher Paradigm*©™® that kicked in.

CONFIDENCE & SELF-ESTEEM

Confidence and self-esteem are not the same thing, although often erroneously linked as synonymous. Self-esteem is more the equivalent of self-respect. It is earned by doing something that in turn registers on the psyche with self-approval.

Confidence is developed through experience as a learner not a knower, as a listener and not a teller, as an observer and not an obtrusive evaluator.

Self-esteem is colored with the biases we hold for other people and can be quite disruptive if we are not self-aware. Simply put, self-esteem is how we feel about ourselves, or would like to give the impression we feel, and is therefore value intensive. We can have high self-esteem and low competence, or low self-esteem and high competence. Self-esteem and competence are not necessarily correlative. The point is to be weary of mixing the two.

This collection of essays endeavors to establish this fundamental premise: failure is as much a part of success as confidence is a product of experience. We all make mistakes; we all register failures; we do so because we are all human. If in our life's adventure, we flunk an academic course or flunk out of school; are fired from a job; are rejected by a loved one or find ourselves very much alone, we are on the cusp of being introduced to ourselves, perhaps for the first time.

Chances are we have been living on automatic pilot. It is time to focus and pay attention evaluating where we are and how we got to this place and space, and what we plan to do about it, now. It is often when we hit bottom that the road less traveled to self-confidence is the road we are already on.

Every experience is a learning experience telling us something about ourselves and where we are, saying:

You are in the wrong place and space with the wrong people to realize your true potential. It is time to move on to where the culture and circumstances better fits your talent and temperament. It is telling you that the time is now.

Good luck in that endeavor.

THE MOST IMPORTANT SALE YOU'LL EVER MAKE!

James R. Fisher, Jr., Ph.D.

© November 26, 2012

"When young, we trust ourselves too much, and we trust others too little when we are old. Rashness is the error of youth; timid caution when old. Manhood is the isthmus between the two extremes, the ripe and fertile seas of action when, only, we can hope to find the head to contrive, united with the hand to execute."

Caleb Colton, Nineteenth Century English Clergyman

"Trust men and they will be true to you, treat them greatly and they will show themselves great."

Ralph Waldo Emerson, Nineteenth Century American poet and essayist

IMPORTANCE OF SELF-CONFIDENCE

*"**With confidence**, you can do anything your mind envisions."* This is the opening lines of *Confident Selling* (1971).

"Confidence is the antidote to fear; fear rooted in self-ignorance. With self-understanding comes confidence followed by tolerance for our own false steps and failures. As we face down our fears, we rise above obstacles we once thought were utterly beyond our control."

Now, why would I say that? Why would I write about confidence, fear and control in the same paragraph? The simple reason is that I have learned:

- *If I thought it, the deed was already half done.*

This could be taken as arrogance to the extreme. There is a litany of reasons to discourage us from doing what our hearts and minds tell us we can do.

- *That is the problem; people are afraid to believe in themselves.*

Therefore, they do not take that first step. They wait for approval from others. They wait for someone to push them over the line into action. They wait until the line becomes a wall. They hang out with people who say they are where they belong while envying those with the confidence to move on. They wait for confirmation that they are on the right track when they are not on any track at all.

- *You know who these people are. They hang out together.*

They are waiting for the right time to make a move. They are waiting until they have enough education, enough money, enough support, enough love and affection to take the risk.

- *They wait until one day they run out of life.*

They are *the gonna be's* and the *gonna do's* and are always going to do these things tomorrow. They never make it because they never made the most important sale in their lives, belief in themselves come hell or high water.

BUSINESS OF CONFIDENCE – THE GROUND FLOOR

Confidence often identifies with one's hero or some special person. Reading is not only a gauge to explore the unknown but a window to knowing the self.

BUSINESS OF CONFIDENCE – IDENTITY

Someone may ask you, *"Who are you?"* Then before you have a chance to answer, they ask you another question, *"What are you?"*

The questioner could be a parent, friend, wife or husband, brother or sister, boss or teammate. We sometimes confound others as well as ourselves as to who we are or mean to be.

Identity is personal and is largely the product of what we do (our work), what we enjoy doing (our leisure), who we hang out with (our friends), and what organizations we belong to and support (church, school, club), for these indices are metaphorically stenciled on our subconscious.

Ask yourself these two questions: Who Am I? What am I?

How you answer will give you a sense of your comfort level with the person you are.

BUSINESS OF CONFIDENCE: WHAT IS CONFIDENCE?

Confidence is not having a sense of superiority; confidence is being engaged.

- *Confidence is the ability to act to completion on something of value to you and to others.*

Confidence is not about half measures, not about looking for approval, or reasons to succeed. Likewise, it is not about finding excuses to abort the chase because it is too difficult.

- *Confidence is about commitment and involvement. With them, you are already half way there so stay the course!*

It doesn't mean going to the "right schools," having the "right teachers," having the "right pedigree," working for the "right company," or hanging out with the "right crowd." It can be all or none of these. They are incidental to the process. Nor is it about pursuing the *favorite career-of-the-day* or doing what everyone says you should do.

- *You know in your heart what you love to do, so do it with a vengeance!*

Confidence is being well acquainted with your own history, with your failures, your successes, your false steps and disappointments, your embarrassments and your triumphs. Confidence is not mechanistic but natural, a process of growth that flows encountering peaks and valleys but is never stationary.

- *Yes, one's confidence dips and vacillates, but that only strengthens one's resolve.*

Confidence has a lot in common with moral courage rather than physical courage. I see young people today building up their muscles and flashing tattoos all over their bodies as billboards of personal identity when it projects just the opposite. It is playing to the crowd identifying with the herd.

- *Confidence is quiet. It is engaged. It has no need for show or need for kudos.*

That does not mean that confidence lacks goals. Indeed, the confident person wants:

- To complete his work to a satisfying degree; his dissertation to a Ph.D.; winning the love of his life; finding the job that he seeks; winning the advancement he pursues; launching his children successfully into life; finding fulfillment in life, love and work.

There are many obstacles to these desires, and they are primarily self-imposed.

Then there are bullies who discourage continuing effort; bullies from the inside and bullies from the outside who disguise themselves as friends and advisers.

BUSINESS OF BULLIES FROM THE INSIDE/OUTSIDE

- *"To have a friend you must be a friend starting with yourself."*

We are more inclined to trust secondary sources, including the views of friends and family more than our own counsel.

We allow ourselves to be bullied. We think of a bully as the neighborhood tough in which everyone cowers. We outgrow that tough during our early years. But we face bullies in the system every step of the way throughout life.

We meet them in teachers and preachers at school and church; in employers and colleagues at work; in pundits and politicians on the tube; in newspapers, magazines and television news, in tweets and text messages from friends and foes; with the counsel of psychiatrists, psychologists, psychotherapists; from family physicians and friends who claim to be in the know as to what is best for us. If this attention becomes our quintessential self, then we are owned by everyone else and reduced to renters of our own nature, strangers to ourselves.

- *When confidence is compromised, there is no chance for the authentic self to surface.*

Many of these secondary sources may mean no harm, but they are not you, and they are not privy to the depth and breadth of your experience. We are also bullied in the military as anyone knows who has experienced basic training in the US Army or boot camp in the US Navy, US Marine Corps or US Coastguard.

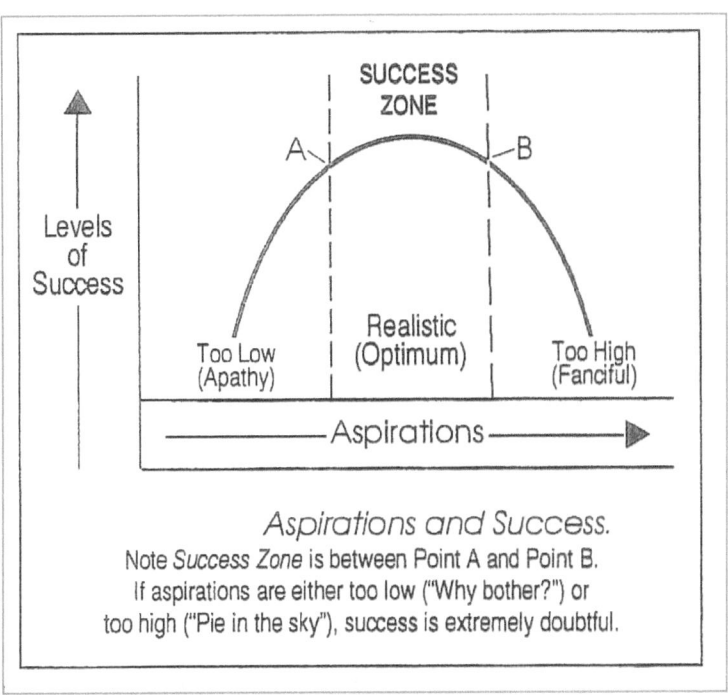

Aspirations and Success.
Note *Success Zone* is between Point A and Point B.
If aspirations are either too low ("Why bother?") or
too high ("Pie in the sky"), success is extremely doubtful.

Strangely, this kind of bullying can put us in touch with ourselves. Some have never before experienced the discipline that is fundamental to a military training encounter. Many have found this regimental and ritualistic training a window to maturity and self-understanding. In the military, you are treated fairly in a regimented protocol to alert you to the dangers and opportunities to military combat.

That said, there are no bullies that equal academic bullies, as academics have little power or prestige other than the power of the grade over the student, which kicks into high gear when a student completes all the course work requirements to a Ph.D. but for the acceptance of the dissertation.

Mean spirited academics have been known to break the student's will, especially if that student is not obsequious, but instead arrogant and opinionated if not also given to challenging the authority of academics.

Consequently, instead of being a quest to demonstrate scholarship, too often seeking a Ph.D. or doctorate in the student's preferred field of study becomes instead an endurance contest forcing the student to grovel at the feet of the dissertation committee.

How else can we explain the high number of students tagged as being ABDs (i.e., "all but the dissertation")? Enduring years of study beyond the bachelor's degree, these students have completed the course work to a doctorate but have been unable to win acceptance of their dissertation proposal, or if they successfully succeeded that hurdle, their dissertation.

In any case, these academics have the power over the student; power the student has willingly given. Once that power is surrendered, the expectation is that the student will be treated with fairness and consideration; will be given guidance and support irrespective of personality quirks so long as the work required has been completed with due diligence and in a timely fashion. That goes out the window as many ABD's can attest if the student is considered a nemesis.

- *Unfortunately, power corrupts, and absolute power corrupts absolutely.*

Too frequently, those in charge in the workplace exploit this power with reckless abandon. For the attention, we have the world that we have today.

- *A factory mentality of academia and industry has no place in the 21st Century.*

Everything is possible despite these limitations if we have the courage to take charge of our life and develop the discipline to map out an agenda consistent with our intuitive strengths or what we do well. Should we do that, not only will we be more engaged, but everyone around us will be enjoying the same synchrony. *Confident Thinking* (2014) concludes with this suggestion:

"It is a time when we can no longer depend on others to decipher the road maps of our mind. Our mind has become homeless. That mind, Milton reminds us, is its own place, and of itself can make a heaven of hell, or a hell of heaven. The choice is ours to make. May you make that connection and soar to grace, greatness and fulfillment."

FEAR, YOUR TICKET TO
A SECOND-HAND LIFE

When I was in industry, we had a policy of holding quarterly seminars. It fell to a different manager to be the host, once per year. Each manager tried to outdo his peers. After one such meeting, everyone was congratulating the host. He took the praise well enough but turned on his adulators with the question: "Why do you think I worked so hard on this?

This was met with dead silence matched only with puzzled expressions. "I'll tell you why," he continued, "It was simply the fear of failure."

This candid admission led to frank exchanges which followed the fear line summed up with the comment, "I think that shoe fits us all. No one likes to get hammered."

Finally, as if an afterthought, I was asked my view. I had a great temptation to fall in line with the others, but I had thought too hard about the idea of fear to con myself now. "What drives me to do my best," I said evenly, "is the effective utilization of my inherent ability."

The reaction was immediate. It echoed around the room with the needling phrase, "How did we ever get a guy like you in this outfit?" Once the nervous laughter subsided, I smiled. "Isn't it just a matter of chemistry, gentlemen, opposite charges attracting?" Even in jest there was a grain of truth as what I was expressing was the complement to the negative, fear, which is confidence.

James R. Fisher, Jr., *Confident Selling,* Prentice-Hall Publisher, 1971.

No country can give itself a new past. But it can alter the future and help change its identity by quitting its self-conscious fixation on its glorious past and embrace its fear of the future.

Dare to ask why this nation is stuck in a very different way than the rest of the world? Could it be fear of the future? Fear is on display in contentious and divisive polarity across the nation as if unable to rise above the immature temperament of six graders squabbling on the playground while leading essentially second-hand lives. How so?

The "spoiled brat" generation is now in charge, euphemistically referred to as "baby boomers."

They are reluctantly moving off stage, leaving something of a vacuum, now in their sixties and early seventies having perfected the habit of living second hand lives by aping each other in dress and manner, speech and morals, attitude and values.

Victor Hugo compared such conformity to prison. In any case, this conformity has made these Americans indistinct from each other as they have gravitated to what is esteemed rather than preferred, leaving their children, the new millennials, confused as to what they believe and stand for. Millennials, consequently, are indifferent to authority and tradition, to institutions and religion, to manners and morals for they look at all this with naked eyes.

While the *"spoiled brat" generation* likely had parents and grandparents who felt it their duty to serve their country in the military, few of this generation has followed that example. Where their parents and grandparents knew scarcity and the pain of constant struggle as the nation limped through the *Great Depression* and then embraced the uncertainties and sacrifices of the *Great War* (WWII), they came into the world in the economic booming years of the postwar that followed.

Their parents and grandparents unwisely attempted to shield the precious egos of their offspring from pain and struggle, self-doubt and failure, discrimination and bias, delayed gratification and disappointment to experience the *Rites of Passage* with no significant obstacles in the way.

Church was unwittingly the casualty of this obsession, which at one time elevated man beyond himself to unite with his God, while conformity and appetite has forced man down to flesh against flesh with desire crushing him deeper into himself. Today, as a consequence of this predilection, we are spiraling out of control.

When you only know plenty and have never had to activate your reptilian brain for survival, you retreat from adulthood as you plan never to grow old or be forced to grow up.

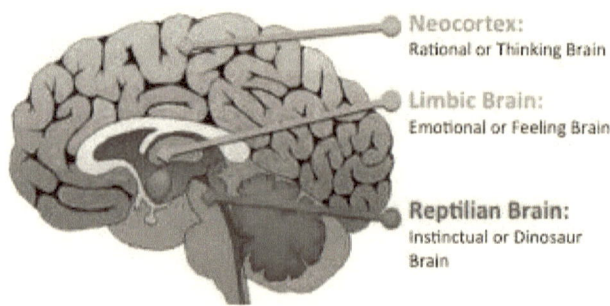

People seem surprised that a member of the *"spoiled brat" generation* would be elevated by popular vote to the *President of the United States*, yet that has happened with the president behaving characteristically consistent with that prototype. In retrospect, the rise of a Donald John Trump to the presidency was as inevitable as the consistency of meteorological tides.

*   *   *

Over one hundred years ago the *First World War* (1918) ended. It was followed by the *"Roaring Twenties"* with a relaxation of traditional social barriers, including an economic run on the banks with wild speculation on Wall Street.

Ninety years ago, the *Great Depression* (1929) hit, throwing the United States and the world of commerce into crippling inflation and massive unemployment that found 25 percent of the American labor force unemployed.

Life became a crushing daily struggle for most Americans while, paradoxically, most families maintained the stability of two parent homes as divorce, crime, and vagrancy were low. Through it all, self-sustaining identification and stoic resolve prevailed against oppressive poverty. Presidential politics (re: US President Herbert Hoover) were blamed for the *Great Depression*, as often happens when a national scapegoat is needed to explain a situation driven by other more complex circumstances.

This led to the inauguration of what would become a four-term president (Franklin Delano Roosevelt) and to the *"New Deal,"* which was essentially a social-democratic agenda that changed the template of American society, and the will of the people.

President Roosevelt pieced together a *welfare system* taking the power and control of survival from the people (*Social Security System*) and corporate pursuits from industry and commerce (*tax concessions*) changing forever representative democracy into a shell game for lobbyists.

To wit, this strategy and policy failed to energize banks, revitalize Wall Street, or, indeed, make a significant dent in either inflation or national unemployment. That would be provided by Europe when *Adolf Hitler* came to power as Germany's Chancellor through the democratic elective process.

Eighty years ago (1939), Adolf Hitler, now operating as Germany's dictator, invaded Poland with Great Britain declaring war on Germany, initiating *World War Two*. The United States would enter the war two years later once the *Empire of Japan* bombed the *US Naval Base of the 7th Fleet* at Pearl Harbor in Honolulu on December 7, 1941. The war, the most devastating in history, decimated Europe and much of Asia leaving only continental United States untouched with such massive destruction.

Seventy years ago (1945) the United States dramatically ended the war in the Pacific and the will of the Japanese people by dropping two atomic bombs on the cities of Hiroshima and Nagasaki in August 1945, killing more than 100,000 people, thus ending *World War Two*.

Estimates of the number of deaths attributed to WWII vary between 50 and 80 million. Meanwhile, the stigmata of that war and the devastation of that atomic bombing lurk in the memory of civilization to this day as if a bad dream. In a curious way, it has led to essentially world peace in the 21st century.

American industry from 1942 to the conclusion of WWII created the greatest war machine known to man. The war effort also led to full employment although Americans had to endure rationing of household goods, along with delayed gratification for such luxuries as new automobiles, boats, household appliances, clothing fashions, construction materials and leisure ware.

Sixty years ago (1958) the economic boom was in full swing and Americans were swimming in cash no longer experiencing restrain or delayed gratification buying houses, cars, boats, clothes, taking luxurious vacations, having children, and then giving them everything they wanted but not necessarily needed, forgetting why or how they came to be so fortunate.

Consumption became therapy for delicate psyches not used to struggle or failure or delayed gratification as the new lexicon was, "See it, feel it, have it, do it now!"

Communities of a thousand new homes in the suburbs seemed to spring up everywhere as if overnight. Most Americans had jobs and good incomes with a compulsion to imitate and emulate the rich and famous with homes that mirrored theirs, but more modestly with attached garages of one, two, or three spaces for automobiles. Paved driveways and manicured lawns were part of the imitation on postage stamp pieces of real-estate. Hugh factories and giant interstate highways of concrete crisscrossed the country over what was once fertile farmland.

Suddenly, with no discernible barriers, parents and their children retreated deeper into themselves to entertain the luxury of worrying about their delicate psyches.

The shrinking of America into a psychological nation was now established. The new priests were psychologists, psychotherapists, mystics and gurus. Paradoxically, rather than this army of palliative prescribers calming anxiety, the attention seemed only to spike anxiety creating a counter dependent industry whose greatest product was the quality of their listening and tolerance for people suspended in adolescence.

Meanwhile, children in school or play now had to be given awards for their participation, as no one must be stained with the stigma of failure, of losing, or unable to keep up with others. Elitism was anathema as the drive was toward relentless mediocrity and cultural sameness.

Grades escalated in elementary and high school, and then even at our most prestigious universities. For no other reason than because we could, Americans came to believe in *American exceptionalism*, failing to realize that Russia lost 20 million (military and civilians) and Germany and the Allies nearly as many (military and civilians), while America lost 400,000 and almost no civilians as no battle was ever fought on the continental United States.

The 1950s marked the appearance of Hugh Hefner who exploited the mood of the times with *Playboy Magazine*, becoming the Marquis de Sade of his generation promulgating his narcissistic Playboy philosophy to an eager affluent audience of self-indulgent males who had too much time on their hands.

Fifty years ago (1968) everything in the United States commenced to unravel. It was as if a knife cut through the fabric of American history separating 1968 and the past from the future. To wit:

In January, the USS Pueblo was captured by North Korea; the Viet Cong launched the Tet offensive in Vietnam;

In April, Martin Luther King, Jr. was assassinated; Columbia University students seized administrative buildings; 367 students were injured in student peace riots in Paris;

In June, Senator Robert Kennedy was assassinated; the *"Poor Peoples March"* descended on Washington, DC to promote economic justice and parity for poor people;

In August, Richard Milhous Nixon was nominated for president at the *Republican Presidential Convention in Miami*; Soviet tanks rolled into Czechoslovakia ending the "Prague Spring"; riots broke out at the *Democratic Presidential Nominating Convention in Chicago* led by the "Chicago Seven";

In October, at the Olympic Games in Mexico City, two American African American sprinters defied tradition at the awards ceremonies with "Black Power" salutes as the US National Anthem was played.

In November, Nixon was elected president; in December, the Pueblo was released by North Korea; and Apollo 8 circled the moon.

In the span of the twelve months that followed, America experienced the *Woodstock Music Festival*, the *Battle of Hamburger Hill,* the *occupation of Alcatraz*, the *collapse of moral boundaries on stage* (with "Oh!

Calcutta!"), *on screen* ("Midnight Cowboy"), *and in print* ("Everything You Always Wanted to Know about Sex but Were Afraid to Ask").

"There are two limiting conditions in our cranial cellular congress to coping with reality. The brain capacity to process information is finite, and the machinery with which to do it is not a conscious unit. When the space requirements of the problems fit the network, things go well; when things don't, they go to hell." **William L. Livingston IV**

Human Coping Limits

Single Problem Bigger
Than Human Capacity

MORE COMPLEX

MORE SIMPLE

Single Human Capacity
Bigger Than Problem

This also marked the genesis of the *Gay Rights Movement;* introduced the era of the *"no fault" divorce;* marked the rise of the *Silent Majority;* and solidified the *Peace Movement* of young people who now burned their draft cards and fled to Canada to avoid serving in the *US Military and the Vietnam War.*

It also marked the explosive growth of the pornography industry that successfully sought shelter under the *First Amendment of the Constitution* leading to a multi-billion-dollar industry.

Forty years ago (1970s), the sanctity of the home was essentially derailed as children became their own parents as parents were now too busy making double incomes to keep pace with the financial demands of their extravagant lifestyles, thus having little time for domestic responsibilities.

Children were given "things" rather than love or time and attention from their parents. No surprise, children came to associate love with material substitutes. Chaos followed.

The abrupt decline of parental authority was in turn manifested in the classroom, which more resembled a war zone than a learning laboratory. Crime was on the rise and out of control with the president (Nixon) declaring "War on Crime" and then "War on Drugs." Neither war proved an effective deterrent.

The unpopular *Vietnam War* led to cover ups, which in turn led to corruption as politicians first deceived the electorate and then themselves which reached a crescendo with *The Watergate Scandal.*

Drugs at all levels of society were now in children's hands as parental discipline was now a charade, while adults came to mimic their children in dress and tastes, manners and behavior.

New forms of bigotry and hatred were hatching as scapegoats to offset personal anxiety and unhappiness. Meanwhile, European and Japanese automobile manufacturers were eating America's lunch, only to have an energy crisis rock the land with OPEC's oil embargo.

President Nixon, forever paranoid, became a law unto himself while Congress stayed the same, missed the changes, couldn't face them, leaving the future up for grabs.

Today, forty years later, the 1970s now a bitter memory, the United States remains a divisive and polarized nation with Democratic and Republican members of Congress stoking the fires of discontent by throwing abuse at each other rather than finding reason for compromise leading to a nation in constant turmoil and gridlock.

Problems have become too complex to consider much less solve.

Problems require facing our fears, our ineptitude, our incompetence and, yes, our lack of initiative and originality. Instead, what is feared is uniqueness; of people of difference; of people who don't see all news as "fake news"; of people who don't have to tattoo most of their bodies to have a sense of identity; of people who don't have to look to experts to tell them what is important and what is not; of people who don't have to follow a diet or belief system currently a bestseller; of people who don't worry about what other people think before they form their own opinions; of people who aren't afraid to differ with the prevailing norm; of people not interested in getting something for nothing; of people who believe in themselves without pretending to have no faults; of people who accept themselves as they are and other people as they find them.

The latter is an expression of "tolerance" that is seriously missing from the conversation of the day. That is because most people are too busy living second hand lives.

A PALLIATIVE TO ANXIETY

James R. Fisher, Jr., Ph.D.
© June 13, 2014

Palliative: to reduce the violence of a disease; to moderate or reduce the intensity of anxiety.

The evidence is overwhelming that we live in an "Age of Anxiety." If one penetrates below the surface of political, economic, business, professional, or domestic crises to discover their psychological causes, or if one seeks to understand modern art, poetry or philosophy or religion, one runs athwart the problem of anxiety at almost every turn. The ordinary stresses and strains of life in the changing world of today are such that few if any escape the need to confront anxiety and to deal with it in some manner.

Rollo May, American psychoanalyst, *The Meaning of Anxiety* (1977)

Stress is the spice of life. Without it you would be a vegetable, or dead. Stress is not something to avoid. It is the extreme of stress or distress that causes so many ailments of modern society.

Hans Selye, American born Canadian physician, *Stress Without Distress* (1974)

Anxiety is a luxury of a self-indulgent culture. It is a culture which has time on its hands. Instead of focusing on living to experience the pleasures that cost nothing, the anxious take themselves too seriously and life not seriously enough.

James R. Fisher, Jr., *Meet Your New Best Friend* (2014)

Someone must have been telling lies about Joseph K., for without having done anything wrong he was arrested one fine morning.

Franz Kafka, *The Trial* (1925)

A CHILD'S VIEW OF ANXIETY

It is no accident this is called an "anxious age." As we have moved away from the comfort of faith in God and the cultivation of a spiritual life, we have move towards melancholy and a moral crisis. We have come to expect the other shoe to fall at any moment, throwing our lives into turmoil. With the move from trust in God, we have departed from trusting ourselves. We don't talk about it. We don't have to. It is revealed in our loneliness, anxiety and sense of abandonment in our increasingly hectic world in which nothing stays the same, not even for an hour.

Ironically, in the modern world, men are slow to give up their boyhood when they have never had a childhood. Instead, they find themselves surrounded with toys that blunt their curiosity, while their games are organized and supervised by adults.

Girls rush their biological clock to prance about as women when they have largely bypassed the insouciance of youth.

Anxiety has become the poison parent of most sins and miseries that haunt the child man and the child woman. In a world where doubt is magnified and disappointment avoided, there is a restless stir and commotion of the mind in search of certainty, which doesn't exist, and thus the dilemma.

Albert Camus (1913-1960) wrote:

I shall tell you a great secret, friend. Do not wait for the last judgment, it takes place every day.

The irony is that this statement proved prophetic as Camus, *1957 Nobel Laureate of Literature*, was cut down in an auto accident at the height of his fame at age 47.

All any of us has is this moment, not tomorrow, not even the rest of the day, so it doesn't make much sense to be too anxious about tomorrow, or about things we can't do anything about, right now! This insight came to me when Rachel, a six-year-old asked me what anxiety was.

"Where did you hear that word?" I asked.

"Mommy's always saying daddy is full of anxiety."

Her father, an attorney, entrepreneur, and sportsman, sleeps four hours a night, and is always on the go. Although successful, he continues to put himself in jeopardy by carrying hanger-on's allowing them advantages they haven't earned and don't deserve, thus the anxiety.

Obviously, money is not the cure for anxiety. If anything, money is the instrument of anxiety masking a sense of identity.

"Anxiety, Rachel, is worrying about something that hasn't happened, and is not likely to occur."

American reformer William Jay (1789-1858) stated it well:

One of the most useless of all things is to take a deal of trouble in providing against dangers that never come. How many toil to lay up riches which they never enjoy; to provide for exigencies that never happen; to prevent troubles that never come; sacrificing present comfort and enjoyment in guarding against the wants of a period they may never live to see.

The words "anxiety," like "stress," "success," "failure," or "happiness," means different things to different people.

Defining it is difficult although it has become part of our daily vocabulary. Is anxiety merely synonymous with stress? Obviously, it involves effort, fatigue, pain, fear, and stress or distress.

Anxiety is apparent with changes in the vital signs of our body. But is it only these things? Or is it also experienced when we lose touch with ourselves and become self-estranged? Think about it! When are we most anxious? It is when we no longer trust ourselves, no longer trust our experience, our history, or our ability to cope with our situation.

It would seem anxiety is a frantic desire to know outcomes before they happen; to enjoy a stress-free life, which is impossible. As Hans Selye points out, *stress is the spice of life, and without it we would be a vegetable.* It is distress that is the culprit, and it is fed by a mania for certainty in an uncertain existence. Just as it is impossible to have a stress-free existence, it is equally impossible to have an anxiety free conscience.

Venturing outside ourselves inevitably produces stress and anxiety, which can lead to distress. It is not uncommon to fear people will see us as the fraud we believe ourselves to be. Actor Leonardo DiCaprio puts it poignantly:

"I want an authentic life. Once I achieved fame, I realized I don't value it at all."

The hardest thing to face is that we forever live in contradiction. There will always be conflict between our projected "ideal self" and our "real self"; between our imagination of reality and the reality of our imagination. Our culture programs us from birth to be inauthentic, pretenders, to take on the guise of what others tell us to value or the persona of our idols.

Those most attentive to this idolatry achieve a successful phoniness. Actors such as DiCaprio know this best. It is a counterfeit marriage of idolatry and passion for images on the screen or tube that are accepted as real to justify the infatuation.

Yet, no condition can be singled out as the "it" to anxiety, since the word implies anything can be the trigger. Psychiatrist Karen Horney in *The Neurotic Personality of Our Time* (1937) writes: *"Anxiety is the dynamic center of neuroses and thus we shall have to deal with it all the time."*

As we see here, a six-year-old child has been made aware of this fact by observing the psychodrama of her anxious parents.

"That sounds stupid," she replied.

"Yes," I answered. "It is stupid."

A child in the womb of the family doesn't feel her security threatened. Horney holds that anxiety is derived from compulsive drives that are born of feelings of isolation, helplessness, fear, and hostility. Anxiety, then, represents a way of coping with the world despite these feelings. The aim is always safety, never satisfaction. The compulsive quality of this is due to anxiety lurking behind repressed feelings. Rachel, up to this point, has had no sense of this. Innocence never leaves the womb, while her parents seem unaware of the impact of their behavior on her delicate psyche.

"Then why do people do it?"

"Because sometimes we act stupid."

People make the complex simple to cope, and the simple complex to problem solve. The clarity of vision escapes us once life takes on age and history. Sociologist Lewis Mumford writes in *The Condition of Man* (1944):

"People whose course of life has reached a crisis must confront their collective past as fully as a neurotic patient must unbury his personal life; long-forgotten traumas in history may have a disastrous effect upon millions who remain unaware of them."

"Do you do it?" she asked.

"Ah yes, many times," I confessed.

The truth is I have learned over time that all my history is important because it is forever contemporary. Nothing is more important than those hidden parts that still survive in me without my being aware of them or their importance. They drive me, and often from rather than towards my contradictions. I ride my anxiety like a surfboard in stormy waters.

"Then you must be stupid, too," she laughed, then paused and studied me a moment. "But you're not stupid. So, you must not have to be stupid to have anxiety."

How could I convey that stupidity is that neurotic distortion between expectations and reality experienced without confusing her? Fear of failing a test in school found me studying hard and earning an "A." Fear of being discovered a coward found me racing down the field to make the opening tackle on the kickoff in a high school football game. For this play, I was touted as a hard-nosed player. Fear of botching an assignment on the job and getting fired resulted in a succession of promotions.

Confronting my anxiety, and accepting the responsibility and guilt feeling involved resulted in increased self-awareness, and with it freedom and an enlarged sphere of creativity. Anxiety is home to the writer, or any person not comfortable in his own skin. Where would art be without anxiety?

On the other hand, anxiety displaced found me critical of my da when his paycheck never stretched from payday to payday. My anxiety was also manifested in being accident-prone. This grew into an aversion for doctors and instant headaches when my parents argued. Later, migraine headaches would plague me the moment I experienced any pressure.

Driven by my anxieties, it was paramount that I be focused and disciplined to the point that I was little fun at all. How could I explain this to this little girl? Competitive success was my dominant drive and the pervasive cause of my anxiety. This would in no way compute with this child who saw me only as "successful." Seeing me as I am for her is yet to come.

"You're right," I said, always surprised, when I shouldn't be. "Smart people are known to sometimes do things that make no sense."

She folded her little arms over her chest, and said, "Anxiety doesn't make any sense to me at all."

Indeed! Someone once said, *"Never trouble trouble till trouble troubles you."* Yet, it is so easy to worry about what never happens, which of course makes no sense. The misfortunes hardest to bear are those that never come. There is much more to anxiety, however, than self-identity and sensible behavior.

DOWNSIDE OF LUCK

People think that if they won the lottery all their anxieties would vanish. A series of lotto winners have complained that it was the worst thing that ever happened to them. On Christmas Day 2002, Jack Whittaker of Charleston, West Virginia won the largest lottery jackpot in U.S. history, $314.9 million in the Powerball jackpot.

Previously, he was already a wealthy contractor. He took his winnings in a lump sum of $113 million after taxes and held an immediate news conference to appear as a jolly saint.

Without hesitation, he split $7 million among three churches, gave money to improve a *Little League park*, bought playground equipment for children, and set up a charitable foundation.

Eight months later, his life and fortune started to unravel. A briefcase was stolen with $545,000 in cash and cashier checks from his SUV. It was parked at a strip club. He not only became a well-known strip club devotee, but also confessed to now being a high-stakes gambler, which is why he was carrying so much cash.

Several thefts to his home, office and other vehicles followed. At one of the thefts, September 2003, an 18-year-old friend of his granddaughter's was found dead. The boy died from overdosing on a combination of oxycodone, methadone, meperidine, and cocaine.

Next, his 17-year-old granddaughter came up missing. In December 2004, Whitaker's granddaughter was found dead on the property of a male friend. Her body was wrapped in a plastic tarpaulin and dumped behind a junked van. The death was ruled an overdose.

In July 2009, Whitaker's daughter, the mother of his dead granddaughter was found dead. Foul play was not ruled out.

He got in a fight at a nightclub, and two men sued him for assault. Other similar suits followed from related brawls. A judge fined him and assigned him to attend weekly *Alcoholics Anonymous* meetings.

In less than a year, he had gone from saint to sinner in his community. One person quipped, "This clown is not capable of handling a $10 bill much less all those millions." His charitable foundation is now closed; his business is in jeopardy; his own health is on the fence. One of Whittaker's friends remarked, "I think it's pretty sad, really. It just goes to show money can't always buy happiness."

UPSIDE OF PLUCK

Rachel is an extraordinary little girl as many young people are. I am convinced that young people like Rachel will redirect our society into a less anxious configuration. The irony of our times is despite the hyped-up technological explosion there is a drab sameness to everything and nearly everybody.

The herd mentality has extended to technology with everyone having an iPhone, laptop or some other mobile. In a way, texting and tweeting have acted like our "worry beads," providing connection with others if only electronically. It would seem we dread being alone while being intimidated with silence.

Anxiety doesn't happen "out there." Anxiety is part of our make-up. It is the friction of ourselves rubbing against ourselves that produces what we call "art." Art brings out our buried demons that wreak havoc with our soul. Art is talking to ourselves with creative verve and is a palliative to anxiety. Nothing is as bad as it seems when it is neutralized by the light of day. Art brings out the sun.

The vicious cycle of anxiety

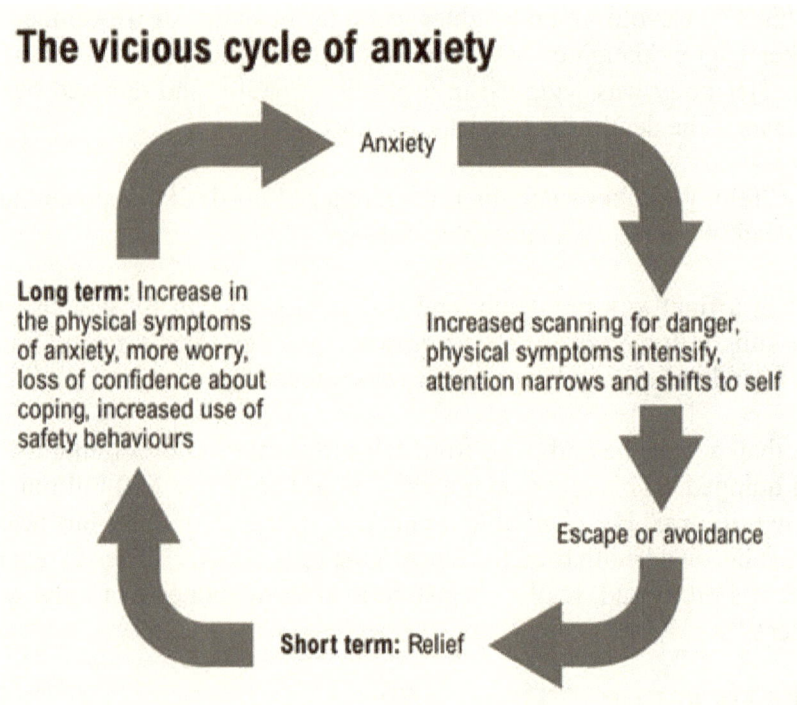

Anxiety

Increased scanning for danger, physical symptoms intensify, attention narrows and shifts to self

Escape or avoidance

Short term: Relief

Long term: Increase in the physical symptoms of anxiety, more worry, loss of confidence about coping, increased use of safety behaviours

Rachel is already writing stories. She loves everyone, finds school exciting, and loves to teach her friends the things she learns. Will society kill that spirit? Will it put her in its cage? Will it blow out her flame of curiosity and egoistic joy, and turn it into sorrow and self-contempt? Will she look to what she doesn't have and isn't rather than what she is and has? Will she balance optimism with doubt and pessimism with reason? Will she wrap her life in confusion and fill her shoes with fretting anxiety, or will she embrace her fears and soar to new insights? I don't know. I can only hope and pray that she does.

She asked me the other day when she came by after ice skating practice, "Who is more creative, you or me?"

I answered, "If this important to you?"

"Yes, why else would I ask?"

Refusing to talk down to her, I explained that comparing and competing are the first forms of anxiety. You cannot be another person or experience what that other person experiences.

"You see, Rachel, you will always see people whom you might consider more fortunate, more able and even happier than you, but that is what you see not necessarily what is there.

"If it is so, feel good about it for them and you will feel better about yourself. Likewise," I continued, "you will see many people less fortunate than you, who are obviously not happy and not as comfortable with themselves. Be kind to them but don't think you know what is best for them. They must find that out for themselves, but don't ever punish them with your good fortune. Chances are they are already doing that to themselves."

Then I added, "To your question of my creativity compared to yours, I expect you will remember this: your creative powers are now at their highest. One day when you are as old as I am, which is quite ancient, you will appreciate your creative powers have greatly faded, and will rely more on your learning, experience and history.

"You can never take your creativity for granted. It is a gift from God. You must feed it and breathe life into it. Otherwise, it will shrivel up and die. That means you must use it. You must read, wonder, observe and ask questions like you are doing now, and never be afraid to challenge anything that doesn't make sense to you."

"I do all those things now."

"Yes, I'm sure you do."

She left a message on my machine yesterday. "I scored four goals in soccer. Just wanted you to know." Then a short pause. "I don't think you're old. I think you're handsome." Thank God for little girls who are blind as well as gifted. [1]

WHEN INNOCENCE TAKES ON THE ROLE OF THERAPIST

During the Thanksgiving weekend of 2004, when Rachel was eight, her family went on holiday to their Michigan lakefront cottage. Rachel's parents arranged for a charitable organization to deliver a twelve-foot Christmas tree, fully decorated, to their home in their absence.

It was the responsibility of the groundskeeper to see that the tree was properly placed in the living room. Unfortunately, once the family had departed, he took off and was out of sight and out of mind. Consequently, the volunteers delivering the tree were unable to place it in the home, deciding instead to leave it at the front door.

As fortune would have it, a violent thunderstorm erupted soon after. Tree limbs and ornaments were spread in a thousand pieces over several acres of manicured lawn, a $1,200 disaster. So, when the family returned from their holiday, the sight, leastwise for Rachel's mother, was at first incredulous, then shocking, finally erupting into vociferous despair.

To put it mildly, Rachel's mother lost it. She was reduced to hysterical outbursts and damning epithets. This greatly upset Rachel. She had never seen her mother in such a state. Meanwhile, Rachel's father, a former police officer who had experience in domestic disputes, took off to avoid his wife's wrath and the object of her fury.

He would later explain to his daughter that once anger reached the level of rage the person's appetite for continuing it was impossible to subdue so long as the cause for it was there. He admitted being that cause, having arranged for the tree's delivery and entrusting his groundskeeper to handle it. This eight-year-old saw the situation in the most drastic terms, that is, her parents divorcing.

A sense of being abandoned, security jeopardized, and peace shattered are common conditions for spontaneous anxiety, especially for a child who is likely to retreat into tearful self-pity. Not Rachel. She took charge.

She instructed her mother to sit down. "Mother," she said, "get hold of yourself! It's only a tree!" Then to put an exclamation point on the situation, she added, "Daddy's left. He may never come back!" She then informed her mother that the tree was something that could be replaced, but not her father.

Her mother listened, whereas earlier she exploded when her husband had said, "It's only a business expense. No big deal!" This response triggered a reminder of his spendthrift ways. On the other hand, Rachel was appealing to her mother's self-interests as well as her own.

When a child fears the breakup of the family, it creates the sense of abandonment, isolation, separation, and helplessness. Consequently, the expected behavior is weeping, not taking charge. Rachel had the presence of mind to appeal to her mother's reason and apprehension. She created a climate in which her mother calmed down; recognizing it was only a tree, while finally realizing what was really at stake.

Within the hour, Rachel's father returned. Peace was tacitly restored in an aftermath of emotional catharsis and apologies. Rachel stepped off stage and allowed her parents to again bond together, but it had been she who acted like the adult in the situation, not her parents, and she was eight-years-old.

A child became the parent, the interventionist and therapist, but who will be this child's parent or therapist when emotional trauma surfaces at some inopportune time in her future?

This is now part of this little girl's history. True, it has put a fissure of vulnerability in her innocence, but at the same time, placed anxiety in perspective.

A FATHER'S TAKE ON ANXIETY

My da was an *Irish Roman Catholic brakeman on the railroad*, who managed only a 7th grade education. He was a wise man albeit life's biblical *Job*. His mother died in *Cook County Hospital in Chicago* when he was born; his father taking off for points unknown never to be seen again.

Reared by his Irish relatives in Iowa, he grew up into young manhood during the "Roaring Twenties," and had difficulty settling down even after he met my mother. She was patient and would in time be his anchor and lighthouse. The 1930s were the years of *The Great Depression*, and then came *World War Two*, rearing four children on a railroad brakeman's income.

He was proud of his work and loved the railroad. During the war, he carried wounded soldiers from the battlefields of the South Pacific from Boone, Iowa to Clinton, Iowa on his *Chicago & North Western Railway* trains heading to *Schick General Hospital*, a *US Army hospital* in Clinton, or hospitals due East. Often, he was so distraught seeing these wounded young men that he could not talk to my mother or anyone after completing his trip.

When the war was over, and life slowed down and became more manageable, he contracted *multiple myeloma*, bone cancer, and a form of leukemia. He died at the age of 50.

It was impossible to miss my da's physical courage, which was on display to the end. He never complained although in great pain and reduced to less than sixty pounds before he expired.

His cage was mental anxiety. Little as he feared death, he seemed afraid of life, afraid to push the envelope. He would give others the benefit of the doubt and not himself; cower to authority figures even when he knew they were blatantly wrong.

To him, everyone was more gifted than he was. I often asked him why.

The incongruity of his humility with my arrogance gave me the courage to venture into the world of work believing no one more talented, only to drop out at the zenith of my career, and eventually, to reenter the much less certain world of words as a writer.

Here are a few of his boilerplate observations that have become etched on my soul:

A man needs only 3 square meals a day, the roof over his head, and the clothes on his back. Everyone, no matter how high they fly, share this in common.

Yet society can take away your table, the roof over your head, and the clothes off your back, but it must kill you to take what you put between your ears.

You are the son of an Irish Roman Catholic brakeman on the railroad. The day you deny that is the day you won't know who the hell you are. That's the only thing you have that is yours. I see college students boarding my trains leaving their parents at the station pretending they don't know them.

You cannot run from who you are, but you can lose who that is.

Don't be too impressed with high flyers. Chances are they have connections you'll never know about.

You have no choice but to find your way with hard work. Don't envy them; don't copy them; and by all means, don't pretend to be like them.

Money is not the root of all evil. It is what people make of money. Everyone likes money. Some will lie to get it; cheat to get it; betray their friends to get it; or steal it. But most people are content to have little of it.

What separates us from the rich is that we are only capable of venial sins when it comes to money, while the rich have a great talent for committing mortal sins in pursuit of it. Don't ever be impressed with the rich.

Most fortunes are built on selling your soul for money.

Your mother expects you to be a big deal. That will never happen. What your mother refuses to understand is that our classless society has a caste system even in this dingy little town of ours.

The haves decide who belongs and who doesn't, while the have nots better know where they belong or they won't be comfortable anywhere.

Whenever you have something to say about someone, imagine that person is standing directly behind you taking in every word. By the same token, when someone badmouths someone not there, be weary. Rest assured that when you're not present, you are fair game.

His good counsel simplified his anxiety instead of giving him reason to venture beyond his self-imposed doubt. He was an honest man who stayed in his Irish Catholic conclave. We had an Irish grocer, two Irish doctors, an Irish dentist and Irish insurance man, two Irish pubs in the neighborhood, lived in an Irish parish, had Irish friends, and even an Irish undertaker. This was something considering the community was more than eighty percent Protestant.

ANXIETY & A LIFE CHANGING EXPERIENCE

There is a saying that when the student is ready the teacher will arrive. This seems less true today. Students appear disinclined to seek pedagogic direction. Likewise, mentors, coaches and counselors in everyday life are less prominent. We are in the impersonal electronic age glued to a cell phone or a computer.

With so much information available, curiosity is being fed by solo flying on the Internet. Active life has been relegated to the back burner. Most experience is second hand or play station reality. If humanity is anything, it is a social group, and social dynamics at every level are critical to developing social skills. The irony is that as we are pushed closer together by the heterogeneity of the population, which continues to grow reducing the distance between us, only to become more insular, not less so, more secluded, and more guided by inappropriate stereotypes than enlightened interpersonal relations.

Self-awareness only occurs when we confront life's obstacles, embrace them and move beyond them to new possibilities. To confront anxiety, it requires moving from the familiar to the unfamiliar, from reassuring safety to challenging freedom, from the content of meaning to the context of identity. Each life is loaded with such possibilities and situations. This was one of mine.

A CASE STUDY

Only in my thirties, after completing an assignment in South Africa, I resigned, retiring from the world of work and moving to Florida.

My executive assignment in South Africa had been to facilitate the formation of a new modest conglomerate of an American subsidiary, a British affiliate, and a South African chemical division.

There were a number of reasons for my early retirement for what, on the surface, might seem a hasty decision. To wit, there was the cultural shock of British colonialism clashing with modest upbringing in a working-class family in Iowa, coupled with the observation of blatant human rights violations of the Bantu peoples, the black majority population, which essentially had few rights. Then there was the passivity of my Irish Roman Catholic Church in the midst of these practices. Added to this was a cavalier disregard of basic ethics by company executives. [2]

This threw my value and belief system into chaos. It didn't help that my wife and four preadolescent children didn't take to life in Johannesburg, exacerbated by the fact that I traveled extensively leaving them to deal, alone, with a strange society.

At every turn, there was the matter of South African apartheid, which reminded me of the Tama Indian Reservation near my home in Iowa. My work was demanding, but that was not the problem. The problem was I came to question my own emotional stability.

My intuition told me the only rational escape from my free-floating anxiety was a full-fledged retreat. I needed a "time out" to regroup and refocus. My life made no sense to me anymore. I resigned and relocated to Florida.

After doing little more than reading and writing for two years, I entered a doctoral program at a local university seeking answers. I was in the program only a short time when a member of my group approached me after an evening seminar. He was a decade younger than me, and we had never spoken to each other before. Straightforwardly, he asked me, "Do you plan to graduate in this program?" It was 9 p.m. and we would talk to nearly 1 a.m. The jest of the conversation was my obvious contempt for academics, disdain for professors who weren't as well read I was, and my palpable scorn for their ignorance of the real world or work.

"What is obvious to me," he continued, "is that with your attitude you are doomed to fail." He now had my total attention. "If failure is in your plans, you are working the strategy to perfection. But if you plan on earning a Ph.D., you're doing everything wrong by intimidating and demeaning your professors.

"As little as you may think of them, they have the power of the grade. As petty as their internal squabbling may offend you, they are masters of this arena. Believe me, they can be as treacherous as I suspect you were in your previous work, perhaps more so. They must grovel for petty raises and petty perks. Pettiness is their battlefield.

"If you were to measure their antipathy for you against your contempt for them, it would not be a contest. It would be like a hot draft from hell compared to a summer breeze. They don't like you, and don't plan on trying.

"You either step lightly, make humble, or they'll crush you like a bug."

"They've never known power, real power as you have. They've never had people part the waters for them when they approach; and they've never made the kind of money you've made. You're the enemy on their turf, and you are showing no respect."

Driving home across the bay, I reflected on his words and my previous career. He was right. I was being an ass. Even though I was quite young in South Africa, I had authority, respect, a generous budget, ample human resources, and total freedom to implement my "intuitive strategy," as my minders called it. No one could explain my success.

It was the major reason I returned to the university: to find answers in psychology and sociology to this conundrum of why I had been so successful yet so unconventional in my approach. [3]

Unknown to my young counselor in the university parking lot that night, I was surprised and frustrated, even angered, to find the university a factory of reification and regurgitation. It had no answers for me. I was like the child looking for the pony in the haystack, only to find I had been duped by false expectations.

Instead of being comforted with my success and affluence, I wondered what my lot in life was meant to be. Was it only to make money, provide security for my family, and then retire with a golden parachute? Or was I supposed to make a difference?

It was on that basis that I resigned, telling my superior, a wise and decent man, that if I weren't doing my job, the company would fire me; the company was not meeting my needs, so I was firing the company. All he could say was that he expected the road ahead of me would be quite rocky, and he, of course, was right.

EDUCATION & PALLIATIVES TO ANXIETY ALONG THE WAY

Retiring young was a life wrenching experience, but there were many mentors, coaches and counselors along the way, some of whom were not at first heeded, people who pointed the most reliable direction they saw for me. In disclosing this now, I would like readers to reflect on their own lives in similar terms and how life has spoken through interested parties to them in their own life's journey.

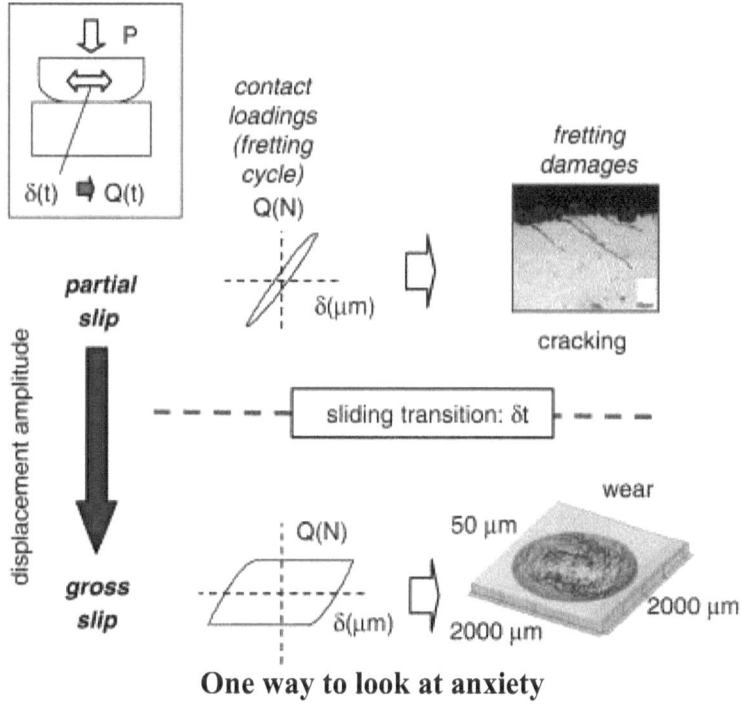

One way to look at anxiety

My mother was my first coach and I write about her in some detail in my memoir as a novel. [4] You have already been introduced to my da. Complementing them were the Sisters of St. Francis at St. Patrick's Catholic School. They made me aware that I had a terrible temper, and that I must curb it or be in constant trouble. They taught me discipline and introduced me to my way with words. To this day, I have a love of books and ideas that they first sponsored.

At our courthouse playground, older boys introduced me to baseball and taught me the game, while a high school athlete, and former student at St. Patrick's taught me the love of basketball. Were it not for the introduction of sports into my early life, I would imagine I would have been more withdrawn. The Sisters of St. Francis encouraged me to play sports as a calming influence on my temperament.

In high school, I had an exceptional math teacher in 3rd and 4th year mathematics. But that is not why he is included here. We took a national test at mid-term of the first semester of my senior year, and I did poorly. This unbeknown to me had troubled him, as he considered me one of his good students. The same test was given again in the middle of my final semester. I was unaware that it was the same test. I did well on it. Afterwards, he explained what he had done, and why, reminding me that I was high strung. "When you become anxious your brain seems to fog up and shut down," he observed. His insight has proven useful to me throughout my life.

At university, taking a core course in literature my sophomore year, I contracted infectious mononucleosis and missed the mid-term, which was on James Joyce's *Portrait of the Artist as a Young Man* (1915). Everyone in the class was much better read than I was, and so I was mainly quiet. My professor chose to have me complete the mid-term on the book as an oral examination. When I concluded it, he asked how I knew the work so well. I said, matter-of-factly, "I am Joyce," meaning that my life paralleled much of what was in the book. He asked me my major. I told him it was chemistry. "You belong in literature, not science," he said. It would take me thirty-five years to heed his words.

WELCOME TO HELL, NEXT STOP HEAVEN!

There is no time in which anxiety, free floating and otherwise, is at greater intensity than those halcyon days of college. Rollo May devotes a good deal of his book *The Meaning of Anxiety* (1977) to academic anxiety and the development of the self. College, compressed into a short number of years, isolated from the real world, and confined to regurgitating ideas, theories, truths, facts, myths and biases, is a time of much anxiety and agitation.

Uncertainty, depression, stress, distress, confusion, and anxiety compete for the student's waking attention. And if that were not enough, these same demons play havoc with the student's dreams while asleep.

When I am in an anxiety prone state, I have a variation of two dreams. One, I am afraid to get my grades for fear I have flunked out. Mind you, I graduated from university a half century ago. The second dream, I have forgotten my class schedule – what class I am supposed to be attending, where and what time – and find myself lost on campus. I encounter students rushing to class but am too embarrassed to ask them where my class might be meeting. I wake up in a cold sweat, and go to my study to write, unable to sleep the rest of the night.

Someone might look at my accomplishments, then at my comfortable existence, and say, "How is that possible?" Soren Kierkegaard had the answer:

To venture causes anxiety, but not to venture is to lose oneself. So, it is too that in the eyes of the world it is dangerous to venture. And why? Because one may lose. But not to venture is shrewd. And yet, by not venturing, it is so dreadfully easy to lose that which it would be difficult to lose in even the most venturesome venture, and in any case never so easily, so completely as if it were nothing – one's self. For if I have ventured amiss – very well, then life helps me by its punishment. But if I have not ventured at all – who then helps me? And, moreover, if by not venturing at all in the highest sense (and to venture in the highest sense is precisely to become conscious of oneself) I have gained all earthly advantages . . . and lose my self! What of that? [5]

Long before I knew Kierkegaard's words, I was stumbling along, ineptly but diligently embracing my resistance to my anxiety. I found it true that the creative imagination is stimulated by accepting anxiety as real with the many lessons it can teach us; that to seek escape from anxiety in search of a safe haven is to find ourselves in a cage.

Each of us has a role in life to play involving the positive aspects of our selfhood. We develop as individuals as we confront, move through and overcome anxiety-creating experiences. There have been many people along my long life that have opened the door of my cage, which I have not always heeded. When I have, the road ahead became easier.

IS KAFKA'S TRIAL OUR OWN?

How often I have heard variations of Kafka's lament in his book *The Trial* (1925):

Someone must have been telling lies about Joseph K., for without having done anything wrong he was arrested one fine morning.

It is a novel of vast symbolism and a psychological study of a system whose leaders are convinced of their own righteousness. To some the court is a symbol of the Church as an imperfect bridge between the individual and God. More pertinent to today, it appears a symbolic bridge between corporate and economic security.

It is a challenge to trust the "system" to produce the leadership necessary to bring about social justice along with comfort and security to individuals collectively in society. This challenge is crass, of course, because it implies that the burden is that of a few individuals and not the majority. What happened to Joseph K happens every day because the passive majority expect their wishes to materialize without any effort on their part.

Plants close, jobs disappear, industries evaporate, communities become lifeless, values change, as well as sacred beliefs, skills become anachronistic, positions become atavistic, and neighborhoods deteriorate or vanish. It becomes difficult to trust leaders who make promises they can't keep. What is a person to do when he has done nothing wrong? But is this true?

We can't change the world to fit us, but we can change ourselves to fit the world. Managing anxiety involves the self-development of the self to an ever-changing world. W. H. Auden captures this in *The Age of Anxiety* (1947):

. . . . it is silly
To refuse the tasks of time
And, overlooking our lives,
Cry – "Miserable wicked me,
How interesting I am."
We would rather be ruined than changed,
We would rather die in our dread
Than climb the cross of the moment
And let our illusions die.

We remain architects of our destiny no matter how much we would prefer giving that role to someone else. In the end as in the beginning, all we have is ourselves to blame.

NOTES

[1] Rachel graduated with honors from a top prep high school. With advanced courses already completed in high school, she will register as a second semester sophomore as she enters college in the fall of 2014.

[2] This tense experience is given a novelist treatment in *Devlin, A Psychological Novel*, which is available on Kindle.

[3] See James R. Fisher, Jr.'s unconventional approach in *Confident Selling*, TATE Publishing, 2014.

[4] The memoir is *In the Shadow of the Courthouse: A Memoir of the 1940s Written as a Novel*, TATE Publishing, 2014.

[5] Soren Kierkegaard, *Sickness unto Death*, Princeton University Press, 1941, p. 52.

THE NATURE OF A "MORAL COMPASS"

© James R. Fisher, Jr., Ph.D.
November 2, 2017

READER WRITES:

Dr. Fisher,

I've read your little book, *"The Absence of Mind in the Modern Self – The Invasion of Media,"* with interest. You point out that the media select facts – true or distorted, verified or not – which suggests a form of propaganda. It is a way of appealing to something in us that we find in adventure movies and novels, and in children's literature.

Media takes us across a line that is hardly visible. What distinguishes selling from education is that selling serves mostly the seller while education serves those being educated. I like to think I have become immune to this evasive strategy.

More to the point, you have often referred to the "moral compass," as you do in this little book. This brings me to my criticism. Your reference to "moral compass" reminds me of what Bertrand Russell once said:

"Everything is vague to a degree you do not realize til you have tried to make it precise."

In other words, to my mind there are widely differing references to the "moral compass." Take for example, *nepotism*. In the Middle East, *nepotism* is considered a virtue for it puts one's family to work. In the West, however, it is considered far less virtuous but something of a pejorative. In that context, ideally, one does not use one's position of authority to favor relatives over merit. Leaving inheritance to offspring aside, which tilts the level playing field, we come back to the ambiguity of your concept of "moral compass" with philosopher Russell's comment, do we not?

DR. FISHER RESPONDS:

Thank you for your most poignant reflections. My surprise is that I've never been asked this question before. I first used the term in *"The Taboo Against Being Your Own Best Friend"* (1996). To wit:

"We are not happy campers. We have lost our moral compass and our way."

Twenty-one years later (2017), I see little evidence that we have rediscovered our moral center, or indeed, our way back to civility.

THE GENESIS OF "MORAL COMPASS"

Obviously, we are looking at the concept of "moral compass" from differing perspectives. My focus is in terms of personal identity and relates exclusively to the individual.

We were both born and grew to maturity in a terrible century, a world of deliberate cruelty, destruction, and the extermination of millions of innocent people which has had no parallel in history. Voltaire once claimed, *"Ideas did it all."* He may have anticipated Karl Marx (1818-1883) and his *Communist Manifesto"* (1848) and Adolf Hitler (1889-1945) and his *"Mein Kampf"* (1925). In any case, *Western Civilization* over the past 100 years has been influenced by ideas taken from these respective ideologies.

Philosopher of the History of Ideas, Isaiah Berlin writes:

(Ideas) *not, as some historians like to believe, social conditions, and the effect of technology on culture,* (when the influenced has been by) *Marxism, Fascism, National Socialism – ideas born in the heads of individuals who bound their spell upon a mass of credulous followers: it is these ideas in the end, and these individuals, who are responsible, without them it is not credible that anything of this kind could have happened* (Isaiah Berlin: *Affirming*, 2015, p. 541).

The focus of my writing has been on the individual with the ideas of that conceptual framework coming out of my experience, reflections, observations and reading. My approach has never been about the collective group, per se, although sometimes the individual has been viewed in that context: e.g., the behavior of the individual in the work group where the dominant culture dictates collective behavior.

Man exists in somewhat of an unconscious state while claiming to be conscious of his every act, when such consciousness often on display is *"after the fact."*

The media in general and advertising in particular – be the claim truth telling or information sharing – has mainly devolved to the status of entertainment as an art form. These disciplines are in the business of manipulating human thought based on an understanding of what effect this or that stimulus will have on them in a marketing, political or economic sense. They lean on the analytics of demographics and behavioral data, as there is no other reliable theoretical substitute. Through mountains of data they distill *catch phrases* that are designed to provoke a plurality of favorable responses and are willing to spend tens of millions of dollars towards that end.

We are a reactive rather than an anticipating animal, although we have the same anticipating mechanism at our disposal as lower animals, which we refuse to use as we prefer to see ourselves as conscious cognitive thinking human beings.

We expect to display *"grace under pressure"* with problem solving aplomb whatever the situation demands. Unfortunately, our failure to take seriously palpable danger is part of our cultural programming. This finds us existing mainly on automatic pilot. Alas, the mechanism we bypass is our *intuition* centered in our reptilian brain.

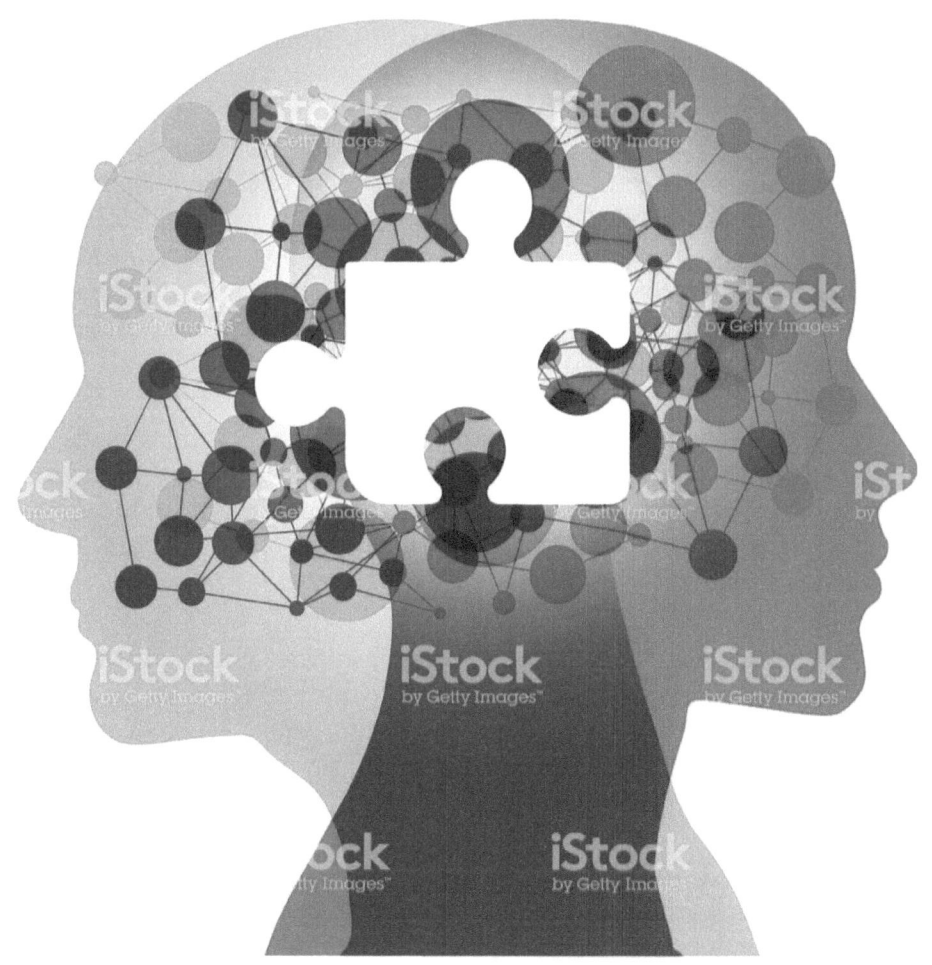

Life is a puzzle for many of us, feeling a piece or more is missing.

We feel danger before we are aware of its presence; we feel a bad relationship before it blossoms into despair; we feel our innate capacity for happiness before we abort it to win popularity with the "in" crowd.

We have had great philosophers since the beginning of time but have been dependent on philosophers of the 18th century's *"Age of the Enlightenment"* ever since.

Philosophers of the *Enlightenment* successfully dismantled the metaphysics of religion to replace it with the *scientific method*, *logical positivism* and *cognitive reasoning*.

Now science has replaced religion with compelling efficiency in exploring physical phenomena while being much less efficient in matters relating to people as persons, the social sciences notwithstanding. Consequently, the individual finds himself in the midst of shifting shadows and misdirecting mirrors unable to grasp reality in an increasingly confusing and hostile social and political climate.

Despite all the disruption over the past 100 years, man has done better than expected when his "moral compass" is on display. Knowing how to act, when to act, how strongly to act, and against whom to act is a gift of this creative center. This is the individual as artist of his own destiny with buoyancy to survive all challenges.

Life is a pragmatic matter in which a "moral compass" allows the individual to identify the ends for which he is working; to discern the subtle distinctions between ends and means; and to recognize possible collisions between equally appealing choices, which cannot be avoided. To not choose between the options available is to have circumstances control the choosing.

None of this is reducible to a simple system. It is the individual reacting to what is real to what is not; what is relevant to what is simply smoke and mirrors; to what enhances progress to what derails such efforts.

Given this assessment, a preoccupation with "things" tends to mask the clarity of what is being pursued. Reliance on second, third and fourth levels of information clouds the mind with spurious data preventing a fundamental grasp of the requirements in the problem solving. The solutions are never in the media; nor are they in books and the latest fad. Solutions are buried in the problem itself, requiring an intrinsic understanding of that problem.

Interestingly enough, once we are comfortable, alone without noise, without the need for compulsive texting and tweeting, without constant checking of our iPhones for the latest social media postings, we are free to grasp reality. We are ready to take the appropriate action demanded in the problem solving; and by extension, ready to reconnect with others in real and substantive ways.

THE MORAL COMPASS & PURPOSEFUL IDENTITY

In June 1993, *The Reader's Digest* carried a brief work of mine, which could have been deemed *"Aspects of Our Moral Compass."* It suggested:

To have a friend you must be a friend starting with yourself. The greatest virtue is kindness. You cannot love everyone, but you can be kind to anyone. Nothing of consequence is achieved without enthusiasm. Positive people attract others while negative people repel. Gossip cheapens the gossiper more than the one gossiped about. Communicate cheerfulness. If inclined to make fun of someone, make it be of oneself. Smile often as it costs nothing. Follow the Golden Rule by doing unto others as you would have them do unto you.

No doubt these are clichés, but they connote values and provide a window to the moral shop of our mind to see who and what we are.

Philosopher Isaiah Berlin claims we are born with certain moral values as a result of all the forces that create us – tradition, education, the views of people we live among, the books we read, and our own thoughts. But can we reject that "self" to which we are kin for yet another self?

Obviously, there exists constant pressure to adopt the identity of the "in" crowd or that of the masses, resulting in the curious predicament of being seen as an outsider if we remain true to our roots. With the flippancy of a chiaroscuro day, we can become a millionaire but remain an imposter to ourselves if we deny our working-class heritage.

We can change our personality as it is impressionistic, and something borrowed. We cannot change our essence as it belongs to each of us, alone. It is something owned. If it is necessary to "blend in" to win acceptance of the group, the price may be self-estrangement.

Evidence of this retreat from self-knowing can be experienced in fits of depression, violent mood swings and boredom. This propensity to gloom and doom has become a boom to the cosmetic, pharmaceutical, psychotherapy, plastic surgery and dermatology industries.

Religion once provided sanctuary from the trauma of self-doubt, but it has lost its efficacy and relevance. The newest boogeyman now is life, itself, as people are afraid of life, afraid to grow up, afraid to grow old, feeling a compelling need to deny death which is simply a part of life.

Drug addiction has become a pervasive norm of popular culture as an alternative to boredom and self-loathing. This may start with the innocence of taking a prescription drug in recreational insouciance only to subsequently become hooked on the remedy and on the road to self-destruction.

We don't become lost and self-hating in a moment. Depersonalization takes time for the gradual erosion of core values and beliefs to drive a person away from self-regard and into a state of being associated with the wrong people in the wrong place at the wrong time. Eventually, the addicted person finds himself in *"nowhere land,"* wondering how this has happened.

There are questions we may ask ourselves when caught in this dilemma:

When did I adopt this new outlook? When did I start to hate what I am and my own people? When did my thoughts spin out of control and my imagination end in fantasy land? When did I uncritically accept my adopted belief system without reflection?

Identity and self-regard spring from a healthy self-monitoring "moral center" with supportive values that are fully operational and self-sustaining.

Anyone who reads biographies and histories of people in their respective situations can see how they wrestled with their times and with demons to reach their eminence.

Challenge and failure humanized them as they dealt with their foibles and follies, the same way they humanize us as we deal with our own. These highly accomplished individuals are not different from us. They are the same as we are only written large. Intuition often plays a role in their lives the same as it does in ours. This was true of Elbert Einstein who dreamed of riding a light beam soaring beyond time and matter and what we call *"space."*

TWO CASES IN POINT

PROFILE OF ADAM

The idea of a "moral compass" has intrigued Adam since a boy as he has always been disinclined to compare and compete with others while quietly doing his own thing to effectively utilize his inherent ability.

The idea of being popular with his playmates never occurred to him, for if they wanted to go to one movie and he desired to go to another, he would separate himself from them, and say he would see them after the flick often to their disappointment and annoyance: *Why would he want to be a party pooper?*

If it started to rain when they were playing baseball, his teammates would find some place to go to chat and play with their baseball cards, while he would go home to read his comics. He would do this without preamble as he never felt comfortable with small talk.

It didn't occur to him that this was odd as it was quite natural to him. His teammates tolerated him as he was, as did his classmates and later coworkers on the job because they knew he would bring his best efforts to whatever he was doing with a complete commitment to excellence irrespective of the activity or the return on that investment.

Once reaching professional status at work after university, he never considered competing against other professionals for raises or promotions. Ironically, since his focus was entirely on the job at hand, he enjoyed perpetual promotions in an array of careers.

Should he become bored at what he was doing, experience a sense of betrayal, or encounter an assault on his character, he would resign posthaste. No amount of money or social pressure could keep him doing what was offensive to him as he trusted himself in finding something more suitable to his disposition, but alas, often at the pain of personal and economic sacrifice.

His "moral compass" has been a reliable guidance system that has defied conventional wisdom and good sense as he is *inner directed* rather than externally dependent.

He would retire early to write books and articles outlining what he has experienced, has learned from that experience, and how that experience has elevated his awareness of the satisfaction and happiness possible when worry, distress and anxiety are put to bed. He would also encourage his readers to think for themselves, creatively and confidently, in their daily pursuits by harnessing their unique talent.

He claims no special talent, never considered himself either especially ambitious or courageous, while being wholeheartedly involved in some kind of activity at every juncture of his life keeping his mind and spirit operating at something approaching his capacity.

PROFILE OF EVE

Eve never met a stranger. She warms up to everyone she meets as if a long lost relative. She is kind, gentle, courteous, generous, humble, perspicacious and perennially cheerful. She goes out of her way to make others feel good about themselves helping them wherever she finds them: at work, in the shopping mall, in the community, or in her home.

It is never about her but always about others with whom she is socializing or working. She delights in bringing a smile to a face that was earlier frowning. She is modest to a fault while being talented at whatever she does. She is exceptionally intelligent but wears this attribute with disarming charm. She is a learner not a knower; a listener not a talker; a problem solver not a worrier. She is the most mature adult you will ever meet, and you will feel this before it reaches your consciousness.

She has a zest for life that is contagious. Everyone she knows considers themselves her best friend. She came from a loving family where her parents were "Born Again" Christians and practiced their faith openly and unapologetically. She was an obedient and loving daughter but once out of the nest she took on life in a much less doctrinaire way and became her own person on her own terms and her own way. This has confounded those confined to absolutes be they of church, state, social class, or of a certain political persuasion, ethnicity or race, as reason not bias guides her actions and choices.

Given this description, the reader might assume that she is malleable to a fault. Not true. There is steel in her spine. Cross the invisible line in her construction that violates the sanctity of her person, and you will experience her wrath, a vitriolic that you will never forget. Her "moral compass" is unobtrusive but totally engaged. While it is not rigid, it will sanction no violation.

To meet her, you would find it hard to imagine her ever getting mad, upset or calling a person out. But lie to her or betray her trust and you will experience her animus and the thunder of her displeasure.

ADAM & EVE AS ONE

The "moral compasses" of Adam and Eve may appear to be quite different, but are they? Eve is clearly a cognitive person with a strong affect while Adam is an intuitive person with an equally strong affect but tainted with self-righteousness. Adam rejects the herd mentality with a vengeance and moralistic disdain while Eve is simply amused by those inclined to such counterproductive dalliances.

Eve is gregarious with a strong social conscience while Adam is most comfortable alone with his books or in the company of Eve. Adam is pensive and quasi-narcissistic whereas Eve never takes herself too seriously. She enjoys games and popular music as well as situation comedies on television whereas Adam has no interest in any of this. He prefers complex mysteries on television with many fault lines with the greater the twists and turns the greater his satisfaction. Such mysteries, however, put Eve to sleep. They both enjoy reading but not necessarily the same books. Adam is driven never having learned to relax, that is, until Eve came into his life. She has introduced him to the comfort of simply hanging out.

Adam and Eve have been married for many years, both with active "moral compasses" with dispositions to act and react to situations and stimuli consistent with their respective differences. What these guidance systems have in common is that they are centered on, activated by and responsive to external stimuli.

Adam and Eve have remained loving, committed and supportive of each other despite their different approaches to life. Why do they get along so well? They respect and trust each other, give each other lots of space, constantly talk to each other every day, sharing their high and low points, while enjoying each other's company in such diverse activities as shopping for groceries or traveling about the world.

Another common bond is that they were both born and grew up in the culture of the American Midwest with Eve's ancestors coming from Norway and of the Lutheran faith, while Adam's ancestors came from Ireland and Norway and were Roman Catholic. Not enough can be said about a common heritage contributing to a sustainable relationship.

In summary, Adam and Eve *are each other's best friend; committed to doing no one harm be they rich or poor, educated or not, and of whatever race, religion, and ethnicity or belief system; for they trust themselves and therefore can trust each other.*

I hope this helps; and I thank you for challenging my reference to the "moral compass."

JESUS, PAUL & FREUD

James R. Fisher, Jr., Ph.D.
© March 5, 2015

JESUS

Jesus or Joshua, if you prefer, means "savior." The Western World divides history into before and after Jesus. Jesus taught the human race how to live. Would the Christian faith collapse if historians and theologians could prove that Jesus never lived, or that he didn't rise from the dead?

None of the *Gospels* states that Jesus was born in a stable. It is also extremely unlikely that he was born in Bethlehem. Even the census taking for tax purposes that has Mary (with child) and Joseph on the road to their ancestral home may be spurious as well, an invention of the four authors of the Gospels.

Apostle Paul's "Letters" have a distinct set of beliefs for Jesus as Paul was writing for Gentiles, not for Jews. One of the beliefs of the *Gospels of Matthew, Mark and Luke*, called the "Synoptic Gospels" because they use similar source material and replicate each other, has Jesus dying on the Cross before the Passover, which is clearly in dispute in the *Fourth Gospel* according to John.

The Gospels are intent on blaming the death of Jesus on the Jews, which had the effect of Christianity starting out as a Jewish heresy. Religious persecution of dissident groups within Jewry is unknown in Jewish history with absolutely no evidence of crucifixions, which were common practice of the *Roman Empire*, occupiers of Palestine in the first century.

Christianity invented the idea of the embryonic church being persecuted by the Jews with the central focus on *The Crucifixion* while there is no evidence in the first century writings of Josephus to suggest such a Jewish practice.

Crucifixion was a common practice of the Roman Empire in dealing with criminals, crucifying tens of thousands in this manner.

Jesus as the mythological Christ was born in a stable, instituted the *Christian Eucharist*, was crucified on the Cross, rose from the dead, and founded the

Christian Church. There is no way to verify any of this other than the putative *Four Gospels in the New Testament.* Scholars from nearly every perspective have come to view these documents as being mainly mythologies.

Jesus of Nazareth, the Shepherd of His flock

Christians today are sustained by the body and blood of Christ in the *Sacrament of the Eucharist. The Fourth Gospel* makes no mention of the Eucharist or the transubstantiation of the bread and wine of the Catholic Mass into the body and blood of Christ.

Jesus comes alive as a recognizable Jew in the first century of the Common Era (C.E.), and only as a Jew. For in none of the gospels does he utter a word or demonstrate a behavior to suggest that he was other than a teacher and holy man among his Jewish people.

Jesus was a Galilean *Hasid* or holy man. He wrote no books. He has been found more real to me in *Searching for the Real Parents of My Soul* than that provided by my Christian training or through the eyes of my Christian belief system. The gospel writers, like all good writers, say more with what is left out or left to the imagination. There the words can be made flesh and dwelt amongst one; there the mystical Jesus can become real in one's consciousness.

PAUL

Paul wrote about Jesus during the winter of 50 – 51 C.E., approximately twenty years after Jesus's death, personifying Jesus as an extension of his own manic, compulsive, twisted self, urging those who would listen to abstain from sexual immorality and all forms of pleasure in the name of Jesus, who was the Messiah.

St. Paul the Apostle alluded to be the *Architect of Christianity*

Yet, Jesus was comfortable around the dregs of society. This included prostitutes, deviants and sinners of every description. He also enjoyed the pleasure of food and drink and showed none of the ascetic inclinations legendary of his cousin, *John the Baptist*. Paul was a crankier side of Jesus.

The majority of Paul's hearers would be *Gentile Greeks*, who had very different ideas about God and gods than that of the Jews. Therefore, Gentiles would have had no trouble turning Jesus into God. Indeed, these *Hellenistic Gentiles* took Paul, and his acolyte, Barnabas, to be divine beings, Barnabas to be Zeus and Paul, as his messenger, to be Hermes.

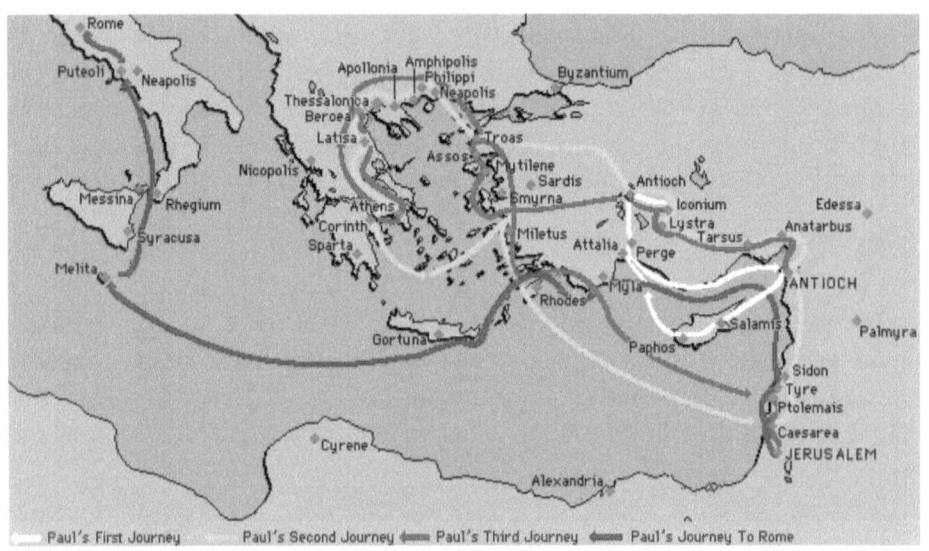

St. Paul's Life & Missionary Journeys

Paul's message was ingenious: Jesus had risen from the dead, and for those who believed, they would one day meet him in *Paradise* in everlasting life. That took the pressure off the poor, the disadvantaged, and the exploited for suffering at the hands of the rich and powerful, for they would be awarded with eternal bliss forever in the next life – *for the first shall be last and the last shall be first.*

There is little to no evidence that Jesus instituted the Eucharist. This is Paul's invention. Paul is not interested in the historical Jesus. Nor is he self-conscious for his proselytizing zeal to convert all to Christianity even though mythology shadows his Jesus. On the contrary, he enhances his message because it cannot be challenged. It is the death of Jesus that matters. The risen Jesus means everything to Paul as it indicates death has been defeated.

Jesus as described in the *Gospels*, and Jesus as interpreted by Paul are often worlds apart, especially in the *Fourth Gospel*.

Paul has an agenda that he makes up as he goes along adjusting to challenges and circumstances, failures and setbacks, but always with a visceral vision of establishing a universal Church. This makes Paul the inventor and founder of Christianity, not Peter.

Yet the gospels have Jesus declaring, *"Peter you are my rock and upon this rock I build my church."*

St. Peters Basilica today is a monument to those words in the center of Rome in all its majestic splendor, which belies this fact, as St. Paul's *Cathedral Outside the Wall* is beyond the Seven Hills of Rome and is modest by comparison.

Matthew, Mark and *Luke* tell us all that we can hope to ever know about the man Jesus. *The Fourth Gospel of John* makes no attempt to replicate their claims, but instead chooses to tell his story of Jesus in metaphor, in rich commentaries, subtle interpretations with embellishments and in an unabashed entertaining impressionistic style.

Paul writes much about himself and is the only gospel autobiographical writer for he is incapable of anonymity. His personality breathes through his every word, which is ecstatic, quarrelsome, changeable, contradictory and conciliatory. He can be feisty and engaging, intimidating and humble, all in a single *Letter to the Gentiles*. He is always playing to make the convert, to make the sale. The moral, religious, ethical and psychological contradictions within these writings become the grand strategy that mirrors the principles of human nature and God-like requirements as he sees them.

Each generation reading Paul has felt the power of his writing, individually, which has made it unsettling and therefore changeable in the minds of readers as a group as the world in which they are engaged is changing.

In this current era of evolutionary biology with human behavior being reduced to post-Darwinian mathematical algorithms, and religion seen totally false in every literal sense, Paul had the wisdom of spreading his Christianity at the individual level that then metastasized to the cultural or group evolutionary level to claim more than a billion souls 2,000 years later.

Paul's genius is like a surfer riding the waves of his time that become today the same waves that they were 2,000 years ago, if we believe in thermodynamics. It was Paul, after all, who singularly wrestled Jesus from the Jews and its Jewish laws, diet, circumcision, its provincialism, and xenophobia, and then from the last remnants of Jesus's own family, Jerusalem Christians.

Paul was a native of Tarsus in Cilicia, Asia Minor, a city in modern Turkey today. He was also a citizen of the Roman Empire. Tarsus was a sophisticated cosmopolitan city and Jews of that city were Hellenistic. It was a melting spot of the Jewish idea of God and the Greek idea of good. Paul lived and worked in the Gentile world, whereas Jesus lived his entire life in the Jewish world.

Paul like Freud was a far more gifted writer and poet than he was a thinker or philosopher. Again, like Freud and other great writers, he was able to project the conflicts in his own mind unto others in the wider cosmos.

It was quite a challenge for a Jew born in the Diaspora to get the attention of the polytheistic Gentiles to know and aspire to become part of a monotheistic faith called Christianity. Paul's confidence came from knowing that in his Hellenistic world there was an inbuilt thirst of the human race for God, the same thirst and compulsion that expressed his own will and motivation.

At some point in his young life, Paul rejected his Hellenism, and became a Pharisee, stating, *"I was born of the race of Israel, of the tribe of Benjamin, a Hebrew born of Hebrew parents. In the matter of the Law, I was a Pharisee."* (Philippians 3:5 -6)

From the beginning, Paul was in conflict with *James* the *brother* of *Jesus*, and *Jerusalem Christians* who saw Christianity as the New Israel, and therefore a Jewish religion.

Jews outside the pages of the *New Testament* have no history of religious persecution, no inquisition, no *Mount Calvary*. In contrast to the *Jerusalem Christians*, Paul came to view Christianity's only possibility for survival as a new religion for Gentiles.

James didn't see it that way; nor did Peter. Tension between Peter and Paul was inevitable as their temperaments and personalities were bound to clash. Paul was combative, impatient, a man of action. Peter was conciliatory, indecisive and patient placing his confidence not in ideas or action, but in the *Torah* and the *Jewish tradition*. Like James, he saw the new religion as the New Israel, believing it would all work out in the end.

Author A. N. Wilson in *"Jesus, A Life"* (1992) believes Paul may have come face to face with Jesus, perhaps in the *Garden of Gethsemane* as one of the arresting Pretorian guards. Wilson imagines that that confrontation came to haunt Saul (not yet Paul) afterwards until his conversion on the road to Damascus.

Jesus, although he had his clashes with Pharisees, seems to have had much in common with them in terms of his views on Judaism. Moreover, Pharisees were some of the most virtuous men who had ever lived to that time. They believed God smiled on virtue and frowned on vice. Paul thought otherwise.

This was made famous by Paul as he clearly took the side of the sinning Publican over the virtuous Pharisee in that defining epistle.

Whereas the Pharisee believed virtue was its own reward, and he was a virtuous man, the Publican admitted that he lacked virtue and was a sinful man, and asked God to be merciful to him a sinner (Luke 18:9 Jerusalem Bible).

This story resonates to this day as a morally anarchic story. The Pharisee and the Publican is not a moral fable against self-righteousness. It is a nihilistic charter from the *Gospel of St. Luke*.

The Pharisee believed an exemplary moral life would lead to future blessedness. Not true according to this story. It denies the commonsense love of virtue absolutely. It denies its roots and branches. What matters in the story is God's capacity to forgive. Sin, not virtue, is the focus of this story.

Since the Pharisee has no sin, he cannot get into touch with God. It is the Publican, the contrite sinner, who is welcomed into God's house.

The test of a good life, this story is saying, is not virtue, but a childlike dependence on the mercy of God. Paul took this idea to the bank with Christianity his vault. *Roman Catholicism*, which became universal Christianity, has exploited this dependence throughout its social, theological and political history, and into the 21st century.

The Gospels which are written from a Gentile perspective see the Pharisees as petty and conservative when actually Pharisees were quite radical.

Whereas the Sadducees were content with the *Torah* as a fixed and finished guide laid down in the Scriptures, the Pharisees applied it as a living document to deal with ever changing contemporary life. They believed the will of God could be discerned in everyday life, not through religious dogma or ritualistic observation, but in an honest assessment of what is and is not right, what is good and what is not, what is ethical and what is dishonest.

From everything we know of Paul from his epistles and letters, this strand in the teachings of Jesus as shown in the *Four Gospels*, which are close to that of the Pharisee's virtue, would be nearly maddening to Paul. His *Galatian Letter to the Romans* makes this clear:

God's forgiveness is not dependent upon human virtue at all, but rather on a free outpouring of divine love for God and the human race in all its frailty.

Paul doesn't see man as strong, but weak, as dependent, not independent, as wanton and depraved, as collectively needing a guidance system, not capable as an individual to make prudent choices in terms of love and will.

Paul as a Pharisee was scandalized by Jesus's laxity in his view of the Law (Torah) and in his indifference to ritualistic observations. Mark has Jesus saying, *"The Sabbath was made for man, and not man for the Sabbath"* (Mark 2:27). For Paul the Torah was equivalent to Kant's categorical imperative (see *"Grounds for Metaphysics of Morals,"* Chap. 2, Part 1).

Actually, it was probably propitious that Paul was not like a tree, rooted, stable and firmly in place, but more like a river ever in motion yielding to and circumventing obstacles of uncertainty to oblige the forces of nature. Were he to have been as rooted as *James* and the *Jerusalem Christians,* chances are the Christianity we know would have been assimilated into Orthodox Judaism and lost forever.

Paul decided to focus on the Gentiles, which meant altering the implicit sense of Jesus in the four gospels as necessary to successfully engage the non-Jewish world to his purposes (see A. N. Wilson's "The Mind of the Apostle," 1997, pp. 229-239).

Why he did this rather than proclaim his own vision is reminiscent of people in general, and individuals in particular who can take someone else's creation and work it to their advantage but are otherwise stymied when faced with a *carte blanche* situation. *The Epistle to the Romans* is a case in point.

This book by Apostle Paul is one of the most influential books ever written, giving a picture of man's relationship with God which is compatible with the sayings of Jesus in the Gospels. It had great impact on *Augustine of Hippo*, *Martin Luther* and *John Calvin*. It provided clues as to how the intellectual and social world of the West would develop against such concepts as original sin and man being saved only through faith, alone. The power of the epistle has God cancelling out sin through love.

That said, the faith of Paul is not the faith of the Galileans or Jerusalem Christians, who had been Jesus's closest personal friends. Wilson writes:

(Paul's faith*) grew out of a hatred, a fascination, in the end a possessive love for one strand in Jesus's teaching which they (the other apostles) seem to have missed: that is the strand contained in the parable of the Publican and the Pharisee.*

Peter saw James and the other Galileans envisioning Jesus as the last great Jewish prophet speaking quite literally within the main body of Judaism, not outside the Torah and Jewish tradition. It was from confrontation with this body of *Jerusalem Christians* that Paul decided that Judaism had to be overturned.

His personality is central to this advocacy, as he was a man tormented with conflict, in constant war with his colleagues as adversaries; his mind at odds with the Law and grace, God's righteousness and man's fallen nature, and at loggerheads between interpreters of Mt. Sinai and Golgotha.

The Cross of Jesus became Paul's cross, and then that of Christianity. He had been a bitter persecutor of Christians, which led to intolerable guilt, ultimately to be expiated in a miraculous conversion, followed by internalizing Jesus altogether as his personal savior.

That enlightening experience was then projected on to the human race, which he saw as neither righteous nor just, but lost and sinful requiring saving.

PAUL AND FREUD

Centuries later, Sigmund Freud's mission was not the hereafter but the existential now. Even so, he showed much in common with Paul. Modernity was consumed with the crippling effects of guilt and repressed anxiety on human consciousness as Western society was experiencing the *Industrial Revolution*, which cut the past and what was understood as reality from the future which was not. People were making material progress but fixated with debilitating depression and stultifying disquiet.

Freud, the Jewish psychiatrist, formulated relief through a talking cure rather than a ritual of prayer and good works. For Paul, it was salvation through Christ and the forgiveness of sins. For Freud, it was sanity and the ability to get out of bed in the morning and have some kind of life.

Paul and Freud were moralists of a difference. With the liberation of repressed demons that Freud insisted we all possess, coping mechanisms could be proposed to lead to self-awareness and the triumph of *Eros* or the life instinct over *Thanatos* or the death instinct; thus neutralizing man's capacity for being his own worst enemy by improving the possibility of him becoming his own best friend, or moving from *self-destruction* to *self-realization*.

It was an interpretation like Paul's of the Jesus message ripe for the times.

Whereas 2,000 years ago, man was obsessed with the *idea of God*, a century ago when man declared *the death of God*, his existential ego took center stage with depression, anxiety and what Freud came to call "hysteria" rushing in to fill the void. Freud's "talking cure" was quickly derailed with man escaping into self-indulgent psychosexual satisfaction. We have been stuck in narcissism ever since.

Western society, especially the United States, embraced Freudianism as the palliative they were looking for, to change without changing at all, the medication to quell their pesky free-floating anxiety with a balm of free-floating expression. Few realized they were embracing a new religion of sand castles in the air. Not too strangely, the answers to man's dilemma were wrapped in Apostle Paul's and Psychiatrist Freud's own troubled psyches.

By a curious juxtapose of ideas, one about Jesus and his message; the other about the libido and its taunting demands; one steeped in theology and the other in psychology; one monotheistic, the other atheistic; but the message of both ringing clearly false today.

Paul is saying man is not capable of morality; Freud is saying man is helplessly consumed with lust and equally incapable of morality. Paul is saying Jesus as God is the answer; Freud is saying a *healthy ego* and his *Reality Principle* is.

Jesus writing in the sand

They are saying righteousness is not enough; that man can abstain from murder but carries within himself the forces of destruction. *The Law of Moses* can tell us to be chaste in a negative sense, but it cannot banish the demons from our souls. Freud unwittingly has introduced us to our demons and now we are obsessed with them. Paul locked Jesus out of Christianity and now it is what this faith needs but is impossible to acquire. It bears repeating:

Paul and Freud took on the world to reflect their own personal torments and made them ours.

Jesus in the Gospels teaches us that morality and virtue are not enough. And even though Jesus didn't find these values that important in his own life, his message made it clear that the yawning gulf between the perfection of God and the imperfection of man could never be bridged by a mere set of religious observations or rules.

There was no pomp and circumstance to the Jesus ministry, no baroque rites and rituals, no cathedrals or castles in the air, no priests draped in majestic gowns or members of powerful hierarchies. There was only a charismatic teacher named Jesus writing with a stick in the sand.

Paul and Freud, on the other hand, interpreted their message in terms of observations and rules. Paul is saying:

The mere existence of the moral imperative cannot save us because we are all exiled from our true homeland with God. Jesus did not offer a way to be morally better but to be Sons of God.

Paul wasn't concerned with a proven historical Jesus as Jesus was internalized as his redeemer. In Romans (8:12; 8:21, 22; 8:39), Paul expresses his discovery of Jesus outside the realm of history into the *"unsearchable riches of Christ."*

That was once true of many who called themselves Christian. As Christianity has come to lose its simplicity, it has come also to lose something greater, its validity and relevance. It started with Paul and his interpretation of the gospels.

For Paul, the *Synoptic Gospels*, the first three gospels of *Jesus as Christ*, is not Christianity as a religion, but religion in a deeper more significance sense. The three gospels of the *New Testament* were written by Matthew, Mark and Luke, men who had learned to look at things in Paul's way.

That was not true of the *Fourth Gospel*, the Gospel of John. The Synoptic Gospels make no claim to history; the Fourth Gospel implies that sense.

The Synoptic Gospels are lenses focused on the person of Jesus through the eyes of *Paul of Tarsus*. Paul focused on Jesus and saw him as a man in whom God Himself was at work. John in the Fourth Gospel saw Jesus as totally a Jew governed by the Law of Moses with a Jewish orientation and perspective. His Jesus had no interest in going beyond the borders of Judaism to embrace Gentile pagans.

In the belief system of Paul, which became the belief system of Christianity, the Synoptic Gospels exemplified Jesus as God-like love in his own person. This was in defiance of the cruelty of men and in the indifference of nature. For Paul, the principle of life itself was love. To live without "agape," without unconditional love, he saw morality itself as a sham. Religious observance in Paul's lexicon was synonymous with the word, love.

For the modern reader, looking 2,000 years back, the perception of love as perceived by Paul would be close to incomprehensible. Likewise, his hymn to love wrapped in the mystical Jesus was that of a visionary governed by the quality of his imagination. We are not an imagining people.

The events of Jesus's life take shape after they pass through Paul's eyes of faith. Since he is the architect of Christianity, the same is likely to be true of those who call themselves Christians today.

Likewise, much as the world might deny it, there is little that shapes the sensual materialistic mind of the times that hasn't passed through Freud's prism of consciousness. He is presented here as foil to our own misgivings looking through a mirror darkly.

Most readers are not likely to be that familiar with the *"Freud, the Father of Psychoanalysis,"* although his roots go back less than one hundred years.

German moral philosopher & Father of Psychoanalysis

For my generation, we looked into the mirror and did not see a face but a retinue of maladies that blocked our consciousness as our eyes were blurred with the ideas of neuroses and psychoses. These ideas emanated from men schooled in Freud's psychoanalysis. They have bombarded our psyches unrepentantly ever since. Freud explained our deepest terrors to us with his explanatory models, which we took to be true with little evidence and even less proof. By the same token, the Synoptic Gospels explained Jesus to us that was Paul's sense of the man. It was not John's Jesus as shown in the *Fourth Gospel*, yet Paul's Christianity persists, while Freud has regressed into history, although his instruments have never been more in evidence. Paul's world is that of theology and religion; Freud's of psychology and morality. Close examination suggests they are the same.

THE MOST DANGEROUS MAN!

James R. Fisher, Jr., Ph.D.
© June 9, 2015

"There are three classes of people in the world. The first learn from their own experience. These are wise. The second learn from the experience of others. They are happy. The third neither learn from their own experience nor the experience of others. These are fools.

"A man of the best parts and greatest learning, if he does not know the world by his own experience and observation, will be very absurd, and consequently very unwelcome in company.

"He may say very good things; but they will be probably so ill-timed, misplaced, or improperly addressed that he had much better hold his tongue."

Lord Chesterfield (1694 – 1773), English Statesman and Man of Letters

The most dangerous man is out of sync with his times for he is able to penetrate the noise and sense of how it listens.

He is guided by a vision that is not revealed to his cognitive mind but occupies his spiritual comprehension, a wisdom that seems conscious but is not; a sense of things which otherwise seem senseless.

He is the undeclared enemy of convention and all those who are guided by that tradition.

He is a student of history which means he is a student of his times.

Many ignore him, but when they can't, they twist his words back to corroborate their own thinking, and if that fails, they are bent on destroying him for he is a danger to them and all that they hold dear.

He looks at the world as it is and does not fear the fact that it is changing.

They look at the world as it was and deny the fact that it is changing.

He admits he does not have answers but can clearly see that conventional wisdom is not wisdom at all, but the mind of a fool unhinged from the reality of what is collectively being experienced.

He has never been trusted because he has little interest in second, third and fourth sources of information, information with which the collective "they" find precious and the résumé of their guiding actions.

He understands them because he records how their actions listen, and uses this to articulate some sense of what he sees on the horizon and why he sees it as so.

They ask him, "Is this your vision?" He answers, "No, it is yours!"

They ponder this and decide he is a madman, a danger to himself and others and must be dealt with in the spirit of what it considers rational, wise and final.

They justify this mindset because he says such inflammatory things as "The Islamic State of Iraq and Syria" (ISIS) was inevitable as it represents the blunt edge of the future turned back on itself."

They ask him what he means by this. He answers with a question, "How else can you explain ISIS?"

They answer collectively, "That is a stupid question!"

"Stupid or not," he replies, "How can you explain, then, that one hundred thousandth percent of mankind has crippled the world?"

Confidently, they reply, "Because they are a terrorist group!"

He asks, "What is a terrorist group?"

They walk away from him in disgust, shaking their heads, now more fearful of him than ever before because he is a madman with an agenda, an agenda that they don't understand.

One of the group says flippantly, "He's a terrorist."

All eyes light up. "Yes, yes, he is a terrorist. He is one of them!"

Then they ponder what should they do. How can they control him, dispose of him without acting like terrorists themselves?

Someone says, "Isolate him, place an embargo on him, taint his name, and spread rumors about him; turn his family against him, his employer, his friends; turn society against him."

Then someone remarks questionably, "Until he becomes like us?"

"Yes, yes," the mob says in unison, "Until he becomes like us, sane, responsible, understandable, agreeable."

Then someone from the back, yells, "And predictable!"

"Yes, yes!" A roar erupts from the crowd, "And predictable like us!"

No one learned anything from **the most dangerous man** because no one got inside of what he was saying; no one was listening. They only heard the echo of their own fears.

* * *

Two thousand years ago, the *Roman Empire* was unraveling, an empire that could not see the hand writing on the wall. Each time it crushed a rebellion it won by losing. The more it tried to dictate the future through control the more it sponsored chaos. It failed to see the world was changing and unwittingly sponsored and then paradoxically generated new enemies.

The most dangerous man of the first century of the Christian era was a man named Paul, who was betrayed by his own people who did not understand him and was beheaded by Rome. He died a failure and was meant to pass into oblivion, but he wrote what he felt, what he saw and what he believed, not certain if his words would survive, but they did.

Paul had the distinction of being seen as *the most dangerous man* by the early *Jerusalem Christians* as well as by the Roman Empire. They both thought they had gotten rid of their nemesis. Instead, this peculiar little man changed the world for the next two thousand years (see "Jesus, Paul and Freud" in these pages).

The most dangerous man now walks among us, but nobody knows him. He asks questions that have no answers in the current lexicon. He is comfortable being seen as a madman.

SELF-UNIVERSITY, THE NATURAL WORLD OF THE AUTODIDACT

PROFILES OF AUTODIDACTS

"CHICAGO" WAYNE SANDER, ENGINEER

DR. DONALD FARR, ENGINEER/PSYCHOLOGIST

CHARLES D. HAYES, AUTHOR/PHILOSOPHER

DR. DAVID LEE STAMP, PROFESSOR/SCIENTIST

James R. Fisher, Jr., Ph.D.
© September 21, 2014

SELF-UNIVERSITY, THE MODERN PROMISE OF PLATO

A number of coincidental things have recently tumbled into place and penetrated my consciousness, thanks to e-mails and the Internet. They concern something common to us all and revolve around the concept of the autodidact.

PROFILE OF WAYNE SANDERS, ENGINEER & PERENNIAL STUDENT:

Wayne Sander writes:

I am sure this article would not otherwise rise to the level of attracting your attention (or many others outside this area). But since we share a small bit of the same geographical history, I thought you might enjoy a brief respite from your all-encompassing intellectual pursuits. This was a tribute to me in the long newspaper:

"OSHER STUDENT CLOSING IN ON 200th COURSE!"

"Chicago" Wayne Sander's upbringing in a Midwestern Mississippi River town to a blue-collar family that valued hard work and skilled labor over higher education, gave no indication that one day he would excel at not only higher education, but education for pure intellectual recreation.

"The narrative I grew up believing was that college and university was for spoiled rich kids who were too lazy – and probably incompetent – to earn an 'honest living,'" said Sander.

As such, he put in only enough effort to maintain a C average in high school. "Seven years later, with a wife and two small children, working a seven-day rotating shift in a chemical factory, the truth regarding the value of education finally revealed itself.

Without the benefit of further education, I was destined to a lifetime of relatively mindless work, employing a biorhythm-destroying schedule that was only sustainable with copious quantities of black coffee and Alka-Seltzer."

So, with only one high-school science class and minimal math under his belt, Sander concluded that the way out was a degree in engineering. "As ridiculous as that aspiration now seems, we sold our little house, my treasured T-Bird and took our modest savings to embark on what most considered a 'fool's errand,'" he said.

Four and one-half years later, he proudly accepted his degree in mechanical engineering from *San Diego State University*, having worked full-time for all but one semester. He continued to finish a graduate degree at night, while working as an engineer by day. Along the way, he decided that in his retirement, he'd like to return to campus, possibly as a part-time faculty member. He did in fact return – decades later – but again as a student, completing a second graduate degree at age 70.

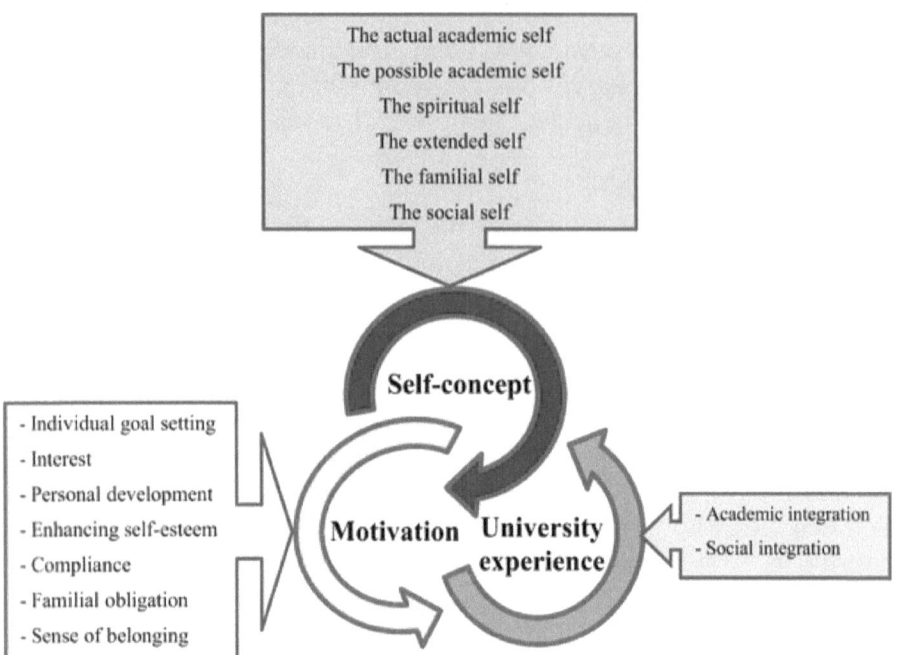

The actual academic self
The possible academic self
The spiritual self
The extended self
The familial self
The social self

Self-concept

- Individual goal setting
- Interest
- Personal development
- Enhancing self-esteem
- Compliance
- Familial obligation
- Sense of belonging

Motivation   University experience

- Academic integration
- Social integration

"Directly following completion of that degree, I actually fulfilled my earlier aspiration by accepting a position as an affiliate professor in *SDSU's College of Engineering* as part of a program called *Project Lead the Way*," said Sander.

"It's where high-school science teachers are taught to teach introductory engineering classes as part of their curriculum. It's also designed to attract female and minority students to the engineering field. A great program.

It was during this on-campus exposure that I discovered the *Osher program*. It's a virtual smorgasbord of educational offerings … a myriad of previously unexplored and surprisingly fascinating subjects. It's also addictive."

Addictive indeed. *The Osher Institute at SDSU* offers intellectual adventure for students' age 50 and better, and Sander took his first course in the spring of 2006. He has since breezed through 195 more, on topics ranging from philosophy, history, and human aggression; to democracy, morality and musical theater.

"My first semester was incredible in the offerings and the level of instruction," said Sander. "The three most memorable that semester were *The Dawn & Twilight of Science*, a four-session class by Bruno Leone, a spellbinding lecturer and concert pianist. Here is truly a world-class lecturer, the likes of which were absent in my previous exposure to higher education.

"Also offered that semester was a course entitled *U.S. Supreme Court: Who Elected Them Anyway?* It was conducted by Gary LaFleur, a knowledgeable and gentle lecturer who destroyed my mostly negative stereotypical biases about attorneys.

"And an unforgettable course entitled *Impolite Subjects; Sex, Religion & Politics* by Rolf Schulze.

It's the only class I 'had' to repeat. A memory is indelibly etched in my mind. It was toward the last of the six-session course. One class member, a frail, stern-looking lady with her grey hair tied back in a bun, resembled a second-grade teacher I had – one that my grandfather had told me 'She was an old lady when I was in the second grade.'

This widowed lady raised her hand and softly said, *'You know, a one-night stand now and then is nice, but I really miss the continuing companionship of a committed partner.'* A very poignant sharing with our class by a woman whose name I can't recall. One who earned my everlasting respect for both her bravery and for this program that allowed and encouraged her to crack open the window to our rarely shared humanity."

Bravery. Humanity. Friendship. Camaraderie. Potlucks. Adventures. Even a reunion of long-lost college roommates. It's all waiting to be found at the *Osher Institute*.

By the way, "Chicago" Wayne is not from Chicago. He chose the nickname as a result of his attempt to teach his wife's infant grandson new words. The little boy found the word hilarious. *"Each time he heard it, he nearly fell off his chair. But he also thought it was my name,"* said Sander. *"So, in that family I became 'Chicago.' But because it's distinctive and has three explosive syllables, I found it useful for dinner reservations where they call your name. In addition, hostesses and others – regardless of interaction frequency – never forgot your name."*

With or without the Chicago portion of his name, Wayne Sander has already become a legend at *SDSU's Osher Institute.*

PROFILE OF DR. DONALD FARR, NASA SCIENTIST & PROFESSOR

Dr. Don, as I call him, like Wayne Sander, grew up in my sleepy little Mississippi Valley town of Clinton, Iowa.

He went to high school at the North End of Clinton, or Lyons, and graduated from *Lyons High School*, while Wayne Sander and I graduate from *Clinton High.*

All three of us graduated the same year, all three from working class families, and all three have had international careers.

Like Wayne Sander, Don expected to labor in some factory. Once out of high school, he joined the *Curtis Lumber Company*, a Clinton industrial plant making finished products out of wood and shipped all over the world.

The Curtis Lumber Company was like a vestigial organ from another time.

In the early twentieth century, Clinton was the lumber capital of the world turning sawdust into gold as logs were floated down the Mississippi River to Clinton from Minnesota and Wisconsin and sawed into lumber and finished products.

When the lumber forests were depleted, the mills in Clinton shut down, and scores of millionaires left town, but not *Curtis Lumber Company*. It is still making sashes and doors, cabinets and other finished products.

As it wasn't in the stars for Wayne Sander to be a laborer in a factory, the same was true of Dr. Don. He went into the *US Navy*, and the navy sent him back to school. At first, he wasn't overjoyed, wanting to go back to be a sailor, but gradually made the transition and saw it as his lot in life.

DR. DON WRITES:

"I got my *BS at San Diego State University*. Then, I helped to form *The National University*, started a new graduate program (*Engineering*

Technology) and completed my *Masters* (Industrial Technology) there while teaching a class, lecturing in several other colleges, all while working full time as a researcher at *General Dynamics* in San Diego, CA. I then went on to complete my *Doctorate* (Engineering Psychology-Human Engineering) at *California Pacific University*."

Dr. Don went on from there to become a NASA scientist in ergonomics designing and testing the internal accommodations for comfort and efficacy of the space capsules for astronauts, working for NASA more than thirty years.

Then, despite several physical maladies including a broken spine, eye disease and diabetes, he found the time to teach, and to work as a volunteer to *Operation Gratitude* (for American military personnel stationed abroad).

In order to keep up with his discipline to effectively mentor graduate students at several universities, he maintained an ambitious e-mail "Memories" network of several hundred correspondents stretched across the globe. This included many former residents of Clinton, Iowa, collating and dispersing these messages daily to interested parties. It was time consuming work, and often energy sapping, while at the same time dealing with pesky health issues, but it was important to him to never forget his roots, and the community that launched him into his productive, many faceted life experiences.

Like Wayne Sander and yours truly, now in our 80's, Dr. Don has not slowed down. He says he enjoys helping people, and must "keep on, keep'n on."

He and Wayne Sander personifies the wisdom of Shakespeare:

"It is one of the most beautiful compensations of this life that no man can sincerely try to help others without helping himself."

AUTHOR/PHILOSOPHER CHARLES D. HAYES, THE ULTIMATE AUTODIDACT

In the early 1990's, I received a manuscript from a man in Alaska, who told me he worked for *British Petroleum*, and had written a book, and was wondering if I would give it a look.

This kind of thing happens often to people who write books. I often ignore the request or write a curt note that I wish the prospective author well. That was not the case with this manuscript.

I started to read it, made notes and comments on the margins of the pages, finally reading the complete manuscript, then sitting there, pausing and saying to myself, "Wow, can this guy ever write!"

It went beyond that. Charles Hayes was obviously well read and an original thinker with a clear point of view, and a passion for ideas and a will to express them.

I shared my regard for the writing with my wife, BB, and said I was going to send the book back with my marginal comments.

"You will do no such thing!" she declared, but then more softly, *"Jim, he won't have any idea what you're saying because nobody can read your handwriting,"* which was true.

So, I typed my comments, which amounted to a small book in and of itself.

"Do you think he will be offended?" I asked her.

She looked at me with that beautiful twinkle in her eyes, and said, *"You'd die to have someone do that with your writing."*

It was true. It was also true that it has never happened.

That was my introduction to Charles D. Hayes, a self-confessed high school dropout, an *ex-US Marine*, a former *Dallas, Texas police officer*, a petroleum worker, and a guy I suspect reads as much if not more than I do.

That first book was *"Proving You're Qualified: Strategies for Competent People without College Degrees"* (1995).

He followed that with *"Self-University"* (1996) and then *"Beyond the American Dream: Lifelong Learning and the Search for Meaning in a Postmodern World"* (1998). This book received recognition by the *American*

Library Association's CHOICE magazine as one of the most outstanding academic books of the year.

Although seeing this as an inclination to gain the respect of academia, I feel his focus should stay beyond academia as it has little to teach him. For me, he is like the monks of the *Middle Ages* cutting away the dogmatic fixation of institutional protocol to boldly explore unchartered virgin territory.

Charles Hayes followed this book with a little red book as a reminder to those with the initiative to grow titled *"Training Yourself: The 21st Century Credential"* (2000). This was followed by *"Portals in a Northern Sky,"* (2003, a novel), *"The Rapture of Maturity: A Legacy of Lifelong Learning"* (2004), and others including the before mentioned *Proving You're Qualified: Strategies for Competent People without College Degrees*; *Self-University: The Price of Tuition is Desire and Your Degree is a Better Life*. He also has a bevy of Amazon.com Kindle essays which reflect what he calls his "unabashed liberal" perspective.

Although I've never met author Hayes, I feel I know him as he writes honestly and with integrity, along with passion and insight, dedication and energy promoting the idea that education is not something you get but something you take.

If you happened to be an Internet explorer, you will find his work has been featured in the *LA Progressive*, *USA Today*, and the *UTNE Reader* on *National Public Radio's "Talk of the Nation,"* and on *Alaska Public Radio's "Talk of Alaska."*

DR. DAVID LEE STAMP, SCIENTIST, PROFESSOR, INVENTOR

In 1958, after accepting a job with *Nalco Chemical Company* of Chicago, leaving my position as a chemist in *Research & Development* at *Standard Brands, Inc.*, in my hometown of Clinton, Iowa, who should show up at my door than the little brother of Don Stamp, with whom I played four years of high school football, basketball and baseball. I was trying to sell my old jalopy, and little brother David showed up with his father looking to find a vehicle for him for college. They decided to take a pass on my modest heap.

Sixty-one years later, David, now an emeritus professor, a text book author, and inventor shows up at my Tampa, Florida home with that same winning smile and quiet assurance that I remembered those many years before.

He claimed to have known me well, not personally, but as a high school athlete with him as a fan. I had no idea that he had been an athlete; in fact, an outstanding one. He won the *State of Iowa Indoor High School* high jumping contest and was an All-American swimmer at *Clinton High School.*

With a self-deprecating smile, he confessed, "I won a full scholarship to *Iowa State University*," then with a shrug of his shoulders, "managed to flunk out my freshman year."

Although we were from the same hometown, he much younger, essentially strangers to each other, this admission was quite startling. Such candor was not remembered of his high achieving family in athletics and academics. Why was he telling me this?

With his disarming personality and engaging candor, my suspicions melted away quickly with his openness and casual acceptance of things as they are. Here was a person who accepted himself "as is" without apology and others as he might find them. This became more evident as he told me his story.

"You know if you have had a near fatal accident on a motorcycle, it can tear up your mind so bad that it can take years to muster the courage to get back on a bike. What you must do is take that first step and sit on a stationary bike. Well, that was me with education."

A series of manual labor jobs followed his abysmal attempt at college, working in construction with concrete and working in the roundhouse making boxcars for the railroad. Then the *US Selective Service Draft* got him, and he was in the *US Army.* He came out of the army with the *US G.I. Bill*, and took a course at the *Clinton Community College*, then another course, working construction all the time, but studying like a monk from 7 to 11 p.m. every night.

Then, after laboring over a short letter to the *Iowa State University Registrar* for seemingly forever, he decided finally to mail his request to be reinstated as a student at the university. The thought of applying to any other university never apparently crossed his mind.

Within two weeks of the mailing, he got the good news that he could reenroll, which he did posthaste. Now with a wife and children to support, he had to find work to supplement his *G.I. Bill.* That said, he knew his regiment of studying from 7 to 11 p.m. every night must never be interrupted. With some ingenuity and serendipity, he found a way, and was off to the races, now academically.

Propelled by this motivation and industry, he was rewarded first with a B.S., then a M.S. and finally a Ph.D. in the physiology of plants with only two B's and the rest A's for his academic efforts.

With a doctorate degree in hand, he took a position as a professor in his discipline at *Oregon State University*, while also acting as an adviser to undergraduate students experiencing some of the same difficulties he once endured.

For his work in the physiology of plants, he wrote several scientific papers for journals and acquired two patents. He also was co-author of a textbook that is still in circulation in his discipline.

From *Oregon State*, he was recruited by *Texas Tech University* where he was in turn enticed by headhunters to join *Stauffer Chemical*. Eventually, with other colleagues in his discipline, he started a seed company in Nebraska, which he left when he decided to retire at the age of 64.

His wife died in 2012 and now he roams the country visiting his five children and eleven grandchildren. His son lives in the *Tampa Bay* area and the reason for his visit with me. He plans to go cross country now to visit his daughter who lives in *Idaho*.

You could never meet a kinder, quieter or more modest man who puts you at ease while releasing new oxygen into a room. I still feel his presence as I write these words.

FINAL THOUGHTS ON AUTODIDACTS:

Longshoreman turned philosopher Eric Hoffer never went to school. He became blind as a child, his sight not restored until he was nineteen. Once he could see, he discovered a voracious appetite for the printed word.

I've read most everything he's written or has been written about him.

Humanness came of age when man asked the first question. Social stagnation results not from a lack of answers but from the absence of the impulse to ask questions

Eric Hoffer

In 1950, he collected his thoughts in a handwritten manuscript, and looked to see who published most of the books he read. It was *Harper & Row*. So, without preamble, he sent his scribbled handwritten manuscript to that publisher.

The book was published in 1951 as *"The True Believer: Thoughts of the Nature of Mass Movements."*

I read the book in 1958 and found it thought provoking although different. At the time, I had no idea that he was utterly self-educated having had little formal education experiencing blindness when he was a child with his sight not returning until he was nearly an adult.

Then in the late 1960's, Hoffer appeared on *CBS Television* with pundit Eric Sevareid. It was a fascinating two-hour free flowing conversation. Instant fame followed. The tag, "true believer" became part of our language to describe the "herd mentality."

Hoffer is every man. Yet, I doubt if he would be inclined to take two hundred eclectic courses like Wayne Sander, or to collect impressive college credentials like "Chicago" Wayne or Dr. Don. I see him more like Charles D. Hayes, a consummate autodidact.

He was asked where he got his ideas. Was it from auditing university courses, listening to esteemed lecturers, or attending seminal seminars?

He gave that lower diaphragm chuckle of his, answering with a twinkle in his eyes, "You might say I am like the fellow who stands on a street corner just waiting for the right guy to come by." He was referring to the authors of the books that lit his fire. I can relate to that.

It has been a stunning discovery of mine that I don't like the intimacy of a discussion group, as clearly does Wayne Sander. That said, it should come as no surprise having always preferred to study alone that I took academic studies as a necessity to be credentialed but was never of academia. Nor do I like crowds while paradoxically loving the ignominy of the teaming city surrounded by possibly millions of strangers.

This is offered simply to point out that we autodidacts are not a homogeneous group.

Given these idiosyncrasies, people, from every quadrant of the globe are visiting the blogs and websites of autodidacts because the visitors see these are real people having real experiences with something interesting, perhaps even vital to say.

MEISTER ECKHART (13th century mystique) writes:

A human being has so many skins inside, covering the depths of the heart. We know so many things, but we don't know ourselves! Why, thirty or forty skins or hides, as thick and hard as an ox's or bear's, cover the soul! Go into your own ground and learn to know yourself there.

We live in an eternal now, which in and of itself is always new. These autodidacts have been introduced to you the reader in the hopes that they will in turn introduce you to yourself.

THE END OF SINCERITY?

James R. Fisher, Jr., Ph.D.
© April 30, 2014

When I was an undergraduate student at the *University of Iowa*, after a physics lecture, Rex Jamison invited me to have coffee with him.

Rex was valedictorian of his high school class at Story City, Iowa. He was also number one in my class at Iowa as well. He would go on to become a *Rhodes Scholar* at Cambridge in Great Britain, and subsequently to graduate from *Harvard University's School of Medicine* at the top of his class.

Rex and I were acquaintances taking many of the same courses, living in Hillcrest Dormitory, and often involved in bull sessions on various topics.

At the time, rather a devout Irish Roman Catholic, and known to attend mass and communion several times a week, I suppose you could say I wore my religion on my sleeve. Rex was not religious.

One night the bull session turned to religion and Rex had the floor. He challenged me among all our friends to justify the tenets of *Roman Catholicism*, the relevance of *Papal Encyclicals*, which were the basis of *Papal Infallible Authority* and the ubiquitous canopy of the church's dogmatic teachings. As a debater, it was evident that I was no match for him.

Rex's prominence as a high school debater was apparent as he systematically reduced my religious belief system literally to intellectual confetti. He never let up even when my responses were reduced to whispered stutters. I felt naked with all my clothes on.

Therefore, I was surprised when he invited me for coffee after our class in physics one day. I couldn't imagine what he wanted from me as my only contact with him was when he had an audience; when he could hold court with his peers and demonstrate his intellectual superiority by punishing one of us with his. It was an unkindness that I sensed, even at that time, was part of his character and a cover for something that was obviously missing that I didn't know and had little interest in finding out.

- 163 -

He was not a good listener, and always seemed to have to be "on." My wonder was how he could feel "on" with only me as his audience.

After our second cup of coffee, he looked into my eyes deeply, and said to me, "Jim, teach me how to be sincere."

Sincerity...

I thought he was kidding, so I laughed and said, "Right!"

"I'm serious. I watch, hell, I study you. Did you know that?"

"Noooo," I said. That felt weird. He studied "me," me of all people, a person he had destroyed before our peers.

"Yeah, I do. You listen to others. You listen to me. I tried to make you mad the other night when we were discussing religion, and I could see pain in your eyes, sincere pain, not phony pain, not contrived pain. I got to you, but I couldn't stop. I also saw anger, and I thought *he's going to hit me*, and you started to stutter, yeah, stutter! That was the damnedest thing. You're a mountain compared to me and could have crushed me like a bug, and what do you do? You stutter!

"Now, that's sincerity, and I want to learn how to attain it. Teach me! Be my rabbi."

"Rex," I said evenly, "sincerity can't be taught. Sincerity can only be felt. It doesn't come out of the head. It comes out of the heart. It is not about dominating or being submissive. It is being comfortable within your own skin, not to impress or be impressed, but to simply enjoy being you. That is all, nothing else, nothing more sophisticated or more earth shocking than that."

"Really?"

"Yes, really!"

He gathered up his books, turned and left, looked back and said, "I'll owe you for the coffee, okay?"

We never had a conversation again. He went on to be a successful nephrologist at Standard University, writing many world acclaimed papers in his medical discipline, speaking at distinguished conferences throughout the world, and inventing procedures that are used by medical professionals across the globe.

THE END OF SINCERITY?

I thought of this conversation when Adam Silver, the Commissioner of the National Basketball Association (NBA), told a press conference that Donald Sterling, the owner of the LA Clippers, an NBA team, would be banned for life from the NBA, exacted a $2.5 million fine, and could never again step into an NBA arena.

Donald Sterling's crime was having said some outrageous and despicable things about African Americans in general and NBA players and former players, such as Magic Johnson in particular using disparaging language to his former mistress, which she recorded.

He made these remarks in the privacy of his own home, not knowing that she was doing this. But the remarks were of such a shockingly racist nature that the NBA Players Association, of which more than 80 percent are African American, as well as NBA fans throughout the league, demanded the commissioner come down hard on the LA Clippers' owner, and they were not disappointed.

If fact, I don't imagine most NBA players or fans expected the commissioner to be so draconian, or his wrath to be so personal against the Clippers' owner. The commissioner made it emphatic that his ultimate objective was to strip Donald Sterling of ownership of the LA Clippers with an early sale of the franchise.

To accomplish this, the commissioner needed three-quarters of the 30 NBA franchise owners to vote for such an action. He claimed it was within the NBA constitution to exercise such an action.

FIRST AMENDMENT RIGHTS –
WHERE IS THE NBA IN ALL THIS?

Donald Sterling has a history or racism and has paid fines before for his shameful bigotry. What makes this different? Charles Krauthammer on the "Bill O'Reilly Show" of Fox TV claims the groundswell of reaction to this tape recording is evidence of the huge shift in public opinion in the past 50 years.

That said, what is disturbing to me is the invasion of privacy, the violation of free speech, and the overwhelming emotional piling on that everyone seems to be engaged in without a moment's reflection on what it may mean – down the road – to everyone else in terms of freedom of speech.

So, Donald Sterling is a despicable human being, but even a despicable human being under the *United States Constitution* has certain rights, among which are found in the *Bill of Rights* with the first amendment of those rights the *Freedom of Speech*.

Can the NBA franchise owners vote a franchise owner out of his ownership because he made some racist remarks in the privacy of his own home?

If this emotional madness is taken to its logical conclusion, and Donald Sterling is forced to sell because of these remarks, what does that say for the rest of us who are not billionaires, not millionaires, indeed, working paycheck to paycheck?

Can we lose our jobs, lose our homes, or be ostracized from our community if a son or daughter, brother or sister, uncle or aunt, or other friend or relative uses an iPhone to record what we say in the privacy of our own home about anything or anybody?

Is there no sanctuary where we can express ourselves, vent our spleen, damn the world, damn the boss, or our company; damn our cat or our dog, our next door neighbor, or anyone down the street who gets our dander up for any imagined or real slight?

If that is the case, more people will be like Rex, finding it impossible to understand sincerity, because sincerity will have died, for no one will be able to afford to say what they actually feel or think; nobody will come to trust anyone to keep a personal confidence of their most private thoughts. It will mark the end of spontaneity.

By punishing a reprobate such as Mr. Sterling for his sick mind and hostile spirit who happens to be an NBA owner, could we be punishing us all in abstentia?

THE FISHER PARADIGM©™®

An Organizational Development (OD) Instrument

Intellectual Capital & the Power of People!

James R. Fisher, Jr., Ph.D.
© February 10, 2010

NOTICE

A Noun. In grammar, it is any class of words naming or denoting a person, place, thing, action or quality.

Intuition. It is the direct knowing or learning of something without conscious use of reasoning. It is immediate understanding.

Webster's New World College Dictionary (2001)

ABSTRACT

The Fisher Paradigm©™® is a diagnostic tool of organizational development (OD). It is primarily an intuitive rather than cognitive model. There are no algorithms to master, no mathematical verifications to compute, yet it is an authentic tool of this discipline.

OD grew out of a need to bring some order and comprehension to the complex organization, which grows more incomprehensible with the passing of time.

Management attempts to give it direction and purpose while management itself becomes increasingly anachronistic.

OD is currently being underused if not misused as a subset of human resources management (HR).

The function of HR is instrumental (operations) while that of OD is terminal (cultural).

HR is dedicated to the management of things (hiring, placement, training & development), while OD is an assessment tool of organizational health and the integrity of organizational leadership.

HR is an insider discipline with its client senior management. OD is an outsider discipline with its client the collective, which is the organization.

HR reflects the values of senior management. OD assesses the culture and integrity of the organization vis-à-vis its mission.

HR is primarily cognitive; OD is cognitive and intuitive.

HR reflects position power. OD reflects the mindset and moral authority of the organization. Position power meets operational and tactical requirement. Moral authority sees that the organization stays the course consistent with its professed objectives.

HR revolves around expediency of demand and is driven by instrumental values, or the means-to-ends commitment of resources.

OD revolves around the mindset, or shared culture and history of the organization. It is expressed in the unconscious behavior of its members which are either consistent with or inconsistent to its stated mission and objectives.

The main task of OD is to demonstrate mnemonic obligations through intuitive leadership. The past gave integrity and purpose to the organization. Corporate memory is corporate identity. OD assesses this identity as to whether it is functional, dysfunctional, or in crisis.

The corporate memory draws on the will of workers to commit to a common purpose. This depends on qualitative values (culture) and spiritual vitality (motivation). This leads to the counterintuitive idea that the less instrumentally driven the organization the more terminally relevant it is. Permit me to explain.

Total reliance on vertical thinking and cognitive reasoning has placed the organization at risk. This is demonstrated in crisis management, circular argument, and critical thinking employed exclusively to solve problems. In an imperfect world, it calls for the complement of lateral thinking, intuition and creative thinking.

OD engages intuition while still utilizing its cognitive arsenal. The Fisher Paradigm©™® suggests that the unconscious is key to moving beyond rational explanatory limits.

INTRODUCTION OF AN IDEA

We are in a 2,000-year-old cognitive funk. It is doubtful the empirical evidence of The Fisher Paradigm©™® will prove convincing to the obsessively cognitive.

Yet, I would suggest that most leaders are using this paradigm but are unaware of the fact. The efforts of this brief are to encourage the skeptical to apply its wider use. It is a diagnostic tool everyman as well as trained professionals use every day.

The rationale for its use is based on the idea that everything revolves around learned experience. Formal education can either enhance or impede relevant experience as a product of cultural programming. Learned experience has two components:

(1) *Immanence* – something "inside the individual."

(2) *Transcendence* – something "outside the individual."

Consciousness contains more than what it is assumed apparent. There is something felt which has no language. The feeling can be misinterpreted because of cultural programming. The inclination is to explain feelings rather than to acknowledge and use them to advantage.

We talk too much and think too little. Instead of allowing feelings to speak to us, we rush to describe them. This has resulted in an explanatory society. It imposes limits to understanding.

We seem obsessed with what has occurred rather than why it has occurred, missing what is bombarding our senses to tell us. Consequently, we are better at developing explanatory models than determining causation; better at generating data than producing ideas; more inclined to deductive rather than inductive reasoning; more given to *critical thinking* (something known that has worked before) than *creative thinking* (something not known and therefore never experienced before); more disposed to defend sacred biases than to interpret them in terms of modern challenges; more apt to search for rather than to create solutions; more driven to imitate success than to create our own reasoned assessment of a situation.

We are in constant flux and desire stability, continuity and predictability which is dictated by an instrumental means-to-an-end focus. Our senses constantly alert us with feelings that confound this arbitrariness, but we summarily reject them because they are abstract and not concrete; they are impressionistic and not replicable; they are considered whimsical and not "scientific."

The fact remains with all the science we still cannot predict human behavior and therefore are constantly surprised when it confounds our instruments of detection with unexpected and often bizarre regularity.

That said, we prefer *rule-of-the-thumb justifications* to thinking through our problems; to assume what is evident rather than to question its validity because we have been programmed with culturally biased assumptions. Meanwhile, our senses struggle to breakthrough this barrier:

"Did I really sense what I believe I sensed, or am I fooling myself?"

When faced with this dilemma, the tendency is to reject intuition and instead mount an exclusively cognitive action plan falling back on what has worked before, is an accepted practice, and what is expected to work again.

This has proven reliable and predictable for inanimate machines but not necessarily for man, a machine with a conscious conscience and a rather elaborate emotional construct.

Management is comfortable with HR because it is primarily a cognitive discipline with its policies and procedures, its statistical models and algorithms, its graphical designs, its engineering matrixes and modalities, which are easily grasped and justified in terms of clear numerical and tangible objectives. This is corporate speak and HR has perfected it in terms of assuaging management's anxiety. This is not true of OD.

OD does not consider itself a tool of management but as an assessment tool of the health of the organization in terms of internal stress and strain and its ability to meet and successfully function in a climate of external accelerating or unanticipated demands. OD focuses on the workplace culture.

The organizational culture follows this formula:

The structure of work determines the function of work; the function of work creates the dominant workplace culture; the workplace culture dictates the prevailing organizational behavior; the organizational behavior establishes whether an organization is to vegetate, flounder and expire, or survive and thrive.

Since management and the organization's history play into this scenario, management's role cannot be overlooked. To state it another way, the architect of the organization's culture is management, and therefore cannot be given a free pass when an OD intervention is contracted.

Unfortunately, too often OD gives management such a pass, attempting to find other justifiers for the intervention; or OD lacks the tact to partner with management in a scheme that will redress the problem situation with a plan with management's involvement. This will take some effort requiring the translation of possible intuitive constructs into cognitive verities. Management would prefer to confine its role to commitment, feigning being too busy to be involved in the actual intervention. Thus, OD involves a selling job as well.

THE CUBE AS ILLUSTRATION OF THIS PHENOMENON

A cube has six sides, but we can never actually see more than three. Our *immanence* or "something inside" tells us there are three faces, not a cube itself. But if we embrace our *transcendence* or "something outside" in clear subjective reporting, we know we are looking at a cube. We don't say, "I am looking at three faces and deduce I'm looking at a cube." So, it is not false to say that our perceptions contain more than meets the eye.

Immanent transcendence contains within itself the ultimate significance of learned experience, that is, being able to demonstrate enough courage to embrace what we know is there but cannot see.

OD practitioners with diverse backgrounds in such dissimilar fields as psychology and engineering, banking and literature, personnel and manufacturing possess a rich inventory of *immanent transcendence* with which to work.

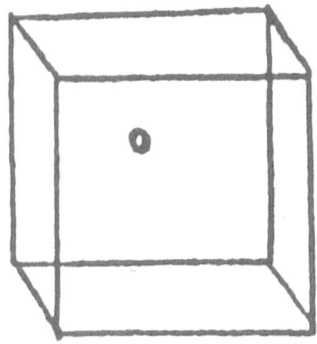

Where is the circle?

But alas, possession of these attributes is not nine-tenths of the law. It often requires penetrating the barrier of our cultural programming.

The individual grows from the "outside-in" rather than the "inside-out." Parents, teachers, preachers, friends, relatives, peers and so on define the individual and what that individual perceives as true, just and right before learned experience kicks in to refute or confirm that programming.

To become oneself, and discover one's essence, rebellion is often displayed as Einstein demonstrated in challenging the 300-year reign of Newtonian physics. More recently Nobel Laureate Richard Feynman playfully reinvented quantum mechanics and grew to be at odds with the very community that idolized him.[2]

Both these accomplished scientists relied more on their internal dialogue than the constraints of their cultural programming to define themselves and orchestrate their minds to new scientific truths.

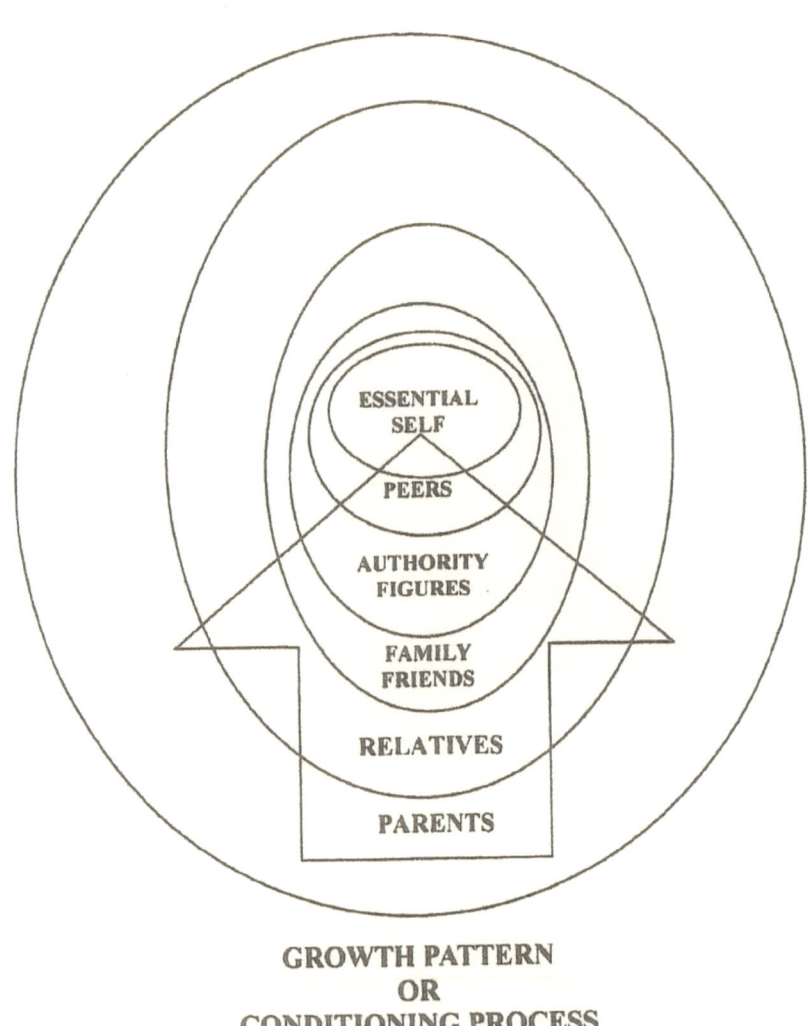

**GROWTH PATTERN
OR
CONDITIONING PROCESS
WE GROW FROM THE "OUTSIDE"..."IN".**

The Fisher Paradigm©™® acknowledges this barrier and proposes a model meant to engage insight, promote intuition, and integrate this into conceptual understanding. Such understanding is only possible when *transcendence* is realized.

The Fisher Paradigm©™® promotes this understanding by postulating that learned experience centers around three discrete spheres of influence:

(1) *Personality*
(2) *Geographic*
(3) *Demographic*

These are offered as profiles recognizing that these spheres are constantly bombarding our senses comparable to the three invisible surfaces of the cube, that is, they are always there but not seen.

CASE IN POINT:

Few would argue the discovery of the "DNA fingerprint" has been one of the more remarkable discoveries in recent times.

James Watson and Francis Crick were co-discoverers of the DNA molecule. That enormous breakthrough was managed through conventional painstaking laboratory research. This is well documented in Watson's bestselling book, *"The Double Helix"* (1969). The methodology was representative of what we expect from scientists.

Not so for Kary B. Mullis, *Nobel Laureate for Chemistry*, 1993. Mullis departs from the furrowed brow stabbing in the dark of this mystifying lot to be more like everyman.

His discovery was that of the polymerase chain reaction (PCR), which redefines the world of DNA, genetics, and forensic science. Known more widely as a surfer, a bar hop, strip club patron, and veteran of Berkeley's rebellious 1960s, he is perhaps the only *Nobel Laureate* to ever describe a possible encounter with aliens.

A scientist of boundless curiosity, he refuses to fit the mold of "scientist," or to accept any proposition based on secondhand or hearsay evidence, preferring to embrace the chiaroscuro of life in all its shades and patterns, not from a distance but as part of him.

In his book *"Dancing Naked in the Mind Field"* (2000), he challenges us to question the authority of scientific dogma and every other kind of authority as he reveals the workings of an uncannily original scientific mind. His words fit comfortably in the Fisher Paradigm©™®. To wit:

Suddenly, I knew how to do it. 'Holy shit!' I hissed and let off the accelerator. The car coasted into a downhill turn. I pulled off. A giant buckeye stuck out from the hill. It rubbed against the window where Jennifer, my girlfriend was asleep. I found an envelope and a pencil in the glove compartment. Jennifer wanted to get moving. I told her something incredible had just occurred to me. She yawned and leaned against the window to go back to sleep.

"We were at mile marker 46.58 on Highway 128 (Malibu, California), and we were at the very edge of the dawn of the age of PCR. I could feel it. I wrote hastily and broke the lead. Then I found a pen. I confirmed (my intuition). I must have smiled. I could still smell the buckeyes, but they were drifting a long way off. I pulled back onto the highway, and Jennifer made a sound of approval . . . About a mile down the canyon, I pulled off again.

"The thing had just exploded again. Not only could I make a zillion copies, but they would always be the same size. I had just solved the two major problems in DNA chemistry. Abundance and distinction. And I had done it in one stroke. I stopped the car at a nice comfortable turnout and took my time working my way through the consequence. Everybody on Earth who cared about DNA would want to use it. It would spread into every biology lab in the world. I would be famous. I would get the Nobel Prize."[3]

The Fisher Paradigm©™® is common yet rare. It is common because the innate capacity for intuition is there for everyone, rare because intuition goes against societal cultural programming in this cognitive age.

If anything, society kills the intuitive drive, as the process of unabashed intuition is too incomprehensible to contemplate. This is displayed in the Washington Post's crass assessment of *"Dancing Naked in the Mind Field"* on the book's back cover:

"Kary Mullis, perhaps the weirdest human ever to win the Nobel Prize in Chemistry, has written a chatty, rambling, funny, iconoclastic tour through the wonderland that is his mind."

The critic focused on the person demonstrating little interest in or curiosity about how a highly trained scientist, Mullis, stepped out of the stereotype of a scientist, and what is perceived to be science, to make this incredible breakthrough.

Dancing naked in the mind field, indeed. Mullis was considered by his scientific colleagues to be a flake, if not incompetent for the ways he behaved against how he was expected to behave as a scientist. Thus, he was not only able to think outside the box but beyond the limits of what the Scots like to call "the multitude."

Mullis was a free man in an age of conformity, which ironically has become more perverse in the scientific community than in such self-regarded institutions as theology, philosophy and academia.

THE FISHER PARADIGM©™®

The Fisher Paradigm©™® looks at the organization whole from its *Personality* (character), *Geography* (baggage) and *Demographics* (make up), then assimilates this wholeness into intuitive insights as complement to more conventional criteria.4

From insights gleaned, the inclination is to move quickly to a more rational mode. This is resisted. Thinking with the whole body is fundamental to this OD process. Once intuition of the Fisher Paradigm©™® registers empirically on the mind, the temptation is to say, *"Why didn't I think of that before?"*

Many have said that of the Mullis discovery. This doesn't make it any less cogent. It was said, incidentally, of my *"Six Silent Killers"* (1998), where I claimed passive and defensive behaviors were like social termites in the infrastructure of the complex organization destroying it from within without anyone noticing.

Currently, there is a popular medical show on television called, "House." Dr. House is a contrary sort, temperamentally infantile, given to polarizing his group on purpose by sending them off to analyze complex cases with their superior medical knowledge, only to step in at the last minute and solve the case with a *eureka like insight*, something of which the group had not considered.

There are three basic spheres of influence in every group dynamic: between the person, the place and the thing. These spheres may be derived from:

(1) *Personality* (person) *Profile*, that is, personal eccentricities, culture, and circumstances;

(2) *Geographic* (place) *Profile*, or situational dynamics on the ground, and in terms of time and circumstances;

(3) *Demographic* (things) *Profile*, which relates to a certain population, but also to the age, gender, race, religion, education, status, experience, competence and circumstances of the individuals within that population.

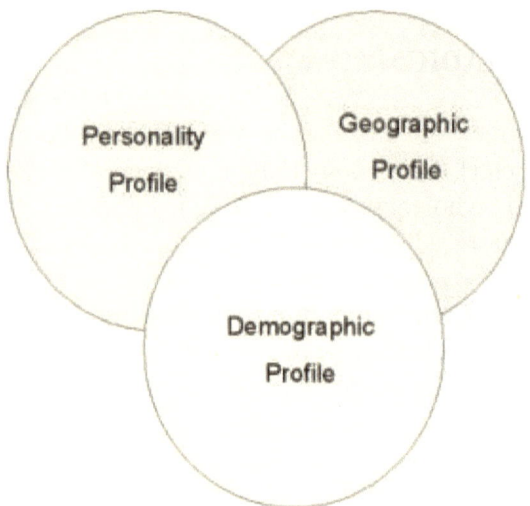

Each of these spheres of influence is constantly in a state of dynamic motion and interaction within the other two.

Where they intercept is the domain of intuition, which alerts the observer to what is really happening.

The observer allows empathetic understanding to surface to consciousness in the form of insight.

For this to occur the observer becomes the observed. The subject and object become inseparable in the dynamic.

Landscape painters often use this device. They observe a scene they are interested in painting. They study it, absorb it, and allow their senses to gradually reduce the distance between what is seen with the eye and what is experienced and perceived imminent and immanent with the whole body. When subject and object become as close as possible to one and the same, landscape painters put brush to canvas but not before. Indian mystic philosopher Krishnamurti was fond of telling this story:

A painter would go to a certain hill in his country overlooking the bay, where a rather unique tree stood on a prominence against the majestic horizon.

The painter would place his canvas on his easel, sit down on his folding chair, unpack his paints, and study the tree, often for hours, then fold up his paraphernalia without touching paint to his canvas and leave.

A stranger observed this several times in passing, and was finally prompted to approach the painter as he was about to leave, and ask:

"Are you a painter?"

"Yes, indeed, I am a painter. Why do you ask?"

"Well, I've observed you many times coming to this place, setting yourself up to paint, but never painting."

"You have observed correctly."

"Why is that?"

"Why is what?"

Now somewhat disturbed as if the painter was playing with him, the man blurted out, "So, if you are a painter, why do you not paint?"

"Oh! I see your problem," the painter said with a smile. "You see, I cannot paint the tree until the tree and I become one, but alas, that has not yet happened."

The man pulled at his beard as he walked away, wondering what he had just learned.

OD operates in somewhat of a similar fashion. The mind is like a heat sensor. An OD practitioner is contracted to solve some organizational problem. Before that problem can be defined, however, like the painter, the OD practitioner must absorb his sense of the place and space of that organization.

The OD practitioner must train himself as to how the organization "listens," and not how the organization believes itself to be. He must become one with his assignment which is to become the embodiment of all the organization's contradictions and conflicts, all its surface and buried issues; in other words, to be a completely and unobtrusively unbiased observer, while sensitive to how the organization actually operates.

OD moves about in no certain patterns penetrating the distracting camouflage that has been erected consciously and sometimes inadvertently to distort the listening.

This wandering about appears as if OD doesn't have a clue, which of course it doesn't; that OD is wasting precious time and money, which it isn't. OD is in the process of becoming one with the organization, not only cognitively but intuitively as well. Eventually, OD, if it has the patience and believes in the process, will experience insights that often erupt out of the blue providing understanding of the problem solving to follow.

Take the familiar story of Archimedes and his principle as reported by Plutarch:

*Archimedes, as he was washing, thought of a way to compute the proportion of gold in King Heiron II's crown by observing how much water flowed over the bathing stool. He leapt up as one possessed, crying eureka! (I've found it"). After repeating this several times, he went his way.*5

The Sicilian mathematician (ca. 287 – 212 B.C.) was the classical absentminded professor, a brilliant thinker often oblivious to the real world and its expectations. He died while tracing a geometric diagram in the dust, as Rome was conquering Syracuse. So absorbed was he in his speculation that he didn't hear the command of a Roman soldier to rise; the soldier, infuriated, ran him through.

Personality Profile

Behavioral
Profile
(Person)

- Personality
- Culture (values)
- Appearance/Identity
- Action

CIRCUMSTANCE

Rationale for the Fisher Paradigm©™®

The Fisher Paradigm©™® is more art than science, more impressionistic than cognitive. Reality is complex, ambivalent, ambiguous, and elusive, as much a matter of play as plan. Given this, the Fisher Paradigm©™® doesn't separate cause from effect, subject from object, thinking from feeling. It is consistent with "Thought and Extension" as proposed by Spinioza.[6]

Spinoza infers natural order must be undivided to be comprehended. Archimedes, tracing the geometric diagram in the dust, was one with the diagram and not separate from it, outside the box and the limits of the world around him, yet very much a part of that world.

The fundamental features of that order, as we perceive them, emerge from within that order, not separate from it. The observer isn't considering the subject observed from a distance but is integral to it.

The Fisher Paradigm©™® abandons the bucket theory of the mind, as in the philosophy of Descartes and other empiricists, according to which, in perception, ideas arrive through the senses into a receptacle, or bucket, where they are processed. This is a limited picture.

Geographic Profile

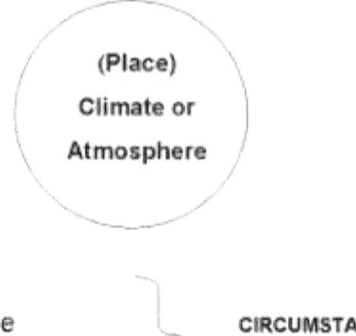

(Place)

Climate or

Atmosphere

- Situation
- Time/Place   } CIRCUMSTANCE
- Psychology
- Sociology

The Fisher Paradigm©™® encompasses Edward de Bono's *lateral thinking*,7 which insists that linear logic and cause and effect analysis reinforce the box and offer no opportunity to think outside it. The emphasis, de Bono claims,

Demographic

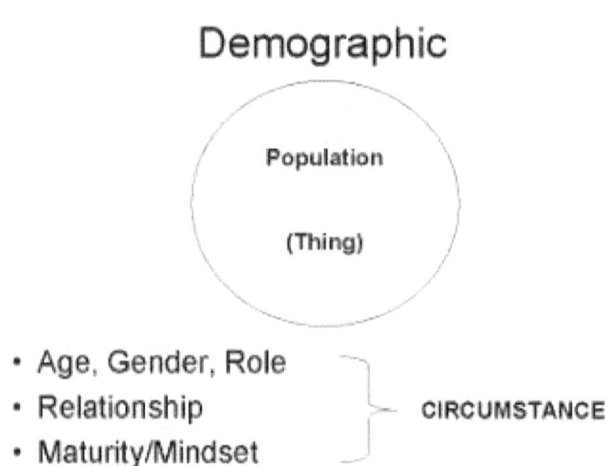

Population

(Thing)

- Age, Gender, Role
- Relationship   } CIRCUMSTANCE
- Maturity/Mindset

is to lionize *critical thinking*, which is limited to the box, or what is already known, whereas *lateral thinking* introduces the possibility of *creative thinking*, which doesn't search for answers but creates them out of experience and what lies beyond.

While the Fisher Paradigm©™® shows evidence of following the prospects of creativity, it does so by thinking with the whole body, not simply the mind.

That said, there is no perception without activity and thought. All perception is in an interaction with a timeless reality, a reality more often intuitively sensed than cognitively understood, especially as it relates to persons, places and things.

An organization has a personality, a certain geography and encompasses specific demographics.

It is a mistake to see the organization simply as different. OD recognizes that each organization has its unique collective conscience composed of individual sensibilities with a mindset that either enhances, neutralizes, impedes or drives it with the desired action.

The emphasis on intuition separates OD from other disciplines. OD's power is self-conscious. Its authority is in calibrating the organizational mindset (culture) in terms of comfort, complacency and contribution.

This is critical for the reasons expressed earlier relative to the *structure of work* (see page 156) and the subsequent culture.

Trying to understand OD as a straightforward naturalistic discipline of action and answers is bound to disappoint and paint an ambiguous picture.

What people are doing is not what OD must see, but what they are not doing and should be doing. OD must see beyond appearances. This means OD accustoms itself to the fact that structure and function are not always what they seem.

An organization that is devoid of conflict, confrontation or disharmony is not a dynamic and healthy organization, but quite the opposite. *Managed conflict not harmony is the glue that holds the organization to its task.* Moreover, when the components of an organization are behaving as well as they possibly can, the whole organization will not behave as well as it can. This is counterintuitive to *Machine Age Thinking* but is absolutely essential to organizational thinking. Conversely, when the organization is behaving as well as it can, none of the parts will be. Why? They are sacrificing individual achievement for collective success.

PRESENTATION OF OD IN EVERYDAY LIFE

Recently I accompanied my wife to a large department store in a discount mall. As she was trying on clothes, I watched a man, woman and child shop. The man was six-foot, athletic looking, dressed in shorts, tee shirt and sneakers. He had a trim physique and prominent calves that suggested a jogger. His salt and pepper beard gauged his age at about 46. The woman was tan, trim and athletic looking in a blouse, shorts and sneakers, age about mid-twenties. The boy was dumpy, about thirteen, a little on the heavy side dressed in jeans, sweatshirt and sneakers.

The man kept bringing clothes for the boy to try on until the cart was overflowing. The woman didn't participate but maintained a bored expression with folded arms across her chest, constantly looking at her watch, forcing a smile whenever the man looked at her. When my wife acquired her purchases, I said, "Wait! Look at that couple and the boy. Tell me what you see."

"I see a family shopping. Why?"

"Look again," I insisted. "Study them a minute. Now tell me what you see."

"This is ridiculous," she said, "I could stalk them if that's what you'd like, and it wouldn't change anything. So, tell me! What do you see?"

"I see a father and his son, and a woman not the mother. The boy is from up north, visiting his father and his trophy wife, and she would like to be elsewhere."

"Okay, smarty pants," she said, then walked over and started a conversation with the woman, who was even younger looking up closely.

"Handsome boy!" my wife opened. "What is he 12, 13? You don't look old enough to be his mother."

"I'm not," she answered tartly and then recovered quickly. "Donny is my husband's son visiting us from Chicago." Then to put a lid on the conversation added, "We have no children." With that, my wife politely withdrew.

"How did you do that?" she asked shaking her head.

"You already know," I answered. "You were just too busy shopping."

It involved marrying the mind to the moment to become one with what was being observed in terms of the three spheres of influence to understand what they implied together. It is the clash of these spheres that produces the chain reaction to intuition.

(1) *Personality Profile* of the three was discrete – father enthusiastically interacting with his son, the woman isolated calculating how much all this would cost;

(2) *Geographic Profile* – father and son in one space shopping with a vengeance, woman in another space with folded arms looking at her watch, wanting to be somewhere else;

(3) *Demographic Profile* – father clearly of an age to have a teenage son, not the woman; the man and woman in comparable physical health, not the boy. But it was the boy's pale complexion, given this is Florida, which spelled separation.

The Fisher Paradigm©™® is designed to advance intuition. It provides an intuitive framework for gauging and interpreting problems in impressionistic terms that OD practitioners, executives and change agents can understand and aptly apply without confusion. A more in-depth discussion is provided in the Fisher trilogy:

(1) *Personality Profile – "The Taboo Against Being Your Own Best Friend"* (The Delta Group Florida, 1999) deals with the adverse effects of social, cultural and psychological conditioning, which program people away from their essence (*essential self*) towards the many masks they wear with their personality.

At the organizational level, the inclination is to look for answers in all the wrong places. An organization has a collective essence (*organizational self*) as well but is inclined to *search for excellence* rather than *create excellence* out of what is right under its nose.

There was literally a craze to "search for excellence" in the 1980s, imitating and duplicating the operations of highly successful companies, believing this was the key to their futures. It was a model that disregarded the company's culture, history and value system. Many companies later regretted their complicity in this mass retreat from their own cultural identity.8

(2) *Geographic Profile – "Six Silent Killers: Management's Greatest Challenge"* (CRC Press, 1998) describes the social termites that burrow silently into the infrastructure of the organization only to be discovered too late for damage control. These social termites are dissonant professional workers.

Are the workers the culprit? No! The toxic culture of the workplace is the culprit. It spawns passive behaviors, cover ups, malicious obedience, defensive postures, and obsessive compulsive complaining. It poisons the collective will to cope and to embrace its resistance to survive. It finds 100-year-old companies expiring at a record rate because they no longer have the energy or will to reinvent themselves.

(3) *Demographic Profile – "Corporate Sin: Leaderless Leadership & Dissonant Workers"* (1stBooks Library, 2000) unmasks the problem. The *Industrial Revolution* is more than 150 years old, yet most workers are still managed, motivated, mobilized and manipulated as well-paid serfs. Something is wrong when a society is blessed with the most able-bodied workforce in history but insists on managing and leading these workers as if they cannot find their way. We are in the digital age which is changing everything, but the way and how we work lags in sophistication. This denies the fundamental change in the balance of power from exclusively position hierarchical power of management and the arrival and new eminence of the knowledge power of workers who have vital answers. It has led to corporate sin where both workers and managers share in the guilt.

The Fisher Paradigm©™® is not theoretical but empirical. I have been practicing this paradigm for more than forty years. The chronology of my OD experiences, which follows is representative of what led to this epiphany.

THAYER MAXWELL & HOW INTUITIVE OD FIRST SURFACED

Three weeks into my new job with *Nalco Chemical Company* as a chemical sales engineer, and a comparable time away from the security of the research laboratory with *Standard Brands, Inc.*, I was told by my district manager, "I don't think you're cut out for this type of work."

Only the previous week when asked by my area manager to critique his calls, I told him they were mainly social calls; he didn't ask for an order; didn't give reasons to change suppliers; gave a canned speech, and made Nalco out to be the greatest thing since sliced bread.

This was the first time my young family of a wife and two children, 1 and 2 had been out of Iowa. My wife hated Indiana, was homesick and complained, rightly so, that I was making less money than I previously made in the lab.

The words of my boss stung me like a slap in the face. "We'll give you some accounts to service," he said. "You're solid technically, but you should find something else within the next six weeks." From somewhere in my reeling mind I asked if I could call on competitors' accounts. "If you like," he answered with annoyance as if my departure were already a *fait accompli*.

One of the first competitor's accounts I called on was Philco in Connersville, Indiana. The plant is seven acres under a single roof and manufactures refrigerators.

Betz Laboratories, Nalco's chief competitor, has serviced this account "challenge free" for years. The front desk secretary informs me that she has not seen a Nalco salesman since joining Philco three years before.

Someone escorts me to the office of Thayer Maxwell, the plant superintendent. The office is a glassed-in bullpen in the center of this huge factory. Mr. Maxwell is not there. I sit for nearly two hours with a cadre of folks coming and going, always looking for the superintendent, and always leaving frustrated.

The desk, chairs, cabinets and tables are overflowing with cigarette butts in dented steel ashtrays, coffee stains everywhere, on papers scattered across the superintendent's desk, on broken floor tiles and even on the glass walls of the bull pen.

Corroded pipes and plugged condenser traps, boiler sludge samples, and severely damaged heat exchangers glare at me from the four corners of the office. These red rusted casualties of operations are haphazardly wedged against the door, on chairs, tables, and on top of papers on the superintendent's desk, even under the desk. It makes me think of the "morgue of machine parts" – a picture of total chaos.

The extent of my knowledge of Nalco, at the time, is a three-week intensive technical training course on water treatment technology at Nalco's Chicago headquarters.

I know little actually about Nalco's products and nothing about selling. Finally, Mr. Maxwell comes in, lights a cigarette, props one leg over the desk, smiles, and says, "Okay, sport, you've got five minutes. What you got for me?"

Where it came from, I'm not sure. Nalco's Chicago laboratories, pilot plant operations, and technical service personnel impressed me during my training. It was like being indoctrinated into a new faith. I believed in Nalco only on the strength of this limited exposure. I found myself saying to the superintendent without flinching, "I'm here to save your job."

Mr. Maxwell throws his head back and laughs heartedly, "So you're the answer to my prayers? Well, I've got to hand it to you, sport. You've got spunk."

Relief registers on his face as his voice tells me he's not angry, only amused. I move to be on the business side of his desk, and he follows me. He sits and I take out a piece of paper and start drawing a flow diagram of a facsimile of a steam generated power supply system from memory of my Nalco technical training.

A red marker is used to indicate areas where I assume, he's been having chronic problems as revealed by the scattered samples across his office. This is a systems approach, not a product approach. I show him no flashy literature. I don't talk about my fabulous company. Instead, I explain the how, the why and Nalco's approach to dealing with his troubles, fanning my eyes across all the spent casualties in the bullpen attesting to this fact.

I talk chemistry and give him the A, B, C's of the trouble-free application of what I am confident Nalco's products and technology can provide. When I finish, he thanks me, lights another cigarette and heads for the door.

"Mr. Maxwell," I say, the timber of my voice rising, "your operation is in trouble now." I look around the room. "Now!" I repeat. Then continue, "I've been sitting here for the better part of an hour and have heard nothing from your people coming in and looking for you, but about breakdowns in your steam generating systems across the plant."

I pick up a blocked piece of pipe. "This is packed with suspended solids, carryover from your boilers. This is not normal. This shouldn't happen. Give me a three-month trial and I'll prove it."

My mind is not thinking of what's in it for me, but solving a problem, a problem I believe is correctible based only on a three-week tutorial and nothing else. Perhaps my naked intensity was disarming. I don't know. But he stopped, took a drag on his cigarette and said,

"You never meet a stranger do you, sport?" I ignore his comment.

"I know I can fix this." I look about the bullpen at the metallic cadavers.

"Blanket order for three-months, eh? What are we talking about in money?"

I have no idea. I have never made a survey, never calculated an actual chemical dosage. I answer without answering his question, relying on what has been my focus.

"A lot less than it's costing you now in breakdowns, lost production, and missed schedules, but we'll have to survey the plant first. We will have to devote a full day to this." The "we" implies I'll need Nalco's technical expertise. I'll need the area manager.

"Okay, do your survey. Have my girl give you a purchase order number. Now let me get back to work."

In terms of the Fisher Paradigm©™®, not yet defined in my mind, this is how the Philco situation was perceived:

(1) *Personality Profile* – managerial neglect is apparent as well as confusion in operational directives with the emphasis in putting out fires not having the time or inclination to deal with causes which has resulted in the panic of crisis management.

(2) *Geographic Profile* – the office and traffic define chaos.

(3) *Demographic Profile* – the focus of plant engineering is on crisis maintenance, not preventive maintenance. Ten names on the "in-out" board of the bullpen wall indicate an overworked maintenance engineering staff as complement to 1,200 factory employees. From failed samples the impression is unmistakable – power plant operations are a foreign concern to this crew.

Thayer Maxwell & How Intuitive OD First Surfaces

Intuition

- **Personality** – Disorganized, not in control, spinning wheels
- **Geographic** – Bullpen of failures
- **Demographic** – Focus on crisis maintenance, not preventive maintenance

⟹ I AM HERE TO SAVE YOUR JOB!

F☯ Paradigm

THE TRIGGER TO THIS INITIAL INTUITION

My lab experience in combination with Nalco's technical training gave me the confidence that identifying and treating chronic problems would lead to success. I had no doubt about that. The technical level is the most comfortable level because it is totally dealing with things. I had left the security of the laboratory and was in the realm of people.

People are totally another matter. Everything I saw and felt (re: persons, places, things) told me the superintendent was overwhelmed, possibly incompetent.

Meeting him I sensed his need and exploited it. I didn't understand what I was doing. Perhaps I thought I had nothing to lose, given my boss's ultimatum. When I called to inform my boss of the sale, he checked with Philco's purchasing to confirm the order. Skepticism was not limited to him.

The area manager surveyed the plant with me the next day, shaking his head in disbelief as he calculated the astronomical daily chemical dosages required.

The situation was made even more incredulous when asked by the superintendent to survey Philco's other two plants in the city and include them in the billing. It was the biggest order in the district's history by someone who had never sold in his life, had no training in sales, and was to be given his walking papers in less than a month.

Compounding the irony, Nalco didn't expect its salesmen to be productive until completing a three-year comprehensive technical training program in the field and acquiring their professional engineering license. Nalco's philosophy, at the time, was that you wowed the customer with your technical knowhow, and then delivered customer friendly service with your sophisticated knowledge of Nalco's many product lines. I had neither.

Intuitive OD, which I was using and would continue to use with consistent success made me out to be lucky rather than skilled, which also seems apparent in the following episode.

It is worth noting, at this point, that I've never thought of myself as a "people person," as I prefer to live and thrive in the narrow confines of the privacy of family. Yet, my natural empathy for and understanding of people has been the arbiter of my long and successful career. *I am a listener more than a talker; a feeler more than a thinker.* Moreover, it wasn't until much later that I came to understand that I was an introvert rather than an extrovert, despite being active in many sports and professional organizations. It could also be said, although the organization is my laboratory, and the source my discovery of the Fisher Paradigm©™®, that I have never been comfortable in any organization. Perhaps the quintessential mindset of the "outsider" provides a perspective that otherwise might not be available to the observer.

THOMAS CROWN AFFAIR

Two years later still with Nalco, after a stifling hot summer day in Terre Haute, Indiana, I find myself on the campus of *Indiana State University*. The temperature is nearly 100 degrees Fahrenheit as it has been so for several days.

The campus is situated in the heart of the business district of this community of 75,000. The summer session is in full swing, but classrooms and dorm windows are open, furniture is spewed out on the campus lawn, and many professors are lecturing outdoors in the stifling heat.

Several chemical trucks with toxic hydrochloric acid are rigged with hoses and acidizing pumps. This means air conditioning condensers have "frozen up" and are down. This is due to calcium carbonate scaling in the condensers because of improper chemical water treatment.

Acidizing will put these units back in service but only temporarily. Confident in my chemical water treatment technology, I drive to the office of the physical plant.

"Mr. Thomas Crown, Superintendent, Plant Engineering" is stenciled on the frosted glass door.

I knock and he says, "Come in." The office is a workplace with a drafting board with white-lined blue pages of architectural drawings, and on the wall framed B.S. and M.S. degrees in mechanical engineering from *Purdue University.*

There is also a picture of several children of various ethnicities smiling down from the wall, and on his desk is a framed picture of an attractive woman and three boys, seemingly age's three to six. Tacked to the wall directly behind the desk is a child's stick figure drawing that says, "Hi daddy! This is me! This is you!"

An American flag is on a stanchion to the left of the desk and another kind of flag I don't recognize is to the right near the corner.

I'm able to take all this in because Mr. Crown busies himself cutting his nails and doesn't look up for nearly a minute. When he does, I explain my business noting the activity on campus, and saying this is the perfect time to establish a sound chemical treatment program.

"It would not only be cost effective but could eliminate the inconvenience or need for periodic downtimes to acidize the condensers."

He listens attentively, and then gives me permission to survey his facilities across the campus and to come back with a recommendation.

Six hours later I return proposing a chemical treatment program including a $10,000 consulting agreement for a year for monthly technical service calls.

"No way Jose! Board will scream to high heaven with such a proposal. We don't pay consulting fees."

I ask for an hour to refigure another option. He agrees. Once the new proposal is in his hands, he says, "Be here at 8 o'clock sharp tomorrow morning. We'll see if we can do business."

The next morning, I arrive with high expectations. As soon as I enter his office, he shouts in a thunderous voice, "Get your ass out of here before I kick it from here to Lafayette."

I hesitate, stunned, but more out of panic than anything. He is a big man, but so am I. "I mean it, God damn it," he bellows, "this new proposal costs as much as the original only you buried the goddamn costs in the chemicals."

I wasn't thinking of the Fisher Paradigm©™® or of the three spheres of influence. I wasn't thinking at all. Yet I must have been processing information subconsciously because I stood there. I didn't leave.

Mr. Crown ranted until his throat was so dry, he couldn't speak anymore. I looked at his tired eyes, deep dark circles etched around them in half-moons. I wondered if he'd been to bed and decided he hadn't.

He slumped forward in his chair, stretching his massive arms over his head, and then through his thick black hair. Suddenly he noticed me standing, waved me silently to sit, and then collapsed forward on his desk. A lapel pin on his jacket became prominent as it bunched up around his bull like neck. It was a *Lions International Club* pin.

"You're a Lion?" I asked. The lids of his eyes lifted, a minute sparkle in them. In that moment I made the connection of the pin, the unknown flag in the corner, and the picture of the children of diversity on the wall. "Lions do a lot for kids," I continued fatuously remembering something about sponsoring children hospitals.

For the longest time he studied me but said nothing. I stared back silently, uncomfortably, my nervous energy crying to fill the vacuum with words, but I resisted. Nearly an eternity of two minutes transpired.

"You know 'bout Lions International?" he asked finally sotto voce, fingering his pin, his voice little more than a whisper.

I shrugged. "Not much. Know of its eye bank. Have a daughter with eye problems." I felt my answer disappointing. I was wrong.

Instead he broke into a big grin, an upturn smile lined across his face. "Giving city a new ambulance tonight."

"Wow!" I heard myself say.

Then he launched into a spirited history of *Lions International*, his face flushed with pride. The exercise was cathartic for us both. I jumped when he banged his fist on the desk. "Tell you what! How 'bout being my guest at the Terre Haute Club tonight? We're having a dinner for the mayor and his staff."

I cowered. "Sure," but actually I wasn't. What's going on here? The guy has gone from rage to rapture just like that! I'd never studied psychology. Something told me, however, to stay cool and quiet during his rage. It helped coming from a home where my da often lost it. I was audience to his fury, one with it, not separate from it. I didn't become defensive. I couldn't explain why. I'm not a meek guy. Perhaps I attributed his rage to a lack of sleep, constant system failures, mounting complaints of students and faculty, and perhaps, as well, to feeling a little guilt for deceiving him.

But I wasn't aware of any of this at the time.

At the dinner, he introduced me to everyone as his friend. He did this from the *Lions Club* president to Terre Haute's mayor. As we were leaving, he whispered in my ear, "I sent in a blanket order for that stuff you recommended. They're to rush it overnight. Your boss will be calling you."

He chuckled. "Don't expect to see your family for a few days." Then he added in a friendly voice, "Believe me I know the feeling."

(1) *Personality Profile*: A man is at his wits end with a problem I am trained to handle. His office defines him, efficient, pragmatic, and functional. The workplace is his comfort zone. Deciphering this proves the key.

(2) *Geographic Profile*: High summer heat, acidizing trucks across the campus, furniture on lawns, student-faculty sweltering in the heat conducting classes on campus lawns, open doors and windows indicate major air conditioning failures.

(3) *Demographic Profile*: A student-faculty population of 10,000 unable to function in classrooms or dorms because of these failures spells a crisis situation.

ROLE OF INTUITION IN THE THOMAS CROWN AFFAIR

Someone might argue that I was programmed to deal with an explosive personality having had a father of that temperament. That would not be accurate.

Superintendent Crown was warm and open in his greeting. He was real. Candor was displayed when he admitted he couldn't sell a consulting agreement to the board.

It was clear that for this air conditioning system to function effectively, however, it required high-end technical service. Nalco had two options to provide this service, one via the consulting contract and the other by incorporating the cost of such service in the chemicals.

Thomas Crown Affair

Intuition

- **Personality** – A man under siege
- **Geographic** – Gods of heat on a rampage
- **Demographic** – Summer school student and faculty population at point of rebellion

$\Longrightarrow$ **"YOU A LION!"**

F ☺ Paradigm

The plant survey of the air conditioning system indicated a serious breach in water treatment application and control. This translated into a costly and time-consuming chemical service commitment. Nalco's 400-series matched these demands however deceptively they were presented.

Discussion was expected, but not rage. Intuition told me to weather the rage although I had no such training. I was clueless to the separate spheres of influence. It was all of them clashing like thunder that submerged me into the problem, not only technically but emotionally.

We carry our geography with us. We carry it in our heads and surround ourselves with it for comfort's sake at work. Mr. Crown did this so openly that the clues to the man spoke so loudly I could not hear him, until I did.

CULTURE + TEST KIT = INTUITIVE SYMBOLOGY

Success in Nalco's Industrial Division brings me to the attention of senior management. No one can put a finger on my incredulous success given my unconventional approach. My method has:

(1) Nothing to do with intimidation;
(2) Nothing to do selling the sizzle instead of the steak;
(3) Nothing to do with finessing the buyer with assumptive closes, penalty of delay or scarcity of the product;
(4) Nothing to do with selling benefits to deflect objections.

My method has everything to do with becoming one with the buyer merging complementary interests into a partnership.

The executive vice president of *Nalco's International Division* is so intrigued with my success that he comes into the field to travel with me. At the conclusion of the day, he says, "I'm not sure what you're doing, but we can use it. How'd you like to work for me in South Africa?"

Knowing nothing about South Africa, I ask if I can think about it. I do and am intrigued with the country's history. My job there is to facilitate the formation of a new chemical company composed of our American subsidiary, *The Alexander Martin Company*, Great Britain's *I.C.I., Ltd.* affiliate, *Alfloc*, and *South African Explosives, Ltd.'s Specialty Chemical Division*.

South Africa has no anti-trust laws to prevent this new company from dominating the huge industrial water treatment business. Water is a precious commodity. Water clarification in the gold and diamond mines is critical to profitable business. Nalco has cutting edge technology in this field and is anxious to leverage its product line to full advantage here.

Two brothers inherited the Nalco subsidiary from their father, Alexander Martin. They have no college training in either chemistry or business but have the colonial manners and elocution of the British business elite. Likewise, the Alfloc people are mainly British and derive their business acumen primarily from colonial history and culture. College trained people are mainly Afrikaners, primarily from South African Explosives.

Afrikaners are descendants of the 17th century Dutch and French Huguenot settlers, who fought two Boer Wars with the British.

It is 1968. Afrikaners have had control of the South African government since 1948, while the British still remained the major player in business and industry.

The Afrikaner government had created a policy of apartheid, or "separate development of the races," which was being rigorously enforced. Nearly a million Bantu workers come into Johannesburg every working day from their homes in the South West African Township of "Soweto."

This is the climate in which the three technical directors from the merging companies are now acting, temporarily, as the technical management team. They asked me, "What test kit are we to use in the field?" I study them and sense their defiance – what is this kid doing here telling us what to do?

"Here is my suggestion," I offered. "Go back, consider the needs of the field, build your test kit, and come back in two weeks with a recommendation."

Three days later they return with a Rube Goldberg concoction. It is mainly a South African test kit, the most inappropriate of the three. "Fine, package it and send it to the field." They look at me stunned. "Anything else? If not, good luck!"

It isn't a month later that radical modifications are made to this basic test kit, and Nalco's sedimentation test kit is being used without modification. When Nalco's *Chairman of the Board* comes to Johannesburg and asks to explain my behavior, I have no vocabulary. It was an intuitive decision that I would not be able to articulate until long after I had left Nalco.

(1) *Personality Profile*:

A clash of cultures is felt from the moment customs confiscates my copy of Allen Drury's critical book on South Africa, *"A Very Strange Society"* (1968). This is magnified as I feel the conflicting pull of colonialism with British descendants who look to Great Britain as their homeland to the passionate nationalism of the Afrikaners, Dutch and French descendants, who consider South Africa, home.

Although Afrikaners in this new company tend to be better educated, it is the English speakers who occupy most leadership positions. A subterranean superior-inferior relationship is rumbling between the two groups with the Bantu majority treated as non-citizens.

(2) *Geographic Profile*:

Apartheid divides the Bantu majority into nine native tribe homelands. These homelands have little wealth, commerce or industry, forcing Bantu men to leave their families to live and work in the industrial centers of Johannesburg, Durban, East London and Cape Town.

Apartheid of a different sort exists between the British and Afrikaner as these two groups share little in common but maintain a necessary tolerance of each other as whites represent only 20 percent of South Africa's population.

(3) *Demographic Profile*:

South Africa is a country with a population of 20 million – 14 million Bantus, 4 million whites (2.5 million Afrikaners, 1.5 million British), and 2 million coloreds (mixed race) including Indians, descendants of 19th century indentured workers from India.

This newly formed company, *Anikem Ltd.*, is slightly more Afrikaner than British.

THE VOICE OF INTUITION SPEAKS TO THE OUTSIDER

Before taking on this assignment, I read all I could about South Africa and found the country's history surprisingly parallel to that of the United States. Also, being from Iowa, I could identify with Afrikaners or Boers (Afrikaans word for "farmer") in their down to earth approach to life unimpressed with the pretentious.

Still, my intuition told me I was an intruder. I looked much younger than my years and knew I was not likely to be taken seriously. My intuition told me to put the risk of failure and the burden of success on this new company, not on Nalco. It was after all "their company." It wasn't until later that I realized this symbolic move proved consequential.

Culture + Test Kit = Intuitive Symbology

Intuition

- **Personality** – Cultural/Org Identity Problem
- **Geographic** – A Very Strange Society
- **Demographic** – Clash of Cultures – three attempting to become one!

WHAT TEST KIT ARE WE TO USE? YOU DECIDE.

F ⟨ ⟩ Paradigm

The action elevated the three diverse companies above petty differences into the possibility of a common culture. What could have been a colossal snafu became an opportunity for a promising success.

* * *

Too often when companies merge, the dominant company in the merger assumes its culture should prevail at the expense of the less dominant company's culture. This puts a wrench in the works crippling the transition and often signaling ultimate collapse.

THE FISHER PARADIGM©™® SAVED MY LIFE!

In 1974, I was contracted by the *American Management Association* (AMA) to investigate a riot, which had occurred in Fairfax County Virginia (*this was covered earlier but is key to this discussion and therefore repeated here*).

A white police officer shot and killed an unarmed 27-year-old black man in a convenient store in Herndon, after the young man grabbed the officer's nightstick and hit him with it. This led to a riot.9

My job was to interview senior officers, detectives and command personnel to get a sense of how the *Fairfax County Police Department* (FCPD) operated and how this might have contributed to this debacle.

During this nine-month intervention, I also conducted executive seminars for AMA across the country. In the course of this work, the deputy *Secretary of the State of Iowa* participated in one of my seminars in Kansas City, Missouri. Later, he looked me up when he came to Washington, D.C. and we went to dinner and took in a play.

Washington, D.C. is about twelve miles from Fairfax City where I was residing at the Holiday Inn. A FCPD police officer drove me to D.C. and said he would pick me up when I called. It was after midnight when the Iowa official and I parted. The police officer, however, couldn't pick me up until 1:30 a.m. I said that was okay, as I was a walker.

It was a brisk evening and I found myself walking along Pennsylvania Avenue. There was a November chill in the air, but I was comfortably dressed in an unbuttoned dark blue cashmere topcoat, a pinstriped gray three-piece suit, and wearing black leather gloves.

I noticed three African American youths across the street that were jiving and laughing as they walked parallel to me. I paid them little mind as there are eight lanes of traffic separating us, that is, until they raced ahead, crossed the street, and started hanging out at the corner under the light.

Some time ago, an elderly United States senator from Mississippi was accosted, knifed and nearly died after being robbed. When I was about one hundred yards from the boys, that episode crossed my mind. Without breaking my stride, I processed this information:

(1) *Personality Profile* – three young people up to no good at this hour and I am alone.

(2) *Geographic Profile* – this is no place for young boys to be out at this hour.

(3) *Demographic Profile* – they are teenagers; I am in my late thirties. They are black, slender, one about six feet, the other two about five-six, athletic looking. I am white, six-four, two-ten, and in good shape.

I feel the rush of their excitement (Personality). How do they see me? I sense danger but imagine they sense opportunity.

Somehow (Geographic), my feet continue their aggressive stride. More incongruous still, I have a sense of calm. Why? I can't define it.

I know the three have the advantage (Demographic) especially if they have a knife or gun. I have no weapon.

No weapon? My senses explode. That's it!

Fisher Paradigm Saved My Life!

Intuition

- **Personality** – Three youth up to no good
- **Geographic** – Pennsylvania Avenue at 1:30 a.m.
- **Demographic** – Three teenagers meet phantom policeman

→ **"There goes the fuzzz!"**

F ☺ **Paradigm**

INTUITION AND THE PHANTOM GUN

During my intense one-on-one interviews with plain-clothes detectives, they would invariably squirm and adjust their shoulder holsters when I asked sensitive questions. I am now thirty yards from the boys, still walking with the same authoritative gate.

When I am ten yards from them, I make an elaborate move to adjust my phantom shoulder holster through my open topcoat. Not a boy misses this. They open a path for me to pass. Without looking back, I hear them giggle, "There goes the fuzzzz!"

Not leaving it at that, I hear myself say, "Going to be a little hard to get up for school in the morning isn't it boys?"

They laugh hysterically, "Yeah, man, ssscchoool's what we's all about! Dig it!" They retreat in the opposite direction.

When I explain this episode to my ride at half past two in the morning, the police officer says, "You just might have saved your ass." No might about it as far as I was concerned.

MUTINY MINDED POLICE OFFICERS

In 1975, the *Public Safety Institute* (PSI) was contracted to investigate and dismantle the unauthorized labor union of the Raleigh Police Officers Association, and to defuse its threat of striking the city of Raleigh, North Carolina.

Statisticians, psychometricians, experts on police organization and public safety policy experts were brought in. I was retained as a *"people's person"* with a reputation for OD detective work. In the course of riding with officers, attending roll call during the three shifts, walking around city hall, and interviewing citizens, the spheres of influence begin to materialize:

(1) *Personality Profile*: A clear dichotomy appeared to exist between police command and the ranks of police officers in the patrol division, or between staff and line authority and function. Police officers were spiteful of the police chief and spoke angrily of his incompetence, but were surprisingly civil to me, an outsider – a disconnect.

They demanded the chief be fired or they would strike even though public employees in North Carolina have no such right.

(2) *Geographic Profile*: Raleigh is the state capital, centrally located, and the hub of politics, industry, commerce and education. It has the bizarre feel of an antebellum community, producing a certain time-lapse ambivalence.

(3) *Demographic Profile*: Raleigh is a community of more than 200,000 with several colleges and universities within and around the city, including Duke University and the University of North Carolina in nearby Chapel Hill.

Only 5 percent of the 350 sworn officers are college trained, the rest are high school graduates or have GED equivalences; 80 percent are between the ages of 25 and 35 with an average of five years on the police force, while 60 percent live outside Raleigh city limits. None of the command officers, including the chief, are college trained.

As the situation worsened, the headlines of *The Raleigh Times* blared a daily menu of police officer dissonance, and the demand for a change in leadership, while television nightly news programs echoed the same sentiments.

Meanwhile, I continued to ride with angry patrol officers on three shifts, interviewed command staff, wandered around city hall, and sent out a questionnaire with the water bill. This was not a scientific study, yet the response was more than 30 percent, indicating citizens wanted resolution of this stalemate.

Mutiny Minded Police Officers

Intuition

- **Personality** – Split personality between command & patrol/patrol & community
- **Geographic** – Community near siege
- **Demographic** – Drug of dissonance incrementally injected by night captain

⟹ Former city mgr creates a mess!

F 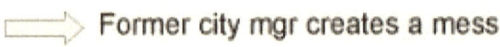 **Paradigm**

INTUITION AS SERENDIPITY

We were several weeks into the intervention and getting nowhere. I had spent scores of hours with police officers, but only marginal time in city hall. Something told me the problem started there.

My previous interviews with the city manager, members of the city council and the chief of police were not insightful. I thought I must dig deeper. So, I wandered city hall some more.

That is how I came to see a distinguished looking man with white hair sitting in an office devoid of trappings reading *The Wall Street Journal*. I asked if I might talk to him. "Sure, make yourself at home," he said with the fastidious gestures and diffident manner of antebellum civility.

For the next two hours I listened to an intriguing story that made everything fall into place.

He informed me he was the prior city manager. His best friend was the previous chief of police. "First college graduate ever to be a Raleigh police chief," he said proudly.

But there was a problem. His friend had an incurable heart condition and could tolerate no stress. To make certain his friend acquired full police chief pension benefits, he made him a sinecure while he rotated the three majors in the department every four months to run the police department, creating three islands of authority, three different and competing police departments, three different work cultures, and three distinct power cells.

After three years in this configuration, the city manager's friend died. He then appointed the senior major of the three as permanent chief, convinced the city council to hire his deputy as city manager, and resigned.

The new chief to solidify his power promoted his favorite sergeant to major over patrol, the most powerful wing of police operations, placed one major in administration and the other in community service – both non-power positions. He then placed his most despised adversary, a captain, on permanent nights running patrol. That proved a fatal error.

This meant that the captain on permanent nights had access to all patrol officers, some 300 strong. As they rotated shifts and came under his wing, he painted the chief as a clown, incompetent if not a crook, and a perfect foil to all that grieved them. I saw this first hand. He used nuance and innuendo, humor and bravado to cultivate the officers' collective dissonance and project their frustration and contempt on to the chief of police.

When I disclosed this scenario in a report to the *Public Safety Institute*, which was in turn published, it took the air out of the siege. Officers could see how they had been duped and used. Order was restored. The union became a social club, and the chief ended his career with dignity.

TECHNICAL OBSOLESCENCE & INTUITION

It is 1980. I am now a Ph.D. in organizational/industrial psychology with ten years of consulting experience. Being an organizational development (OD) consultant failed to be fulfilling mainly because there was no sense of closure.

An OD intervention can uncover chronic systemic problems, and make recommendations, but then the OD practitioner usually moves on, and is not there for the implementing stage. So, I was delighted when an opportunity came to join *Honeywell Avionics* in Clearwater, Florida as an OD psychologist.

My new boss gave me what sounded a lot like an ultimatum, reminding me of my initial days with Nalco a decade earlier. "If you don't find your role here in the first six weeks," he said, "you are history."

Directness is akin to my own personality. I liked the unabashed clarity of my marching orders. He, too, had first been trained in the hard sciences before studying the soft sciences, and was not inclined to beat about the bush when he had something on his mind. His directness established immediate trust as he was to become my mentor.

So off I go to create an OD role and identity in this new environment. It soon became apparent that the spheres of influence were blatantly obvious:

(1) *Personality Profile*:

Engineers here were the elite, treated with deference, which is manifested in a cavalier attitude by engineers toward every other discipline. They are cowboys who can do no wrong. *Human Resources* personnel, where OD is located, are intimidated by these engineers and obsequious to their demands, mainly because they speak a different language and have that hauteur and mystique of having special power.

(2) *Geographic Profile*:

The facility is mainly a government subcontractor with work centered on large defense contracts in space and strategic operations. Program managers are engineers and dictate the tempo of work. All accede to their needs. The ten-acre campus is graced with seven attractive white sun baked buildings including a recreation center on manicured lawns, and complemented by an artificial lake, picnic area and several parking lots in the heart of this leisure driven tourist paradise called Clearwater, Florida.

(3) *Demographic Profile*:

The working population of 4,000 includes 1,000 engineers, 2,400 support technicians and administrative personnel, and 600 production workers. More than 3,000 workers are college trained with 400 with advanced degrees among whom there are more than 30 Ph.D.'s.

After three weeks in the company, I experience the wall between Human Resources and engineering. Engineers requisition courses, seminars, and professional meetings but take umbrage when asked to explain the benefits.

Their elitist attitude says, would you know if I told you? A pervasive duplication of courses is noted. This unnecessarily multiplies costs. I ask HR Compensation to generate a demographic profile of the engineering community.

Most striking in this profile was that pay of veteran engineers continued to increase as the actual complexity of their actual jobs decreased; that 75 percent of these engineers were working on technology developed long after they had left engineering college. Moreover, many engineers received engineering pay for non-engineering work. Technical obsolescence was blatantly apparent, a problem correctible with a continuing organized technical training program.

A memo is prepared that goes out to all chief engineers announcing the formation of a task force to address this problem. No response. A second memo follows to forty of the top engineers who are representative of the range of engineering disciplines and programs. One response.

The single engineering responder is an engineer near retirement, who long ago recognized his declining skills, and claims to be sold on the idea of continuing engineering education.

We meet every week as if we are a full-fledged task force with me mainly the audience to his delivery. All of this is dutifully written up and sent out in memos to the chief engineers and the top forty engineers.10

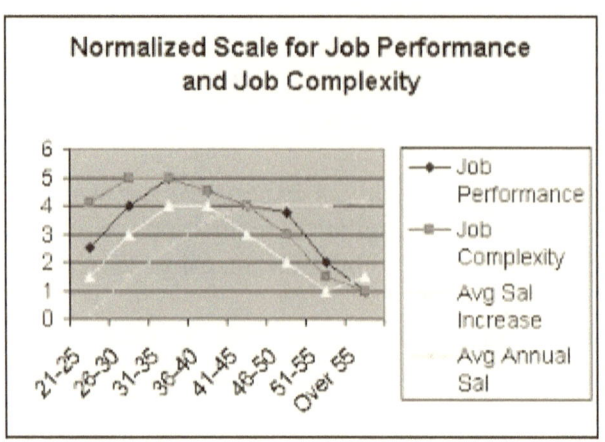

Normalized Scale for Job Performance and Job Complexity

INTUITION AND THE POWER OF THE PEN

Trained as a chemist, I can relate to technical arrogance. Knowing this, and being a writer by inclination, I embellish our weekly sessions with statistics, schematics, graphs and studies and copy everyone on the original listings.

One day a chief engineer joins us. Mention is made of his attendance in the next memo, not realizing his celebrity. Thirty engineers show up for the following session overflowing our cramped quarters. The chief engineer takes over the meeting outlining how technical education might work.

Each gathering thereafter finds greater and more diverse attendance from the engineering community. A holistic view is developing. In time, the chief engineer becomes *Director of Engineering*, and then *Vice President* and *General Manager* of *Honeywell Avionics* with technical education key to his administration.

Today technical education at *Honeywell Avionics* is a highly developed program. Technicians in conjunction with the *Engineering College* of the *University of South Florida* can pursue engineering studies while working on the Honeywell campus. All engineers come to see the benefit of upgrading their skills as no engineer need be left behind.[11]

A BRIDGE TOO FAR

The management team of the *Charles Stark Draper Laboratories* (CSDL) of the *Massachusetts Institute of Technology* (MIT) makes its routine visit to

Honeywell Avionics, Clearwater and asks to see me. They have read an article of mine, *"Quality Control Circles: Motivation through Participative Management."*[12] The CSDL director says he would like me to come to Cambridge to work with his people in team building.

CSDL designs the ring laser gyros that are manufactured in Clearwater. It is evident that a breakdown exists between the design phase in Massachusetts and production phase in Clearwater. This is a $50 million U.S. Navy program.

Before going off to MIT, I create a book out of my published works at Honeywell that cover all phases of OD that relate to operations. I do this with the full realization that MIT is unlikely to take me seriously. I didn't anticipate the elitism would be any less in Cambridge than it was in Clearwater. Yes, this is an anticipated bias, but a protective one.

(1) *Personality Profile*: The nation's top engineers, physicists and chemists work at CSDL. These scientists are perfectionists. If there is a problem, they are certain it is not with them.

(2) *Geographic Profile*: There is a 1,000-mile separation between the design team and production team.

This was before the digital age and the Internet and so that distance was an obvious barrier. What was not so obvious until I arrived at CSDL is that another barrier existed that further crippled this collaboration.

18656

TEAMING

PRODUCTIVITY THROUGH COOPERATION

By

James R. Fisher, Jr., PhD

Honeywell

Human Resource Development and Recognition Department
Avionics Division
Clearwater, Florida 33546

The CSDL facility was designed around twin circular towers joined by a bridge well above the street. This housed the CSDL laboratories and offices on the MIT campus. The design was meant to provide privacy, but it also promoted separation and isolation.

(3) *Demographics Profile*: There is a distinct CSDL pecking order. Physicists are of the first rank, engineers and mathematicians of the second rank with electrical engineers rated above other engineers, and chemists and biologists completing the ranking corps. Many are Ph.D.'s and so academic credentials cause less friction than seniority and status.

The mean age of the group is late thirties, but the mindset is closer to that of the spoiled child.

A Bridge Seemingly Too Far

Intuition

- **Personality** – Quintessential Perfectionists
- **Geographic** – Ergonomics the culprit
- **Demographic** – Too much cognition, too little affect

→ **CREATE AN ARTIFICIAL REALITY**

F 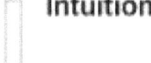 Paradigm

INTUITION AS ANTICIPATION

Although an OD psychologist is not a clinician, per se, I anticipated being perceived as a touchy-feely shrink trained at second-rate schools (state universities), so I put together beforehand a loose leaf book titled "Teaming: Productivity through Cooperation,"[13] composed of articles I had written on team building, transactional analysis in the workplace, leadership style, effective communications, stress management and how to conduct meetings. Armed with 40 books produced by Honeywell's technical services, I journeyed to CSDL.

Once there, I outlined how to use the book, divided people into groups of ten with the balance acting as audience, and then sent them off to plan their respective meetings on topics ranging from conflict management to how to sell an idea. My anticipated rejection never occurred.

They took to the assignment like excited children. Each team tried to outdo the other. In the process, they ventilated pressing concerns and created an agenda on how to address them. The following week, again in teams, they conducted meetings, developed corrective strategies and allowed ideas to surface without interference. Sad to report, but it was quite apparent these well-trained minds had never had an opportunity to demonstrate leadership.

Pleased with their solutions, anxious to implement their ideas, they decided I could now go home.

"Aren't we forgetting something?" I asked. "I don't see Clearwater in the picture."

Busy arriving at consensus on how to work better together they overlooked the breakdown between the design and production teams, between Massachusetts and Clearwater. That was partially my fault. I left Clearwater out of the discussion wanting them to bring up the subject. No one, up to that point, had made the connection that something was awry between the two operations that they might consider and resolve.

"Why don't we have a CSDL team go to Clearwater and observe production and have a Clearwater team come to Cambridge?" somebody finally said. And that is what happened.

The CSDL team learned that their precise design was not reproducible in the factory, and the production team found they could propose suggestions to the lab to make its design more production friendly. One thousand miles was no longer a bridge too far nor were the labs in the two towers across the bridge.

WORKINGS OF THE FISHER PARADIGM©™®

These illustrations are not abstractions. Nor should it be a concern of the reader that the Fisher Paradigm©™® originated in a sales discipline.14 It was in sales I learned the fallacy of the mechanistic A, B, C linear approach to persons, places and things. It was in working as an OD consultant that I learned a company has a personality, geography and demographic profile unique to itself.

These spheres of influence are charged with intuitive insight if we can only erase the lines between *cause and effect, thinking and feeling, observer and the observed* to witness what is happening without bias and allow the small voice of reality to resonate with its need.

The Fisher Paradigm©™® is conceptual, self-conscious and self-organizing. Instead of forcing the world it observes to fit into a presupposed order of vertical thinking (linear logic) or inside the box, it lets information organize itself into horizontal thinking (lateral thinking) and conceptual understanding.

By doing so, persons, places and things find themselves on the same page; they fall into their own unique patterns and find their way forward to move off the dime together.

The quick response is that "the Fisher Paradigm©™® is just common sense," but common sense is so rare. Even rarer is to see a situation whole and integral rather than separate and elemental, to see beyond the cultural blinders that would judge, label and describe "what is," not as it is but as it should be or is expected to be. The workings of the Fisher Paradigm©™® are as much in evidence in the small as in the large as I close with this episode.

BOTTLING PLANT FIASCO

A major bottling company of soft drinks replaced its bottling handling conveyor system with a top of the line electronic conveyor system during a Christmas vacation while 200 employees were on holiday.

The new design was meant to cut operating costs in half and reduce employees by a third. The exact opposite happened.

A productive workforce with virtually no labor problems (*Personality Profile*), situated in a low-tech community (*Geographic Profile*) with most employees otherwise unskilled (*Demographic Profile*) registered shock, then anger, and finally disgust when reporting back to work to find everything had changed.

Management expected employees to be pleased. They weren't. This is important. Workers kept their bad feelings to themselves. They displayed their contempt for the company silently and indirectly in passive behaviors: that is, work slowdowns, failure to repair equipment immediately, failure to report outages in the new system, coming in late and leaving early and doing just enough to get by. Production levels plummeted, schedules were missed, product wastes increased, and costs soared. The company was on the verge of collapse.

In panic mode, an OD intervention was initiated. This included interviewing all the workers. A sense of betrayal and being taken for granted was palpable. Employees wanted to hurt the company, as they had been hurt, failing to realize it was hurting them as well.

The management team was advised to level with employees, to explain the basis of its thinking, and its surprise at the reaction. Teams of management-employees were set up to voice concerns and to ensure this didn't happen again.

Economic challenges had never been discussed with employees before. OD advised that such discussions be initiated as problem solving and brainstorming sessions. These teams looked at cost cutting measures and innovative ways to increase production, improve quality, and reduce waste. Management was at first reluctant to discuss such matters, but found when it did that workers were reasonable, understanding and more enthusiastic than they had expected.

Management had mistakenly read the slow down as employee apathy. Nothing could be further from the truth. Employees felt locked out, deceived and betrayed.

Bottling Plant Fiasco

Intuition

- **Personality** – Solid Workers
- **Geographic** – Low Tech Community
- **Demographic** – Limited skills

MGMT ADMIT FAUX PAS; FORM WORKER/MGR TEAMS; ESTABLISH SKILLS TRAINING; NO MORE SURPRISES

F ☯ **Paradigm**

Intuition was staring management in the face but was ignored. Intuitive OD gave management the eyes to see, but the mind and will to understand are likely to require more time.

Production eventually increased to its former levels with every indication that the new technology would perform as advertised. The workforce was cut by only 10 percent rather than the projected 30 plus percent. Trust was still an issue. Management's challenge now was to earn that lost trust.

NOTES

1 The Fisher Paradigm©™® as of October 10, 2002 has sought copyright protection. The Fisher Paradigm©™® has also applied for trademark registration pursuant to certification for "consulting and advisory services with respect to infrastructure organizational development in commercial, educational, industrial, military, government and religious institutions as well as for individuals therein and separate from same."

In the interim, no one may use it or a variation of it in writing or application without the expressed written approval of the author and *The Delta Group Florida*. Licensing agreements are available as well as application seminars in the innovative use of this design by contacting The Delta Group Florida, 6714 Jennifer Drive, Tampa, FL 33617, Phone/Fax: (813) 989 – 3631, or by email: TheDeltaGrpFL@cs.com

2 *James Gleick, Genius: The Life and Science of Richard Feynman* (Pantheon Books 1992). Feynman was a magician of the highest caliber, architect of quantum theories, enfant terrible of the atomic bomb project, and caustic critic of the space shuttle commission. He forever changed science, and what it means to know something in this uncertain world. He was also a scientist with an intense emotional nature and used it.

3 Kary B. Mullis, *Dancing Naked in the Mind Field* (Vintage Books 2000), pp. 6 – 11.

4 As Emerson insists, experience is crucial. Dr. Fisher's life represents an OD progression: he was reared in an *Irish Catholic home*, educated by the *Sisters of St. Francis* in grammar school (*St. Patrick's*), attended public high school (Clinton, Iowa), *State University of Iowa*, spent five summers as a laborer in a chemical food processing plant (*Clinton Foods, Inc.*), worked as a bench chemist in research & development (*Standard Brands, Inc.*), entered *U.S. Navy* (enlisted man) with the *United States Navy Sixth Fleet* in the Mediterranean during *Eisenhower Administration*, then became chemical sales engineer (*Nalco Chemical Company*). It was at Nalco that he commenced to practice OD without knowing it. Forty years later intuitive OD (Fisher Paradigm ©™) would take shape in his mind. With Nalco, he advanced from a field manager to an international corporate executive, retired (in his 30s), returned to school (*University of South Florida/Walden University*) to earn his Ph.D., consultant (*Psyche-ology, Inc.*), adjunct to several universities, contract consultant (*American Management Association, Public Safety Institute*), OD psychologist (*Honeywell, Inc.*), international corporate executive (*Honeywell Europe, SA.*) and for the past thirteen years, full-time author/consultant/publisher (The Delta Group Florida).

5 Michael Macrone, *Eureka! 81 Key Ideas Explained* (Barnes & Noble 1994), pp. 77 – 78.

6 Oxford don Stuart Hampshire describes this as "the Spinoza solution," *The New York Review*, October 24, 2002, p. 55.

7 Edward de Bono, *Lateral Thinking* (Penguin Books 1970), *Parallel Thinking: From Socratic to de Bono Thinking* (Penguin Books 1994). The author decries the limitations put on thinking imposed by vertical or cognitive and *critical thinking* (cause/effect, linear logic) in a changing world. Thinking "inside the box" (or thinking based on what is already known) is no longer adequate, the author insists, with it necessary for vertical thinking to be complemented with lateral thinking, or conceptual and *creative thinking*.

8 Two years after Thomas Peters and Robert Waterman published their sensational bestseller *In Search of Excellence* (1982), the cover story for *Business Week* (November 5, 1984) was, "Who's Excellent Now?" Many companies rushed to copy the excellence demonstrated by the companies profiled in the book, abandoning their own culture and ways, only to be dismally disappointed and disparaged. *They failed to realize that this was at the sacrifice of their essence, until it was too late.*

9 James R. Fisher, Jr., Master of Arts thesis, *"A Social Psychological Study of the Police Organization: The Anatomy of a Riot,"* University of South Florida, Tampa, Florida, 1976.

10 James R. Fisher, Jr., paper titled *"Combating Technical Obsolescence: The Genesis of a Technical Education Program."* This paper was presented at the World Conference of Continuing Engineering Education in Orlando, Florida, May 8, 1986.

11 Ibid.

12 James R. Fisher, Jr., *"Quality Control Circles: Motivation through Participation,"* paper presented at the National Conference of the Institute of Printed Circuits in Dallas, Texas, October 17, 1981.

13 James R. Fisher, Jr., *Teaming: Motivation through Cooperation* (© 1983 by Dr. James R. Fisher, Jr., Honeywell Avionics, Clearwater, Florida).

14 James R. Fisher, Jr., *Confident Selling for the 90s* (The Delta Group Florida 1992), nominated for a *Pulitzer Prize* in 1992, is comprehensively OD. It is a sequel to his earlier bestselling *Confident Selling* (Prentice-Hall 1971) in which the intuitive OD framework of the Fisher Paradigm©™® was first displayed in its embryonic form.

THE FALLACY OF HARD WORK
IN THE INFORMATION AGE!

James R. Fisher, Jr., Ph.D.
© April 23, 2014

This is a vignette from "Six Silent Killers," a book that probes the cultural biases that have been programmed into the mindset of many professionals. On the other hand, those who have taken charge of their lives, rejecting such programming, are doing swimmingly well in this uncertain economic climate.

"The Work Ethic Lives! Americans labor harder and at more jobs than ever."

This was an attention-grabbing *Time magazine* (September 7, 1987) lead-in to an article which, curiously, insisted that hard work is ennobling, and that people forced to work two and three jobs to live in style is proof positive that the American work ethic is alive. I don't think so. It suggests quite the opposite; that hard work is no longer relevant, much less exalted today (see Jeremy Rifkin, *"The End of Work,"* 1996).

Working hard is like treading water in place, knowing if you ever stop treading you will drown. There is a community of workers in conventional jobs who feel precisely like they are treading water. There is a limit to endurance, then what? Working two or three jobs is avoiding the issue. It is not evidence of a work ethic, but of *unconscious incompetence* or the search for the easy way out.

The formula for success today is to finish high school, then go to college or trade school, whatever is more appropriate, wait to have children until after you are married, and have a full-time job that can support you and your family.

There is no easy way out. Workers who have seen their jobs vanish must either be retrained in more productive work, retire, or go on the dole.

They cannot keep treading water. If they are unable or unwilling to learn new skills, they may well become a casualty of the post-market era. *Conscious competence* demands that workers make reality checks periodically, and that they assess their competence against that reality.

Moralizing is not the answer. *The economics of warfare has no heart.* The question every worker must ask himself is this: What can I do now that I am not doing to get out of the deep water and onto firm soil? Workers are under siege, and this is no time for half measures.

Unfortunately, there is a jaundiced appetite in worker consciousness for a strenuous schedule. Even if a worker is not making progress, he gets social sympathy for working hard: "Isn't it just wonderful how hard Sam (Sally) works? Why, I believe he (she) is working two jobs?"

Workers take pride in boasting about how hard they work. It is much less acceptable to boast of how smart one is working: "I only work 20 hours a week and make a good living. Isn't that great?" Most people would not think so.

First, they would be suspect of your boast; next they would put you down for bragging; and then they would hate you for making them feel a fool. Few are likely to tell friends it is taking them half the time it once took to earn a living. People take exception to those who show themselves as clever, while the same people welcome someone who complains of working hard. They can identify with the latter, but not the former. Why?

Workers hate to make hard choices. The fact that hard choices make it easy for them eventually has little impact on their decisions, nor are they aware that easy choices eventually make for hard lives. Research shows that most careers of workers are accidental, not planned. Most workers fall into their jobs and don't consciously seek out their careers. They stumble into their destinies.

So, workers recite to colleagues how tough their schedules, how many hours they work, how many jobs they juggle, failing to see the imbecility of this. Many workers prefer self-deception to committing to work they passionately believe in. Instead, their energy is engaged in menial diversions.

There is graphic evidence of this. The graduate schools of many American universities are the best in the world, especially in the pure sciences and

Nightmare of the Postmodern American Worker, being pursued by the ghost of hard choices.

technologies. Students who dominate these graduate schools in the more demanding curriculums are foreign students, mainly Orientals. The mathematics, physics, chemistry, and graduate engineering programs, especially in electronic and computer engineering, have anywhere from 50 to 75 percent of their graduate students from foreign countries.

Obviously, one of the reasons for this brain drain is that these curricula require extensive preparation, from grammar school, high school, and through undergraduate school. Europe and Asia excel at preparing students from preschool on for rewarding careers in science and technology. Meanwhile, Americans exalt students with athletic prowess who can throw a ball through a hoop, kick it through a goal post, or hit it out of the park.

If not athletics, Americans exalt students who chase the buck in business or law schools. We produce more MBAs than the rest of the graduate schools of the world combined, and in Washington, D.C. alone there are 65,000 lawyers. American universities have some of the best liberal arts and fine arts colleges in the world, which again draw widely from foreign lands. Schools are here; opportunity is here; but where are the American students?

Chances are they are looking to find a way to acquire a degree with the least amount of psychic and intellectual effort. Or the more cynical approach is to find a way into a prestigious university, preferably an Ivy League university, cough up a quarter million dollars, then coast to a degree. Once the degree is in hand the prestige of the pedigree will speak for itself.

This, of course, is equally asinine as is the bravado of working hard doing two or three jobs. Both extremes give work a bad name. Clearly, such people are not in charge and have contempt for the idea of work. That is not the point of this piece. Work can be *love made visible*, a spiritual and enhancing endeavor as these two Indian Masters suggest:

"Everyone has been made for some particular work, and the drive for that work has been put into his heart."

Julai al-Din Rumi (1207-1273)

"If you wish to work properly, you should never lose sight of two great principles. First, a profound respect for work undertaken; and second, a complete indifference to its fruits. Thus, only can you work with the proper attitude."

Swami Brahmananda (1863-1922)

ALL FALL DOWN!
THE COLLAPSE OF THE
WORKPLACE

IS IT TO BE REINVENTION BY THE SEAT OF THE PANTS?

James R. Fisher, Jr., Ph.D.
© July 31, 2014

Nikil Saval has bravely written a book about the workplace dilemma, putting it in the perspective of what work has become over the last two centuries.

He calls his work, *"Cubed: A Secret History of the Workplace"* (2014), referring to the cubicles or open cages that have become endemic to the modern workplace.

Saval reminds us of an open secret, and that is that three quarters to four fifths of workers today make nothing, touch nothing that is made, *but only track what is made financially and logistically.*

Most workers cannot imagine a workplace other than the open boxes they occupy in tall buildings.

Moreover, people, who work on farms or in our disappearing factories, don't have a clue as to what office workers do, or why they are doing it. In any case, they don't consider what they are doing as being "work," as to what that word "work" means to them.

Alas, most office workers would find it difficult to describe their jobs as work because it is not "hands on," as they don't have to till soil, mine for coal, man a machine, lay brick, pave a road, or even canvass door-to-door in the field, but for some reason tend to feel superior, however, because they probably earn better pay, have better working conditions and can stay clean wearing better threads to work on a daily basis.

In the late nineteenth century, as office workers became an increasing presence, what they really did was not totally clear to anyone, leastwise themselves. They showed up every work day and followed orders.

They acquired "positions" and felt justified in looking down at people who made things, did things, and knew exactly their worth because it had concrete value.

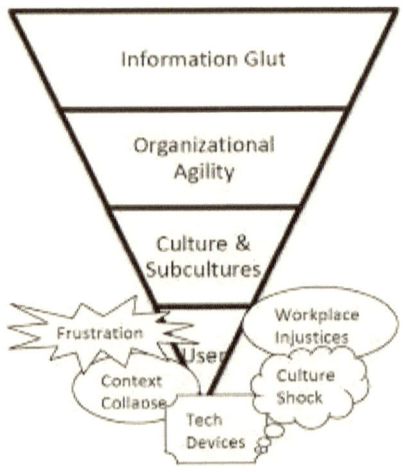

Corporate guru Peter Drucker was to tag these workers as "knowledge workers," a concept that took hold although relatively meaningless. He assigned this term to people involved in planning, directing, designing, negotiating, organizing, recording, or tracking something.

Drucker is a philosopher for corporate executives who read no philosophy.

It was nice to see Saval give a nod to the medieval guilds that combined work and management as a single function and not a division of labor between the two.

A form of the guild was adopted in the 20th century with great success. It was called *Skunk Works™*. The aerospace industry has promoted *Skunk Works* on specific assignments, often out performing groups ten times their size. The term "skunk works" refers to a small and loosely structured group of people, mainly engineers, who research and develop a project primarily for the sake of radical innovation. The term originated with *Lockheed's* World War Two *Skunk Works™* projects.

Nineteenth century Europe created office workers, housing them in large essentially windowless buildings. This ambience managed to diminish them as persons by the sheer size and isolated nature of these structures, which played on the workers' psychology.

In the 20th century, these buildings became skyscrapers. Hundreds, even thousands of workers rushed into these buildings to take residence in diminutive ready-made spaces. The buildings defined the work that these office workers did.

A kind of intimate dependency developed between office workers and their bosses, who kept close tabs on their work.

The closeness of office workers and bosses precluded any possibility of unionization as these workers were less inclined to sue for pay or working conditions, but rather to cue for greater intimacy with their bosses. It was a depersonalizing symbiotic connection.

Prestige could be earned by how many times an office worker was invited into the boss's closed office, often a glass bubble, to discuss a project. Brownie points were powerful incentives.

To give a sense of how well defined this was between the boss and the worker, when I was interviewing for assignment in Europe in the late 1980s for Honeywell Europe, SA., as *Director of Human Resources Planning & Development*, I was waiting to be interviewed by the late Dr. Helmet Hosse, President of Honeywell's extensive German subsidiary operation, when I had to go to the bathroom.

From the corner of my eye, I spied a washroom off the President's office, and moved towards it. The President's secretary nearly made a flying tackle of me as I approached the washroom, yelling in German, "Can't you see that is Dr. Hosse's private washroom?"

Charles Dickens in *David Copperfield* created *Uriah Heep* (1850) with his cloying humility and obsequious manner, as one form of an office worker. Herman Melville in contrast created *Bartleby* (1853), who's enigmatic refusal to work became the haunting mantra, "I prefer not to."

By 1855, a third of all workers in New York City were office workers; by the 20th century more than half of all workers were office workers.

The pre-20th century office worker felt superior to the laboring masses, but ambivalent about his management. This worker was solipsistic, but nothing compared to the narcissism of the late 20th century office worker who thought work was all about him.

This gave birth to the "pyramid climbers" (see Vance Packard's *"The Pyramid Climbers,"* 1962), who sought the right mentor to flatter, the right boxes to fill to attain an inside track to promotion, leaving nothing to chance, but also leaving little time or energy to do the job they were paid to do.

Nationally, early in the 20th century, 80 percent of American workers were in farming, manufacturing or allied fields. These workers did not consider what office workers did as "work."

They saw these workers as an effete mob, effeminate, greedy, decadent, talkative, cowardly, and more interested in being well dressed than having a skill set.

Frederick Winslow Taylor was the author of *"The Principles of Scientific Management"* (1911), and the guru of assembly line time and motion efficiency. At mid-century, his acolytes turned their attention to office work and workers. In doing so, Taylor's methodology is credited with destroying the soul of the worker leaving no scope for the individual worker to think or excel, but to behave essentially as a well-documented and controlled machine.

In the 1950s, time and motion studies were doctrinaire attempting to turn office workers into a replication of the rhythm of the factory.

Drucker was right in sync with Taylor's idea, seeing these workers as cogs in a machine by adding his *Management by Objectives* (MBOs) and *Standards of Performance* (SOP) into the mix. A bevy of work station architects followed.

These ergonomic specialists came on the scene to make office workers as efficient as automatons, the apotheosis of form following function in the skyscrapers that housed these workers.

Millions of workers flocked into these buildings to work in "cells" or "cubes" in open three-walled cubicles, in building now known as *"Taylor's Cathedrals."*

The 1980s, the Dawn of the Office Complex of Cubicles

To earn access to these cubicles (post-World War II), increasingly, you had to be credentialed, which meant you had to submit to IQ tests and personality profiles, to assessment centers, where the nature of your work was created to assess your capability to do the job, followed by a barrage of interviews conducted by executives before winning approval and being hired.

Much of this was tossed out a decade later, especially the IQ tests and personality profiles, as being unconstitutional.

I'm familiar with this process as I endured it when I was hired by *Nalco Chemical Company* in 1958. The company prided itself in screening 200 qualified applicants before hiring one.

Less than two decades after the war, an army of mainly academics created paradigms to make management less draconian and arbitrary when it came to these workers.

Such managerial theorists as Douglas McGregor, Rensis Likert, Robert Blake and Jane Mouton, Frederick Hertzberg, Paul Hersey and Ken Blanchard appeared with their solutions, but alas, none succeeded.

The workplace was evolving more quickly than recipes could be formulated to deal with the changing situation.

Sociologists entered the fray with such books David Riesman's *The Lonely Crowd* (1950), William H. Whyte's *The Organization Man* (1956), and Sloan Wilson's novel *The Man in the Gray Flannel Suit* (1955), which was turned into a popular film (1956).

Anomie and self-estrangement were part of the new vocabulary to describe the loss of social and economic identity of workers who felt little connection between work and themselves.

Meanwhile, with the workplace now more than 80 percent occupied by office workers in cubicles, the ergonomic gurus turned to personalizing these cubicles as veritable oases.

Although workers were now caged in these labyrinth catacombs, each office worker could call his place and space his "home away from home."

These diminutive spaces were cross pollinated with the ergonomically right chair, desk, filing cabinet, and bookcase to be perfect for the occupant.

But then came the dot.com revolution of the 1980s.

Now all bets were once again off.

The bookcases and filing cabinets had to go, as well as pushing paper, and in place was a computer screen that needed constant attention, which meant resolute brainpower to develop and run innovative operational programs.

The work was exhaustive. What to do?

To keep minds fresh and on task, office work of the past was scuttled, and the workplace was turned into a playground.

No more suits and ties, now it was jeans and T-shirts. Executives dressed the same as workers. Everything was loosey goosey, but kept on task, always on task.

Pizzas were delivered, beer busts on campus on Friday nights (workplaces came to be called "campuses"), full recreational facilities including basketball and handball courts, running tracks, weight rooms, and entertainment centers to rival *Disney World*.

The 80/20 rule, which has always held was now more apparent. As much as 80 – 90 percent of the consequential work that was now being done was by 10 – 20 percent of these office workers. Other workers were too busy playing, or thinking about playing, or complaining about not having enough time to play.

Ergonomic gurus promoted the idea of turning these glass cathedrals into open spaces without defined functionality, which meant no cubicles.

So, people got lost at work as to where they should be or what they should do because work had been changed into eclectic paradises with no specific work stations.

Saval goes into this to read like science fiction. Perhaps it is. He shows how the advent of the telephone and the typewriter transformed the office from a spoken to a written culture. The telephone forced people to keep records; the typewriter enabled them to do so. Growth meant upward with office buildings reaching well into the sky as this was cheaper than buying land. Designers did this without any idea how to organize the interiors of these metal framed stationary missiles. Saval suggests the equally metal vertical filing cabinets became a metaphorical "stand-in" for the office itself with each floor of the building stacked up like a separate file.

A current trend, which may prove anachronistic, is to abandon these monolithic vertical cities for flat one-story barracks like buildings in small towns in the countryside and suburban settings, where hundreds of computer screens drone on 24/7 with attentive eyes on the *Wide World Web* of the Internet.

These flatbed suburban structures may prove equally anachronistic as progressive thinkers are playing with the idea that most office workers will soon be working primarily at home, or if not working at home, not working at all.

As this pregnant idea is bandied about, others are thinking of abandoning the whole concept of working at home to simply outsourcing most of a company's work to third world countries, thus reducing the overhead costs, and the cost of benefits, pensions, and other entitlements.

This outsourcing designates these workers euphemistically as "contract consultants," meaning they are on their own nickel.

Little thought has been given to the fact that a short fifty years ago, people worked in one place for one company their entire careers. They felt secure and loyal to that employer and counted on entitlements and benefits as part of that security.

Just as farmers and manufacturers had no idea what office workers called "work" a century ago, these office workers cannot get their minds around the idea of work being that of "contract consultants." They translate that idea into insecurity and even poverty, subject to the whims of employers.

It should come as no surprise that trauma is written on the faces of these workers. For the past two or three generations, nothing even close to this independent self-management has been demanded of workers. What's more, they have not had training to deal with this possibility.

Indeed, the old rules of employment have been turned upside down, and workers have been given no orientation, no training, no insight, and no perspective on what these new demands may entail.

They have not been asked to develop a self-employed mindset, a mindset that cannot be realized instantaneously by osmosis.

This will take special attention, attention that is beyond the pale of the current conversation.

The United States Bureau of Labor Statistics projects by 2020, less than a short six years away, freelancers, temporary workers, day laborers and independent contract consultants will constitute 40 to 50 percent of the workforce. Can most workers fathom much less imagine that?

Regarding freelancers, the bureau also reports that currently as high as 77 percent of these workers have had trouble collecting payment for the work provided. Employers appear to be holding the money as long as they legally can. This should give pause.

"PRINCIPLE OF RECIPROCITY"

James R. Fisher, Jr., Ph.D.
© October 27, 2018

This is an excerpt from second edition of "Time Out for Sanity!" (2014) in a chapter titled "The Refreshing Turf of the Outsider."

Problems become personal and well beyond comprehension when a person moves into adulthood with still the mind and disposition of the child with insatiable needs and wants.

Careerism becomes the critical definer for some who lead double lives going along to get along at work bringing out the worst in them, while in private they lead secret lives that sometimes destroy them.

This is the gravitational pull between *exploitation* and *oppression* where everything is on the table and everyone is fair game. Claude Levi-Strauss calls this pragmatically, *"the principle of reciprocity."*

There are three distinct types of reciprocity that occur in human societies: *generalized, balanced and negative.*

With *generalized reciprocity*, gift giving has no expectation of immediate return.

Balanced reciprocity is the opposite of *generalized reciprocity* in that a specific value of return and under an established time limit is expected, for example, loaning cash to a friend. It can also involve doing a favor to a stranger which can be as simple as a few friendly words, an invitation to one's home, or a helpful suggestion. It entails the risk of rejection of the offer itself, or the risk of rejection of the overture implied by failure to reciprocate and enter a friendly relationship.

Negative reciprocity comes into two forms: *positive reciprocity* and *negative reciprocity* fairness.

Negative reciprocity occurs when an action that has a negative effect upon someone else is reciprocated with an action that has approximately equal negative effect upon another.

Positive reciprocity occurs when an action committed by one individual has a positive effect on someone is returned with an action that has an approximately positive effect, that is, the individual expects an action to be reciprocated by an action that is approximately equal in value. This is a *quid pro quo* relationship: you show a kindness to a person and expect a kindness of equal quality to be returned.

By taking this risk, an individual ends the complete indifference between himself and the other person. It forces on the other a choice of two alternatives, as Levi-Strauss notes:

"From now on it must become a relationship either of cordiality or hostility."

It will not remain neutral.

This was especially pertinent to me when I lived and worked in South Africa. By nature, I am a very private person, and the South African manager director was gregarious to the extreme. We worked closely together in forming a new chemical company composed of my American subsidiary, a British affiliate and a South African specialty chemical company. He assumed the social aspect was an automatic extension of our working relationship. Complicating matters further, we were both young and with similar young families.

From the very beginning, he went out of his way to include my family in his family's activities, which entailed a very active social life, making my family essentially part of his. When I failed to reciprocate, the die was cast. Our relationship went from warm to cool to cold, becoming implicit adversaries for no other reason.

He was by choice "an insider," and loved it, while I was by choice "an outsider," who valued his privacy and had never joined the club, which he could never fathom, and for this reason became quite paranoid. We were never able to bridge the gap.

An original mind is one thing. An independent mind is quite another. A private disposition is still another, each a complication to the other. An imitative mind cues on different sources for its satisfaction, as does a dependent socially oriented mind.

Each of these mindsets has different needs and expresses them in different ways, always looking for reciprocation for satisfaction.

An original mind uses other sources seeing old things in new ways. An independent mind believes in no contributing dependency. To put this in a college student context, an independent mind would prefer to study alone. In contrast, a dependent mind has little interest in originality or independence, restless when being alone, and therefore develops a nervous but carefree symbiotic relationship with others on the fly and serendipity of experience.

A private disposition is often taken as arrogance, while a social temperament is commonly perceived as superficial and insincere. *"The principle of reciprocity"* shows just how difficult it is for minds to meet and remain authentic.

When the pressure is great to conform to a social calculus, and the creative person is not of such a mind, creativity is likely to be buried in compliance, not cooperation. Cooperation is always voluntary. Still, there are frightfully clever imaginative sybarites ready to put their hooks into original thinkers for their own purposes. Reciprocity is always at work, always something for something.

Appalling, yet comic, our culture encourages piggyback thinking, while professing to support originality. This is the subversive side of teamwork. We are well schooled in conformity, in being tentative and circumspect looking for the ideas of others to latch on to. Reinforcing this, we join a new company and are told in orientation, *"we are a family."*

As absurd as the idea of family, it is meant to show mutual respect, establish trust, and put aside differences in terms of the nuclear metaphor of love and togetherness in reciprocal harmony.

David Cooper has something to say about this in *"Death of the Family"* (1970):

"The appearance of love is subversive to any good social ordering of our lives. Far more than being statistically abnormal, love is dangerous; it might even spread through the aseptic shield that we get each other to erect around ourselves. What we are socially conditioned to need and expect is not love, but security. Security means the full and repeatedly reinforced affirmation of the family."

Cooper goes on to point out that there is a certain gluing together of people based on the sense of one's own incompleteness. We seldom think of the work situation in these terms, but it was true for me.

I once told my mentor and boss, the late *Dr. Francis Xavier Pesuth*, my motivation to "behave" was not driven by fear of reprisal but love and respect for him. It clearly made him feel self-conscious, even suspect. When the affirmation of the family has a cold corporate design, it results in people seeing it as the basis of their security. We are not comfortable with the idea of love of work for itself much less passion separate from security. It speaks to Alan W. Watts' *"wisdom of insecurity"* because real security and non-alienated love are threatening to such a corporate structure. Only with unencumbered love of doing is it possible to get past security.

The corporate basis of security permeates all institutions including academia. Scholarship is often a measure of reinforcing the obvious social or implicit biases of academia, reactive constructs that applaud intellectual conventions and condemns constructions that disturb consensus perceptions.

The academic scholar goes on the briefest of limbs only to be cut off from the feeding trough (see Heather MacDonald's *"The Diversity Delusion,"* 2018). Criticism within this framework is a safe profession. It is made of one-part reaction to the work of another, and one-part walking in cadence to the drum roll of the majority. Such conforming scholarship is like an eating frenzy on the carcass of original thought.

From an early age, we hear the bromides, "nothing ventured nothing gained," and "actions speak louder than words." It is the con we play on ourselves that outsiders will have no part. They see ideas of original thinkers are torn to shreds while most fail to appreciate the irony.

We are not aware of this irony because we are too busy being busy. We are on a treadmill not unlike that of our pet gerbil and still see ourselves as superior beings going places, doing things, and making progress. We have the mental equipment to dig deep into our souls and find the source of our light, but for most of us that fun is left to the outsider.

Have you ever felt as if we are all on the same ship without a helmsman steering the course? The lack of original thought supports that impression. Every time "Freud" is mentioned it speaks to this deficiency. We can't seem to ignore him or get past him.

We echo our contempt for him. American sociologist Peter Belau (1918 – 2002) sees this as a desire to fit in, be one of the crowd, resonate with its sentiments, wave the same banner, and grunt with the same gusto, while having little sense of the collective nonsense of it all. Belau writes:

"Power that is exercised with moderation and confers ample benefits in return for submission elicits social approval that legitimates the authority of its command."

That is why most churchgoers are docile, workers dependent, and citizens obliging. Our behavior resounds with the soundless cry: feed me, cloth me, give me access to exchanging bodily fluids, and my soul is yours.

Our debt to Einstein in science, Freud in psychiatry, Skinner and Adler in psychology, and others in their professions, is so staggering that I wonder if they have doomed us to our fate. It is as if we are on a ship of strangers with the only thing held in common is our estrangement.

If you wonder how Watts and Hoffer, and others like them, have avoided this fate, it is quite simple: they were never members of the passenger manifesto, more likely stowaways.

They might be on board for a time, legitimately, as entertaining curiosities but no more, as they are essentially invisible. Because of this they have escaped idolatry, of being placed on a pedestal only to be knocked off it at the insider's pleasure. Outsiders never have to worry about pedestals.

In the worship of intellectual celebrity, there are the "ins" and "outs" and "no accounts." Watts and Hoffer fall somewhere near the "no accounts." It is permissible, even proper to cuss and discuss men of the status of Freud and Skinner, providing you belong. Celebrities are "in" and "out," and then "in" again like the outrages change in academia and politics, and the fads change in the entertainment industry.

Watts and Hoffer are complete outsiders. Misfits can choose to rant and rave to their hearts' content as few are paying attention. Their ranting is a nuisance factor, but occasionally a welcomed diversion to the boring climate of intellectual "ins."

Eric Sevareid (1912 – 1992), the commentator of television's CBS News, discovered Hoffer in reading his book, *"The True Believer"* (1951).

In the fall of 1967, CBS aired the interview called *"Eric Hoffer: The Passionate State of Mind."* The program lasted an hour. Hoffer spoke passionately on several subjects, including the U. S. policy in Viet Nam, the importance of Israel, the failure of leadership in the *Civil Rights Movement*, and the uncanny character of *President Lyndon Johnson*. This was very controversial stuff in 1967.

Despite this, perhaps because of this, the nation was tired of a panoply of insincere optimism from every outlet of the media. Hoffer became a national curiosity, gruff, almost primordial in stature, with a thick German ascent, and clipped comments on America's retreat from its problems. He was a breath of fresh air in the adolescent climate of *spoiled bratomania* that persisted at the time with seemingly nobody in charge of anything anywhere.

The television nightly news featured America's young people's latest angst, pranks, and protests to the point of *ad nauseum*. Hoffer entered the fracas playing understanding *"grandpa America"* to a fatigued and confused nation consoling it with his confidence that "all would work out in the end."

He was a dreamer, but fantasies help when a society is split down the middle with double-digit unemployment and double-digit inflation with a pathological mindset that clings to the cognitive dissonance that it has done nothing wrong.

"Hoffer made millions feel better about their country," Sevareid reflected to explain Hoffer's television success. While this was true, the country obviously had no intentions of changing, which anyone who had read *"The True Believer"* would clearly understand.

One of Hoffer's intriguing metaphors was the railroad. He said American railroads, unlike European's, never broke down because "Americans believe in *preventive maintenance*." No sooner said, then American tracks appeared faulty, unscheduled trains collided, rail bridges collapsed, and the efficiency metaphor proved to be quite leaky.

[In December 2013, we found this slide into the lackadaisical extended to an engineer operating a Metro-North Railroad train into New York City. He went into a curve going 82 mph which was nearly three times the speed allowed. Four people were killed and seventy were injured. His defense? According to his lawyer, he was suffering "highway hypnosis," or in the sense of this essay, operating robotically on automatic pilot.]

This collision with reality did not deter Hoffer's popularity as he was a curiosity. Readers and television viewers found his mass movement and crowd theories entertaining, and his confidence in America reassuring. They read his books that were brought out by an "in" publisher, Harper & Row.

His popularity was even among the normally cautious consumers of the printed word. There was something of an earthier Emerson to his epigrams. They spoke to these independent sleepy minds that wanted to feel better about their country. He dignified peripatetic readers and eclectic thinkers who were tired of the inclusion-exclusion metaphor. They needed to find some sense in the nonsense of the times. One thing his readers had in common despite the evidence to the contrary: they believed the myth that they were their own man.

While Freud and Skinner devotees have become institutionalized, Hoffer's readers have remained floaters. Freud and Skinner have set anchor, confident of their place and space, while Hoffer sees no Nirvana around the bend of the river.

Hoffer passes the shoreline of late nineteenth and early twentieth century that is emboldened with Freud and Skinner markers.

Have these "inside" thinkers arrived? I believe they think they have, but what have they found? Hoffer makes no claim to originality, or to having found anything. He is just moving on the river. He has no universal "nature of man" theory, only a kinship with the giants of the past as student. He knows their ideas are like this river, always changing in profundity, sometimes comforting, often confounding, then contradicting, as they push against what is known to what is not, comfortable as he moves on as the quintessential common man.

When we drop anchor, and cry, "Eureka! I've found it," we are in trouble. It would seem a navigational weakness common to thinkers today and our recent past. In "Fragments of a Philosophy," I write:

"The amateur thinker can be defined as having the ability to articulate the world of ideas in broad terms comprehensible if not immediately applicable to the average man. He is a doer who thinks out of life. Compare this to the preference for technical language of the specialist. Specialization provides a place to hide from the masses in the cloistered abbey of omniscience.

Instead of substance, the average man is offered the dribble of inauthentic syntax to accommodate his vernacular. He is not the audience. He is a distraction. To console him he is given a few new words and terms that become popular without insight or understanding. In Iowa, we call that feeding slop to the pigs."

THE ROMAN EMPIRE ENTERS THE BREACH

"Search for the Real Parents of My Soul"

James R. Fisher, Jr., Ph.D.
© November 14, 2014

Was this the way it was for most people? The time they lived in was an open invitation to a cocktail of self-denial and self-glorification. And if you didn't like the situation you were stuck in, there was always the option of running away from yourself; running away from your opinions; your marriage; from your country; from old values; from trends that had otherwise meant so much yesterday. The problem was just that out there, among all the new; you found nothing of what you were looking for deep down inside; because tomorrow it would all be meaningless again. It had become an eternal and fruitless hunt for your own shadow and that was pitiful.

Jussi Adler-Olsen, Denmark novelist in "The Hanging Girl" (2014)

Three thousand years before *Christ*, people worshipped *Horus*, who stood for light, and *Seth* for darkness with the good god of light winning the battle against the evil god of darkness, *Seth*.

The hieroglyphs recount similar stories 1500 years before Christ and almost every figure in the *Old Testament*. Moses in the bulrush basket was known as Mises in Egypt, Manou in India, and Minos in Crete.

The hieroglyphs also reproduced the story of *Noah and the flood*. The Jewish faith may proclaim exclusive rights to these stories, but many of the *New* and *Old Testament* stories are found in the hieroglyphs.

Horus was born on December 25th by a virgin named *Merci* with the stepfather named *Seb* accompanying her. The birth was predicted by a Star in the East and announced by an angel, who heralded shepherds on the hillside to attend. *Horus* was born in a cave and worshipped by three kings who followed the Star from their homelands in the East. Horus became a teacher at twelve, was baptized at thirty, and then joined by twelve followers or disciples with whom he traveled about performing miracles. He was betrayed by *Typhon*, crucified, and resurrected after three days.

When you look at prominent religions throughout history, there appear a number of generic characteristics similar to the story of *"Horus and Christ,"* including the prominence of celestial bodies to the beliefs of these religions (see J. Warner, *"Is Jesus Simply a Retelling of the Horus Mythology?"* November 6, 2017, *Atheism Writings*).

Whatever your perspective, we now move out of the *Old Testament* and Edward Gibbon's assessment, along with others, into the *New Testament* and this new religion, *Christianity*. For whatever the reader may think or believe, historians agree, Jesus did in fact live and has an authentic if sketchy history.

That said, the irony is, were it not for the efficacy of the *Roman Empire,* a popular theory holds that Christianity might never have gained its prominence. Keep this in mind as we move forward.

* * *

There is a thread that goes through Western civilization that is so fine that while it knits the past with the present and the future, it is so easy to miss how it has been weaved into a single fabric, which is today commonly called *"the West."*

As we have seen thus far, the Hellenistic tradition of Greece greatly influenced the Judaic culture, especially as it relates to the Pharisees, and that influence continued with the *Rise of Rome*, making *Rome* the world's greatest empire (Everitt 2012).

The best estimates of the beginning of the *Roman Empire* are with the accession of Augustus as the first emperor in 27 B.C. Others say the date of Rome's foundation was sometime in the eighth century, possibly 753 B.C. (Everitt, 2012)

Rome is the discernible connection between the *Old* and *New Testament* as we are now introduced to the "clash of cultures" between the pagan polytheism of Rome with the monotheism of Judaism, and the cult of Jesus, which will become Christianity as we move into the *New Testament*.

* * *

During the Reigns of Augustus and Tiberius, Judea had several Roman Prefects according to Jewish historian Josephus: Coponius (6 A.D.), Marcus Ambibulus (7 A.D.), Annius Rufus (14-17 A.D.), "Valerius Gratus (17-27 A.D.), and Pontius Pilate (27-36 A.D.), who ultimately ruled on the crucifixion of Jesus.

Scholars have provided estimates for the year of the crucifixion in the range 30–33 AD, with the majority of modern scholars favoring the date April 7, 30 AD. Another popular date is Friday, April 3, 33 AD.

The crucifixion of Jesus is recorded in the *New Testament* with Christians believing Him to be the *Son of God* as well as *the Messiah*. He was arrested, tried, and sentenced by Pontius Pilate to be scourged, and finally crucified.

Collectively, this is referred to as the *Passion of Jesus' suffering and death by crucifixion followed by his resurrection,* central tenets of Christian theology concerning the doctrines of atonement and salvation.

His crucifixion is described in the four synoptic canonical gospels and referred to generally in the *New Testament Epistles* as well as attested to by other ancient historical sources and confirmed by non-Christian sources (Eddy & Boyd, 2007).

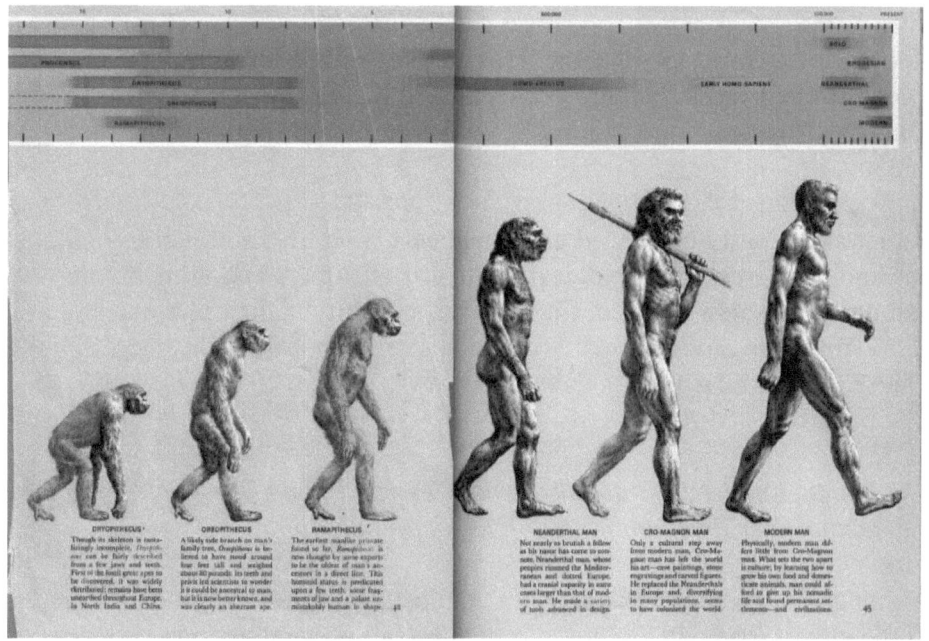

The march of the Homo sapiens from his theoretical origin into the post- modern era.

*   *   *

This sets the stage for the appearance of an irascible figure of no apparent consequence, a figure that will clash with Jesus' disciple, Peter, and Jesus' brother, James, over the direction of the new sect, throwing the modest movement off course to split from Judaism and become a new religion, challenging the *Roman Empire.* This nondescript man was Saul from Tarsus (Ruden 2010).

Saul, a Hellenistic Pharisee and tent maker who some say witnessed the stoning to death of St. Stephen, as he is alleged to have held the garments of the stoners, his associates, whose job was to search out and persecute members of the Jesus cult. Witnessing this stoning, which author Sarah Ruden shows is a slow miserable death, proved shattering to this sensitive and conflicting young man (Ruden 2010).

Later, on his way to Damascus, Saul was confronted by the full horror of his human limitations. *"Saul, Saul, why do you persecute me?"* the voice asked (Acts 9:4).

Known to be epileptic, the shock of this voice put him into an immediate swoon for he lived in humanity and came to realize the hurt done to the Jesus followers, like that done to Jesus in human form, now registered as an assault on God.

Saul was instantly converted and changed his name from Saul to Paul, and became "the greatest theological genius of all time," and arguably the lone architect of the new religion, Christianity, as Christian doctrine came not from Jesus, nor from any of Jesus' "twelve apostles," but from the pen of Paul of Tarsus (Ruden 2010).

*   *   *

The Roman Empire fell into this breach, an empire that rose modestly gaining momentum over time into the colossus that it became.

Although Rome began as a republic, the period from the legendary founding of the city of Rome in 753 B.C. through the fall of what became known as the Western Empire in A.D. 476 represents a continuous history of a culture we call the *Roman Empire.*

That said, starting in 19 B.C., Augustus ushered in a conservative revolution that focused on moral renewal of the Roman state in part by bringing back customs from the past. He enacted reforms concerning religion and social and sexual behavior that directly affected personal freedom as well as what it meant to be a citizen under the empire.

Augustus interpreted the period of civil war prior to his reign as immoral in which Romans had neglected the gods in deference to their personal luxury and pleasure. This aside, his achievements rested with his popularity with the army, securing the borders, improving empire administration, and developing a well-planned method of succession.

The defeat of Mark Antony at the *"Battle of Actium"* (31 B.C.) secured Augustus's power. Augustus then cut the size of the army but retained the goodwill of his disbanded troops by granting them full citizenship, the ability to vote, immunity from tribute, opportunities to relocate throughout the empire, and retirement bonuses for 20 years of service.

After his death in 14 A.D., his stepson Tiberius was easily accepted as emperor being keen to rule much as his father had, continuing the Augustus tradition, while encouraging Romans to move eastward quietly expanding the Roman influence.

This swelled the Roman presence in Judea during the reign of Tiberius (14-37 A.D.,), Caligula (37-41 A.D.), Claudius (41-54 A.D.), and Nero (54-68 A.D.), a period of emperor eccentric steadiness according to historians.

Although each had strengths, none would recreate the golden age of the first emperor's reign. Instead, they are remembered for their faults and oddities, from madness to stuttering, from tyranny to Nero's suicide.

"Pax Romana" (27 B.C. to A.D. 180) represents two centuries of peace that commenced with the reign of Augustus (27 B.C.) and the death 207 years later (180 A.D.) of Marcus Aurelius. It was a period of internal order and indisputable dominance abroad, similar to the *"American Century."* Historian Anthony Everitt, however, finds that comparison between Rome and the United States ludicrous if not dangerous (Everitt 2012).

Rome had its "New Age," as well, ushered in by Augustus in 19 B.C. in what proved to be a conservative revolution. He focused on the moral renewal of the Roman state in part by bringing back customs from the past. He also enacted reforms concerning religion and social and sexual behavior that directly affected personal freedom as well as the definition of what constituted a Roman citizen.

At the same time, there were mounting delusions of grandeur. This included a sense of invincibility and destiny, as well as a preoccupation with empire showing little alarm at increasing dysfunction of Rome at home.

Rome failed to recognize emerging socioeconomic problems such as immigration as diverse ethnic groups which were pouring into Rome, foreigners who resisted assimilation into the Roman culture, instead becoming wards of the state contributing little to the majesty of Rome's already established greatness.

In retrospect, the seeds of the decline were planted in the birth of the *Christian Empire* (*National Geographic* 2014). By the fourth century A.D., Christians were integrated into all facets of Roman society, including the military, judicial, and educational establishments, while comprising only 8 percent of the population.

Troubled by this mounting influence, in 303 A.D., Emperor Diocletian ordered that all Christians renounce their beliefs and sacrifice to Roman gods, starting the final Roman persecution of the church.

A decade later, following the *"Edict of Milan,"* the practice of Christianity was as accepted as that of any other religion. Rome, however, would not become a fully Christian empire until after the fall of the *Second Tetrarchy* (i.e., four rulers), and Constantine's reign (*National Geographic* 2014).

* * *

Emperor Constantine, after a battle field conversion, made Christianity the state religion and prohibited the worshiping of all Roman gods in 313 A.D.

Once established, few could have foreseen that this act, with the death of Constantine in 337 A.D., would mark the beginning of the end of the *Roman Empire* (Womersley 1994).

A series of forces were at work, some familiar, some new, which combined to make Rome's downfall almost inevitable.

Without new territory, the empire lost revenue, burdening an economy that was already straining under the enormous cost of maintaining a vast army, a welfare system at home, saddled with bureaucratic lethargy, and a series of emperors without the force of personality to lead, who instead were likely to be entrenched within their imperial palaces, often located outside of Rome, along with corruption in the Senate, leaving the government marginalized in the day-to-day conduct of business.

The tension between the East and West segments of the Roman Empire had become increasingly destructive as emperors no longer cooperated and instead undermined each other.

Barbarian tribes from the north administered the *coup de grace*, as some traditional tribal nemeses migrated into the empire when the Huns invaded Europe, while Visigoths and Germanic tribes took advantage of the power vacuums and attacked Rome itself.

Rome's empire had grown so large that its borders became harder to defend. Meanwhile, in the east, a new empire of the Sassanid overran Rome's traditional enemy the Parthians. Tribes such as the Goths from the Baltic regions and the Alamanni, a confederation of Germanic tribes from the upper Rhine invaded from the north. Rebels within and without the empire annexed territory and broke away from Rome (*National Geographic* 2014). The western empire started to unravel with the death of Constantine in 337 A.D. with Rome giving way completely to Byzantium in the east in 476 A.D., which marked the end of the Roman Empire.

*   *   *

Edward Gibbon devoted more than a decade to his magisterial *History of the Decline and Fall of the Roman Empire* (1776-1789), which opens with this famous sentence:

In the second century of the Christian era, the empire of Rome comprehended the fairest part of the earth, and the most civilized portion of mankind.

The empire was at its peak, thanks to the spirit of moderation with which Augustus had imbued it. Gibbon praised Augustus' moderation who was content to rest with the republic's conquests, having no inclination to subdue the entire world. Gibbon continues:

Inclined to peace by his temper and situation, it was easy for him to discover, that Rome, in her present exalted situation, had much less to hope than to fear from the chance of arms (Womersley 1994).

Gibbon asked the questions:

What caused the empire to fall from those heights? The barbarian invasions? The rise of Christianity to the status of a state religion?

Yes, he concludes, but that was only the most important aspect of a more encompassing cause. He put his views in a section titled, "*General Observations on the Fall of the Roman Empire in the West*":

The decline of Rome was the natural and inevitable effect of immoderate greatness. (Gibbon 2007)

Too much ambition, too much prosperity, too much power in the hands of the Praetorian guards, too many provincials bearing the name of "Roman," who knew nothing of the Roman spirit. These were the causes, he concludes, of the Rome's destruction.

Chapter 15 and 16 of Gibbon's work are immoderate, as the historian makes no attempt to express himself in politically correct terms. The early Christians, he assessed, were simple and mild folks, but from the first they preached and practiced an intolerant exclusivity.

Whereas the pagans stood ready to add another god to the pantheon, the followers of Christ insisted that theirs was the true and only God.

Gibbon, a nonbeliever, viewed religion of any kind the sanctuary for the ignorant and superstitious masses only. At the same time, he recognized the social usefulness of religion, but only when it was polytheistic, tolerant, moderate in its enthusiasm and modest in its claims.

Thanks to *Paul, the Apostle*, Christianity was none of these things. Christians were immoderately passive. They discouraged active virtues and buried the last remnants of the military spirit in the cloister. Gibbon held a special grievance for the sacred indolence of the monks who he claimed embraced a servile and effeminate age (Womersley 1994).

Yet, he viewed Christians as also immoderately pugnacious, even within their own camp, zealotry could not be held in check. Between the bishops in Rome and the bishops in the provinces, there was a continuing cold war.

Bishops, like almost all Christians, Gibbon observes, were fanatics who for a variety of reasons, zeal, the promise of another world, miraculous claims, rigid virtue, or church organization, were able to transform themselves from a persecuted minority into an intolerant majority.

Christians had been persecuted, Gibbon admits, but the pagan treatment was less intolerable than many believed. He concedes that Nero may have carried things too far. But he reminds the reader that once Christians came to power they were "no less diligently employed in displaying the cruelty in imitating the conduct of their pagan adversaries." (Womersley 1994)

Nero's antagonism to Christian doctrine spilled over into the Jewish faith, leading to charges of anti-Semitism:

From the reign of Nero to that of Antoninus Pius, the Jews discovered a fierce impatience of the dominion of Rome, which repeatedly broke out in the most furious massacres and insurrections. Humanity is shocked at the recital of the horrid cruelties which they committed in the cities of Egypt, of Cyprus, and of Cyrene, where they dwelt in treacherous friendship with the unsuspecting natives; and we are tempted to applaud the severe retaliation which was exercised by the arms of legions against a race of fanatics, whose dire and credulous superstition seemed to render them the implacable enemies not only of the Roman government, but also of humankind. (Womersley 1994)

Emperor Julian attempted in vain to restore polytheistic paganism from the monotheism of Christianity and Judaism. Julian was also known as *Julian the Philosopher* and was emperor from 361-363 A.D. with strong Hellenistic leanings.

A member of the Constantinian dynasty, Julian became Caesar over the western provinces by order of Constantius II in 355 and in this role campaigned successfully against the Alamanni and Franks. Most notable was his crushing victory over the Alamanni in 357 at the Battle of Argentoratum despite being outnumbered.

In 360 in Lutetia (Paris), he was acclaimed Augustus by his soldiers, sparking a civil war between Julian and Constantius. Before the two could face each other in battle, however, Constantius died, after naming Julian as his rightful successor.

In 363, Julian embarked on an ambitious campaign against the Sassanid Empire in the east. Though initially successful, Julian was mortally wounded in battle and died shortly thereafter.

Julian was a man of unusually complex character: he was "the military commander, the theosophist, the social reformer, and the man of letters". He was the last non-Christian ruler of the Roman Empire, and it was his desire to bring the Empire back to its ancient Roman values in order to save it from dissolution.

He purged the top-heavy state bureaucracy and attempted to revive traditional Roman religious practices at the cost of Christianity. His rejection of Christianity in favor of Neoplatonic paganism caused him to be called *Julian the Apostate*, or "a person who has abandoned the religion and principles" of the (Christian) church. He was the last emperor of the Constantinian dynasty.

Unlike Constantine, Julian was moderate and tolerant, "the only hardship," according to Gibbon, "which he inflicted on the Christians, was to deprive them of the power of tormenting their fellow subjects, whom they stigmatized with the odious titles of idolaters and heretics" (*General Observations* 2007).

Julian was a true believer in the pagan gods and not a philosophic skeptic concerning all religions. In Gibbon's view, he should have emulated those who had allowed philosophy to purify "their minds from the prejudices of the popular superstitions" and who therefore rejected Christianity.

Julian was speaking of Seneca, the elder, and younger Pliny, Tacitus, Plutarch, Galen, Epictetus and Marcus Aurelius, whose death in 207 A.D. marked the end of Rome's golden period.

As point of reference, Gibbon is considered to be a son of the *European Enlightenment* and this is reflected in his famous verdict on the history of the Middle Ages:

"I have described the triumph of barbarism and religion."

However, politically, he aligned himself with the conservative Edmund Burke's rejection of the democratic movements of the time as well as with Burke's dismissal of the "rights of man."

Gibbon's work has been praised for its style, his piquant epigrams and its effective irony. Unusually for the 18th century, Gibbon was never content with secondhand accounts when the primary sources were accessible. With reference to primary sources, Gibbon is considered by many to be one of the first modern historians.

In accuracy, thoroughness, lucidity, and a comprehensive grasp of a vast subject, his history is considered incomparable; an English history that may be regarded as definitive. Whatever its shortcomings, *"The Decline & Fall of the Roman Empire"* is artistically imposing as well as historically unimpeachable as a vast panorama of a great period.

Having recounted his melancholy tale of Rome's decline and fall, Gibbon asked if it contained a warning to the present. Might Europe one day suffer a similar fate? Incredibly, he thought not:

The abuses of tyranny are restrained by the mutual influence of fear and shame; republics have acquired order and stability; monarchies have imbibed the principles of freedom, or, at least, of indoctrination; and some sense of honor and justice is introduced into the most defective constitutions by the general manner of the times. In peace, the progress of knowledge and industry is accelerated by the emulation of so many active rivals in war, the European forces are exercised by temperate and indecisive contests (Gibbon, *General Observations* 2007).

The crucifixion of Jesus is recorded in the *New Testament*, Christians believing Him to be the Son of God as well as the Messiah. He was arrested, tried, and sentenced by Pontius Pilate to be scourged, and finally crucified. Collectively, this is referred to as Jesus Passion, Suffering, Death by Crucifixion, and His Redemption as the central tenets of Christian theology concerning the Christian doctrines of atonement and salvation.

His crucifixion is described in the four synoptic canonical gospels, referred to in the *New Testament Epistles*, attested to by other ancient sources, and is established as a historical event confirmed by non-Christian sources (Eddy & Boyd, 2007).

*　　*　　*

This sets the stage for the appearance of an irascible figure of no apparent consequence, a figure that will clash with Jesus' disciple, Peter, and Jesus' brother, James, over the direction of the new sect, throwing the modest movement off course to split from Judaism and become a new religion, challenging the Roman Empire. This nondescript man was Saul from Tarsus (Ruden 2010).

Saul, a Hellenistic Pharisee and tentmaker who some say witnessed the stoning to death of St. Stephen, as he is alleged to have held the garments of the stoners, his associates, whose job was to search out and persecute members of the Jesus cult. Witnessing this stoning, which author Sarah Ruden shows is a slow miserable death, proved shattering to this sensitive and conflicting young man (Ruden 2010).

Later, on his way to Damascus, Saul was confronted by the full horror of his human limitations. "Saul, Saul, why do you persecute me?" the voice asked (Acts 9:4).

A man who lived in humanity, he came to realize the hurt done to the Jesus followers, like that done to Jesus in human form, which now registered as an assault on God. He was instantly converted and changed his name from Saul to Paul, and became "the greatest theological genius of all time," and arguably the lone architect of the new religion, Christianity, as Christian doctrine came not from Jesus, nor from any of Jesus' "twelve apostles," but from the pen of Paul of Tarsus (Ruden 2010).

*   *   *

The Roman Empire fell into this breach, an empire that rose modestly gaining momentum over time into the colossus that it became.

Some historians regard the *Roman Empire* as beginning with the accession of Augustus as the first emperor in 27 B.C. Others recognized that although Rome began as a republic, the period from the legendary founding of the city of Rome in 753 B.C. through the fall of what became known as the Western Empire in A.D. 476 represents a continuous history of a culture we call the *Roman Empire*.

That said, starting in 19 B.C., Augustus ushered in a conservative revolution that focused on moral renewal of the Roman state in part by bringing back customs from the past. He enacted reforms concerning religion and social and sexual behavior that directly affected personal freedom as well as what it meant to be a citizen under the empire.

Augustus interpreted the civil war prior to his reign as immoral in which Romans had neglected the gods in deference to their personal luxury and pleasure. This aside, his achievements rested with his popularity with the army, securing the borders, improving empire administration, and developing a well-planned method of succession.

The defeat of Mark Antony at the "Battle of Actium" (31 B.C.) secured his power. Augustus then cut the size of the army but retained the goodwill of his disbanded troops by granting them full citizenship, the ability to vote, immunity from tribute, opportunities to relocate throughout the empire, and retirement bonuses for 20 years of service.

After his death in 14 A.D., his stepson Tiberius was easily accepted as emperor being keen to rule much as his father had, continuing the Augustus tradition, while encouraging Romans to move eastward quietly expanding the Roman influence.

This swelled the Roman presence in Judea during the reign of Tiberius (14-37 A.D.), Caligula (37-41 A.D.), Claudius (41-54 A.D.), and Nero (54-68 A.D.), a period that historians claim as emperor eccentric steadiness. Although each had strengths, none would recreate the golden age of the first emperor's reign. Instead, they are remembered for their faults and oddities, from madness to stuttering, from tyranny to Nero's suicide.

"Pax Romana" (27 B.C. to A.D. 180) represented two centuries of peace that commenced with the reign of Augustus (27 B.C.) and the death 207 years later (180 A.D.) of Marcus Aurelius. It was a period of internal order and indisputable dominance abroad, similar to the *"American Century."* Historian Anthony Everitt, however, finds that comparison between Rome and the United States ludicrous if not dangerous (Everitt 2012).

Rome had its "New Age," as well, ushered in by Augustus in 19 B.C. in what proved to be a conservative revolution. He focused on the moral renewal of the Roman state in part by bringing back customs from the past. He also enacted reforms concerning religion and social and sexual behavior that directly affected personal freedom as well as the definition of what constituted a Roman citizen.

At the same time, there were mounting delusions of grandeur. This included a sense of invincibility and destiny, as well as a preoccupation with empire showing little alarm at increasing dysfunction of Rome at home.

Rome failed to recognize emerging socioeconomic problems such as immigration as diverse ethnic groups poured into Rome, resisting assimilation into the Roman culture, instead becoming wards of the state contributing little to the majesty of Rome's established greatness.

In retrospect, the seeds of the decline were planted in the birth of the *Christian Empire* (*National Geographic* 2014). By the fourth century A.D., Christians were integrated into all facets of Roman society, including the military, judicial, and educational establishments, while comprising only 8 percent of the population.

Troubled by this mounting influence, in 303 A.D., Emperor Diocletian ordered that all Christians renounce their beliefs and sacrifice to Roman gods, starting the final Roman persecution of the church.

A decade later, following the "Edict of Milan," the practice of Christianity was as accepted as that of any other religion. Rome, however, would not become a fully Christian empire until after the fall of the *Second Tetrarchy* (i.e., four rulers), and Constantine's reign (*National Geographic* 2014).

*   *   *

Emperor Constantine, after a battle field conversion, made Christianity the state religion and prohibited the worshiping of all Roman gods in 313 A.D. Once established, few could have foreseen that this act, with the death of Constantine in 337 A.D., would mark the beginning of the end of the *Roman Empire* (Womersley 1994).

A series of forces were at work, some familiar, some new, which combined to make Rome's downfall almost inevitable.

Without new territory, the empire lost revenue, burdening an economy that was already straining under the enormous cost of maintaining a vast army, a welfare system at home, saddled with bureaucratic lethargy, and a series of emperors without the force of personality to lead, who instead were likely to be entrenched within their imperial palaces, often located outside of Rome, along with corruption in the Senate, leaving the government marginalized in the day-to-day conduct of business.

The tension between the East and West segments of the Roman Empire had become increasingly destructive as emperors no longer cooperated and instead undermined each other.

Barbarian tribes from the north administered the *coup de grace* as some traditional tribal nemeses migrated into the empire when the Huns invaded Europe, while Visigoths and Germanic tribes took advantage of the power vacuums and attacked Rome itself.

Rome's empire had grown so large that its borders became harder to defend. Meanwhile, in the east, a new empire, the Sassanid, overran Rome's traditional enemy the Parthians. Tribes such as the Goths from the Baltic regions and Alamanni from the upper Rhine invaded from the north. Rebels within and without the empire annexed territory and broke away from Rome (*National Geographic* 2014). The western empire started to unravel with the death of Constantine in 337 A.D. with Rome giving way completely to Byzantium in the east in 476 A.D., which marked the end of the Roman Empire.

* * *

Edward Gibbon devoted more than a decade to his magisterial *History of the Decline and Fall of the Roman Empire* (1776-1789), which opens with this famous sentence:

In the second century of the Christian era, the empire of Rome comprehended the fairest part of the earth, and the most civilized portion of mankind.

The empire was at its peak, thanks to the spirit of moderation with which Augustus had imbued it. Gibbon praised Augustus' moderation who was content to rest with the republic's conquests, with no inclination to subdue the entire world. Gibbon continues:

Inclined to peace by his temper and situation, it was easy for him to discover, that Rome, in her present exalted situation, had much less to hope than to fear from the chance of arms (Womersley 1994).

Gibbon asked the questions:

What caused the empire to fall from those heights? The barbarian invasions? The rise of Christianity to the status of a state religion?

Yes, he concludes, but that was only the most important aspect of a more encompassing cause. He put his views in a section titled, *"General Observations on the Fall of the Roman Empire in the West"*:

The decline of Rome was the natural and inevitable effect of immoderate greatness. (Gibbon 2007)

Too much ambition, too much prosperity, too much power in the hands of the Praetorian guards, too many provincials bearing the name of "Roman," who knew nothing of the Roman spirit. These were the causes, he concludes, of the destruction.

Chapter 15 and 16 of Gibbon's work are immoderate, as the historian makes no attempt to express himself in politically correct terms. The early Christians, he assessed, were simple and mild folks, but from the first they preached and practiced an intolerant exclusivity.

Whereas the pagans stood ready to add another god to the pantheon, the followers of Christ insisted that theirs was the true and only God.

Gibbon, a nonbeliever, viewed religion of any kind the sanctuary for the ignorant and superstitious masses only. At the same time, he recognized the social usefulness of religion, but only when it was polytheistic, tolerant, moderate in its enthusiasm and modest in its claims.

Thanks to *Paul, the Apostle*, Christianity was none of these things. Christians were immoderately passive. They discouraged active virtues and buried the last remnants of the military spirit in the cloister. Gibbon held a special grievance for the sacred indolence of the monks who he claimed embraced a servile and effeminate age (Womersley 1994).

Yet, he viewed Christians as profligately pugnacious, even within their own camp, zealotry could not be held in check. Between the bishops in Rome and the bishops in the provinces, there was a continuing cold war.

The bishops, like almost all Christians, Gibbon observes, were fanatics who for a variety of reasons, including zeal, the promise of another world, miraculous claims, rigid virtue, or the church organization itself, were able to transform themselves from a persecuted minority into an intolerant majority.

Christians had been persecuted, Gibbon admits, but the pagan treatment was less intolerable than many believed. He concedes that Nero may have carried things too far. But he reminds the reader that once Christians came to power they were "no less diligently employed in displaying cruelty, than their pagan adversaries." (Womersley 1994)

Nero's antagonism to Christian doctrine spilled over into the Jewish faith, leading to charges of anti-Semitism:

From the reign of Nero to that of Antoninus Pius, the Jews discovered a fierce impatience of the dominion of Rome, which repeatedly broke out in the most furious massacres and insurrections. Humanity is shocked at the recital of the horrid cruelties which they committed in the cities of Egypt, of Cyprus, and of Cyrene, where they dwelt in treacherous friendship with the unsuspecting natives; and we are tempted to applaud the severe retaliation which was exercised by the arms of legions against a race of fanatics, whose dire and credulous superstition seemed to render them the implacable enemies not only of the Roman government, but also of humankind. (Womersley 1994)

Emperor Julian attempted in vain to restore polytheistic paganism from the monotheism of Christianity and Judaism. Julian was also known as *Julian the Philosopher* and was emperor from 361-363 A.D. with strong Hellenistic leanings.

A member of the Constantinian dynasty, Julian became Caesar over the western provinces by order of Constantius II in 355 and in this role campaigned successfully against the Alamanni and Franks. Most notable was his crushing victory over the Alamanni in 357 at the Battle of Argentoratum despite being outnumbered.

In 360 in Lutetia (predecessor Roman name of the French city of Paris), he was acclaimed Augustus by his soldiers, sparking a civil war between Julian and Constantius. Before the two could face each other in battle, however, Constantius died, after naming Julian as his rightful successor.

In 363, Julian embarked on an ambitious campaign against the Sassanid Empire in the east. Though initially successful, Julian was mortally wounded in battle and died shortly thereafter.

Julian was a man of unusually complex character: he was "the military commander, the theosophist, the social reformer, and the man of letters" He was the last non-Christian ruler of the Roman Empire, and it was his desire to bring the Empire back to its ancient Roman values in order to save it from dissolution.

He purged the top-heavy state bureaucracy and attempted to revive traditional Roman religious practices at the cost of Christianity. His rejection of Christianity in favor of Neoplatonic paganism caused him to be called *Julian the Apostate*, or "a person who has abandoned the religion and principles" of the (Christian) church. He was the last emperor of the Constantinian dynasty.

Unlike Constantine, Julian was moderate and tolerant, "the only hardship," according to Gibbon, "which he inflicted on the Christians, was to deprive them of the power of tormenting their fellow subjects, whom they stigmatized with the odious titles of idolaters and heretics" (*General Observations* 2007).

Julian was a true believer in the pagan gods and not a philosophic skeptic concerning all religions. In Gibbon's view, he should have emulated those who had allowed philosophy to purify "their minds from the prejudices of the popular superstitions" and who therefore rejected Christianity. He was speaking of Seneca, the elder, and younger Pliny, Tacitus, Plutarch, Galen, Epictetus and Marcus Aurelius, whose death in 207 A.D. marked the end of Rome's golden period.

As point of reference, Gibbon is considered to be a son of the *European Enlightenment* and this is reflected in his famous verdict on the history of the Middle Ages:

"I have described the triumph of barbarism and religion."

However, politically, he aligned himself with the conservative Edmund Burke's rejection of the democratic movements of the time as well as with Burke's dismissal of the "rights of man."

Gibbon's work has been praised for its style, his piquant epigrams and its effective irony. Unusually for the 18th century, Gibbon was never content with secondhand accounts when the primary sources were accessible. With reference to primary sources, Gibbon is considered by many to be one of the first modern historians.

In accuracy, thoroughness, lucidity, and a comprehensive grasp of a vast subject, his history is considered incomparable in English history that may be regarded as definitive. Whatever its shortcomings, *"The Decline & Fall of the Roman Empire"* is artistically imposing as well as historically unimpeachable as a vast panorama of a great period.

Having recounted his melancholy tale of Rome's decline and fall, Gibbon asked if it contained a warning to the present. Might Europe one day suffer a similar fate? Incredibly, he thought not:

The abuses of tyranny are restrained by the mutual influence of fear and shame; republics have acquired order and stability; monarchies have imbibed the principles of freedom, or, at least, of indoctrination; and some sense of honor and justice is introduced into the most defective constitutions by the general manner of the times. In peace, the progress of knowledge and industry is accelerated by the emulation of so many active rivals in war, the European forces are exercised by temperate and indecisive contests (Gibbon, *General Observations* 2007).

NOTE ***This is an excerpt from an unpublished manuscript, "Search for the Real Parents of My Soul."***

HOTEL DEL CORONADO

The Surreal as Real

James R. Fisher, Jr., Ph.D.
© June 28, 2015

CALIFORNIA DREAMING AS A MINDSET

You only have to be in California for a day or two before subliminally feeling you have consciously left the world of the real for the world of the surreal. You are in Puck's land of *"A Midsummer's Night's Dream."*

California is swimming in debt and daily faces the ultimate possibility of bankruptcy, but everyone seemingly is living as if they have won the lottery with its funny money. Students at *California's great universities* are more preoccupied with matters of diversity than studying for exams; more interesting in binge drinking and partying as if there is no tomorrow than taking the tough courses that lead to substantial careers; more dedicated to creating DNA genders beyond male and female than biology would allow. Optimism here in the face of reality is not a mindset but a religion.

This was apparent as my wife and I left the desert community of Hemet, California and drove south to *San Diego, California*. The *Interstate Highways System* is in pristine condition, the eight to ten lanes are filled to capacity with an ocean of sparklingly new automobiles gleaming in the midday sun carrying the illustrious banners of their automotive brands.

To enhance this dreamlike imagery, the shoulders of these roads rise majestically around these byways with carefully coiffured vegetation (trees, shrubs, sculptured walls and other appointed landmarks) to give the insouciant impression of abundance and solvency.

Once you enter *San Diego*, and travel through the downtown, through the ethnic neighborhoods of Hispanics, Italians, and other ethnic groups, which are larger than the same more celebrated neighborhoods in *Chicago* of which we were familiar, and we might add, are cleaner and better maintained. Appearance is everything when substance is not the focus.

This *Lego Land* mystique is so striking as to put one in mind of a gigantic *Lego Land Exhibition,* or not a real city at all, but a cluster of neighborhoods to mock reality.

We took a two- and one-half hour trolley cruise through the city and noted the veneer of cleanliness, neatness and orderliness of the *San Diego* surface causing one to wonder what was hidden. I've traveled the world and always found the character of a place revealed by its underbelly. We saw no such underbelly in this trolley ride.

The surreal was further enhanced when we took a 2.1-mile ride over an expansion bridge 200 feet above *San Diego Bay*, which connected with *Coronado Island* and the home of the internationally known *Hotel Del Coronado.*

The *San Diego–Coronado Bridge* is a pre-stressed concrete and steel girder bridge over *San Diego Bay* connecting *San Diego* with *Coronado Island*, which is not actually an island but a peninsula as part of State Route 75.

My Beautiful Betty (BB) was apprehensive about driving across this bridge and did so without looking down. I, on the other hand, had a marvelous view of the bay, the luxury boats and yachts and the magnificent ships of the *United States Navy* below, as well as the abbreviated skyline of the City of *San Diego*.

I say "abbreviated" because no building in *San Diego* can be taller than 500 feet as the *San Diego International Airport* is smack in the middle of downtown.

Compounding my irascibility, this airport besides being in the wrong place has only one runway with planes landing and taking off every ninety seconds. Not to worry, the rational has little to do with the dialectics.

For example, there are plans for building a $1.7 billion football stadium in *Carson* outside *San Diego* to be jointly shared between the *San Diego Chargers* and the *Oakland Raiders* of the *National Football League*. It is to be built on the privately financed sale of hundreds of millions of dollars of preferred seat licenses.

Little note is made that Raiders and Chargers are infrequently playoff bound.

Everyone back in Florida told us that the *Hotel Del Coronado* was "a must see." It did not disappoint.

It is magnificent, appealing to the eye, overwhelming to the senses, and intimidating to one of limited means.

I thought the baroque architecture and lavish colors of *St. Petersburg, Russia* were a bit over the top, but in a different style and architecture to be sure, the *Hotel Del Coronado* competes in that same league of gaudy excess.

Google Hotel Del Coronado and you will see what I mean in the lavish pictures presented there.

It cost $24 for two-hour parking, and if you lost your ticket it was $58.

What we didn't know but found out by having a coffee (me) and clam chowder (BB) is that the waitress could electronically stamp our parking ticket and we were given three hours of "free parking."

The coffee and clam chowder cost $34. The coffee, which cost $6 was not as good as McDonald's, but who cares when it comes to *"quality."*

The hotel has shops and boutiques that we wandered through as well as beautiful gardens, and the most impressive beach we had ever seen with its white sand expanding for several miles beyond our vision.

We thought the beaches of *Clearwater, Florida's* white sand were the best, but the city fathers of that city opted to put in huge parking lots with meters that has ruined the previously breathtaking setting.

Wandering through the shops I saw a windbreaker I liked on sale for half price. I gave it a look. The *marked down price* was $200 and looked a lot like a windbreaker I saw at JC Penny's back home for $16.95, full price. Of course, the JC Penny's windbreaker didn't have the *Hotel Del Coronado* imprimatur.

The Hotel Del Coronado is a beachfront luxury hotel in the city of *Coronado*, just across the *San Diego Bay* from *San Diego, California*.

It is one of the few surviving examples of an American architectural genre: the wooden Victorian beach resort.

It is the second largest wooden structure in the United States (after the *Tillamook Air Museum* in *Tillamook, Oregon* and the *Belleview Biltmore* in *Belleair, Florida*) and was designated a *National Historic Landmark* in 1977 and a *California Historical Landmark* in 1970.

When it opened in 1888, it was the largest resort hotel in the world. It has hosted presidents, royalty, and celebrities through the years. The hotel has been featured in numerous movies and books.

The hotel received a *Four Diamond* rating from the *American Automobile Association* and was once listed by *USA Today* as one of the top ten resorts in the world, though it has since been removed from that list. In the mid-1880s, the *San Diego region* was in the midst of one of its first real estate booms.

At that time, it was common for a developer to build a grand hotel as a draw for what would otherwise be a barren landscape. The *Hollywood Hotel* in *Hollywood, California*, the *Raymond Hotel in Pasadena*, the *Hotel Del Monte in Monterey*, and the *Hotel Redondo in Redondo Beach, California*, were similar grand hotels built as development enticements during this era.

HISTORY OF THE HOTEL DEL CORONADO

On December 19, 1880, three people went together to buy all of Coronado and North Island for $110,000. Those people were E. S. Babcock, retired railroad executive from Evansville, Indiana, Hampton L. Story, of the *Story and Clark Piano Company of Chicago*, and Jacob Gruendike, president of the *First National Bank of San Diego*.

A 24-page prospectus with the title *Coronado Beach, San Diego, California*, asserted that "The Coronado Beach Company has been organized with a capital of One Million Dollars ...."

The officers were Babcock, Story, and Gruendike. Also involved with the company, at this early stage, were three men from Indiana: railroad baron Josephus Collett of Terre Haute, lumber merchant Heber Ingle of Patoka, and John Igleheart, a miller, who later became famous through the development of *Swansdown flour.*

The men hired architect James W. Reid, a native of New Brunswick, Canada, who first practiced in Evansville and Terre Haute. His younger brother Merritt Reid, a partner in Reid Brothers, the Evansville firm, stayed in Indiana, but Watson Reid helped supervise the 2,000 laborers needed.

E. S. Babcock envisioned the hotel "would be built around a court...a garden of tropical trees, shrubs and flowers. From the south end, the foyer should open to *Glorietta Bay* with verandas for rest and promenade.

"On the ocean corner, there should be a pavilion tower, and northward along the ocean, a colonnade, terraced in grass to the beach. The dining wing should project at an angle from the southeast corner of the court and be almost detached, to give full value to the view of the ocean, bay and city."

That vision was turned into reality, Southern California style.

Construction of the hotel began in March 1887, "on a sand pit populated by jack rabbits and coyotes."

We heard a lot about jack rabbits in the trolley ride. These vermin were apparently so plentiful that they literally ate away all the indigenous trees and shrubs to the point that hardier and less dietary pleasing vegetation could be imported and planted.

If the hotel were ever to be built, one of numerous problems to overcome was the absence of lumber and labor in the San Diego area.

The lumber problem was solved with contracts for exclusive rights to all raw lumber production of the *Dolbeer & Carson Lumber Company* of *Eureka, California*, which was one of the West's largest. *Planing mills* were built on site to finish raw lumber shipped directly from the *Dolbeer & Carson* lumber yards, located on the shores of *Humboldt Bay*.

To obtain brick and concrete, Reid built his own kilns. He also constructed a metal shop and iron works.

As we learned about the vision of these early entrepreneurs and the difficulties they had to overcome, we could not help but think of the fate of our equally famous *Belleview Biltmore Hotel in Belleair, Florida.*

While many *Belleair, Florida* residences were sleeping, a big vote came down that allowed a developer to demolish nearly all of the historic *Belleview Biltmore Hotel.*

About 90 percent of the hotel is in the process of being torn down, and the plan for the 10 percent that remains is ambitious.

CONTRAST THIS WITH THE DEMISE OF BELLEVIEW BILTMORE

The Belleview Biltmore, Belleair, FL

Planners say the oldest part of the Belleview Biltmore is actually in the best shape. So, the developer is promising to move that whole section of the hotel about 250 yards to the east and turn it into a boutique inn.

The vote came down after a six-hour commission meeting inside *Belleair Town Hall.* Some neighbors argued with all their hearts to save the hotel from the 1890s. Those passionate people saw an important link to *Tampa Bay's* past vanishing as if what was once called the *"White Queen of the Gulf"* were torn down.

But town commissioners also heard from dispassionate experts, who said the structure was too far gone. They testified that repairing the hotel would cost more than $150 million, but the resulting building would be worth just $50 million in today's market.

*   *   *

The "man-in-the-middle" of the debate as to the fate of this great hotel proves how little nostalgia impacts a decision when "father time" dictates the demise of a structure as much as that of a person. Economics notwithstanding, this conversation is touching:

"My mother," the man-in-the-middle says, "when she was alive 14 years ago, I took her by this special place, and she said, 'You know, you were two years old and I walked you through here in a stroller'."

Belleair Mayor Gary Katica said. "We all have those memories. But you know what? Life is a series of adjustments."

Katica told his audience that he loved the old hotel, but it was falling apart and costing the town a fortune in maintenance.

"We listened to the people of *Belleair*, and that's what they want," Katica said. "It's time. When you're costing a town $600,000 to $800,000 a year for six or seven years, that's a lot of money. We start our budget with a minus. Not good!"

A developer from St. Petersburg, Florida, *Mike Cheezem*, is now in the process of buying the property for just under $7 million from its current owners.

His company, *JMC Communities,* says it plans to break ground this summer on new houses and condos. *Belleair* citizens are hoping to learn more about the timetable for tearing down the majority of the hotel, one of the icons of *Old Florida* that was, unfortunately, taken for granted as being indestructible.

THE CONTRAST, WHY INCLUDED HERE

Those responsible for the survival of the *Hotel Del Coronado*, equally of the age of the Belleview Biltmore, when grand was the theme of the late nineteenth century, have made it a constant money maker.

Nothing is cheap at the *Hotel Del Coronado*, and the ambience cries to the rafters that it is for reason. It is not only meant to survive but to prevail.

With that mindset, it is likely that one hundred years from now, through constant refurbishment, dedicated maintenance, and reinvestment, it will sparkle with loving care in perennial rejuvenation with the same vitality and hospitality that is displayed today.

Workers in the parking lot, on the beach, in the restaurants, in the boutique shops, in the clothing emporiums, in the kitchens and engine rooms, in housekeeping and security were not only polite but engaged.

There was an atmosphere of commerce, no doubt, but one indisputably customer friendly. There was a collegial sense of pride and awareness of this magical trophy that it was their duty to protect and sustain.

Our waitress, when we told her we were not a guest of the hotel, said she would stamp our parking ticket so that we would be absolved of the $24 parking fee.

An attendant in the park convinced us that the ticket had been electronically stamped as it looked untouched, while shop workers indulged our questions without pressuring us to purchase their merchandise.

That said, everything about the Hotel Del Coronado was an intoxicating commercial and beguiling as well.

The Hotel Del Coronado sits in an idyllic setting gracefully bordered by a white sandy beach and a crystal-clear water bay as did the once majestic Belleview Biltmore.

That is however where the nature of things becomes transparently different. A thousand voices explained the *Belleview Biltmore* demise while a cadre of folks quietly promote the next iteration of *Hotel Del Coronado*.

INCIDENTAL OF THE SAN DIEGO SOJOURN

San Diego was invigorating, but also tiring as the pace is inhumanly frantic. There is obviously another side to this region that is less frantic, less affluent, less commercially existential, but we discovered it only by accident.

We have a practice of leaving the maid $5 for each day that she serves us. I asked BB, "Do you think the same maid will be here on Monday?" We were then leaving Hemet for San Diego where we had been staying for three days.

"Ask her," she said simply, which I did, as we were leaving Monday morning and always left our gratuity with a note.

As I approached the maid, she told me in broken English Monday was her day off. Handing her our appreciation, she surprised me with a big hug and a kiss on the cheek. That said a lot about California societal stratification and brought me back to reality.

*　　*　　*

The best advertisers of an area are people who have been there previously. This also proved the case for San Diego. Aside from the *Hotel Del Coronado* and the spirited crossing of the *Coronado Bridge*, we did a bit of sightseeing and shopping in the town.

We then left Coronado for San Diego's famous *Balboa Park,* where we had lunch at the *Prado Restaurant*, and spent a few hours in the *"Museum of Man."*

THE MUSEUM OF MAN

Balboa Park is blanketed with museums and one could spent several days touring them all. One of the interesting discoveries in the *"Museum of Man"* was that our ancestral tree starts with the lemur.

Located beneath the ornate 200-foot California Tower, the San Diego *"Museum of Man"* is the city's only museum devoted exclusively to anthropology.

With its Spanish colonial and mission style architecture, the landmark building was originally constructed for the 1915–16 *Panama-California Exposition*. Today, a key focus of the museum is to create and display dynamic and educational anthropological exhibits about people and places throughout the Americas and around the world.

The museum traces its origins to the *Panama-California Exposition*, which opened in 1915 on the occasion of the inauguration of the Panama Canal.

The central exhibit of the exposition, *"The Story of Man through the Ages,"* was assembled under the direction of noted archaeologist *Dr. Edgar Lee Hewett of the School of American Archaeology* (later renamed the *School of American Research*, and since 2007 the *School for Advanced Research*).

Hewett organized expeditions to gather pre-Columbian pottery from the American Southwest and to Guatemala for objects and reproductions of Maya civilization monuments.

Numerous other materials were gathered from expeditions sent by anthropologist Aleš Hrdlička of the *Smithsonian Institution*, who gathered casts and specimens from Africa, Siberia, Alaska and Southeast Asia. Osteological remains and trepanated crania from Peruvian sites were also obtained.

Trepanation is a surgical intervention in which a hole is drilled or scraped into the human skull, exposing the *dura mater* to treat health problems related to intracranial diseases or release pressured blood buildup from an injury.

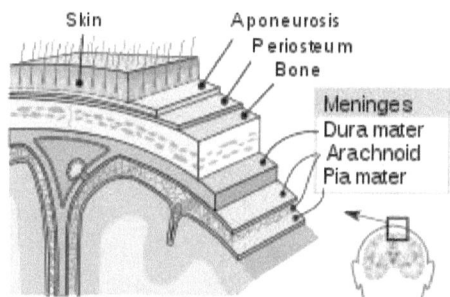

Schematic of Dura Mater

As the Exposition drew to a close, a group of citizens formed the *San Diego Museum Association* to retain the collection and convert it into a permanent museum, with Dr. Hewett as the first director.

Notable additions to the museum's collection after the Exposition included the Jessop Weapons Collection and a rare collection of artifacts from the ancient Egyptian city of Amarna, donated by *Ellen Browning Scripps* and the *Egyptian Exploration Society*.

Between 1935 and 1936, the museum's name briefly changed to the *Palace of Science* in order to correspond with other exhibit buildings participating in the *California-Pacific International Exposition*. During this exposition, the museum housed several special exhibitions from a variety of sources, such as the *Monte Alban* exhibit, which featured many artifacts on loan from the Mexican government.

The name was changed to *"Museum of Man"* in 1942 to emphasize the museum's concentration on anthropology. *"San Diego"* was added in 1978.

The museum was converted into a hospital during World War II, and its exhibits and collections were temporarily moved into storage. Following the war, the museum began to focus its collections on the peoples of the Western Americas. The museum's collections grew substantially from the 1980s through the early 1990s, and today contains nearly 2 million individual objects.

The museum is housed in four original buildings from the 1915 Exposition. The main museum, including exhibits and gift shop, is housed in the ornate *California Building* with its landmark tower, which had been closed to the public for nearly 80 years. It reopened on January 1, 2015, in time for the 2015 centennial of the *Panama-California Exposition*.

The tower contains a carillon and quarterly-hour chimes which can be heard all over Balboa Park. The museum also occupies three other original 1915 buildings.

On the opposite (south) side of the *California Quadrangle*, housed in what was originally the *Fine Arts Building*, is *Evernham Hall*, a banquet room which is also used for temporary exhibits. Immediately adjacent is the *Saint Francis Chapel*, a non-denominational Spanish-style chapel available for private events such as weddings.

The museum's collections and permanent exhibits focus on the pre-Columbian history of the western Americas, with materials drawn from Native American cultures of the Southern California region, and Meso-American civilizations such as the Maya.

The museum also holds one of the most important collections of Ancient Egyptian antiquities in the United States, which includes authentic mummies, burial masks, figurines, and seven painted wooden coffins. The most extraordinary of these is an extremely rare *Ptolemaic child's coffin* — only six others are known to exist worldwide. Total holdings include more than 100,000 documented ethnographic items, more than 30,000 books and journals, and 25,000 photographic images.

PARADISE POINT, BAREFOOT BAR & GRILL

On our next to final night in San Diego, we took my nephew Danny Schall, his wife, Michele, and his two college student children, Elyssa, 19, and Ryan, 21 to Paradise Clove and the *Barefoot Bar & Grill* for true beachfront dining.

The Barefoot Bar & Grill is a local waterfront restaurant coveted for its panoramic views of Mission Bay. This legendary San Diego beachfront restaurant offers a casual coastal California dining atmosphere where the Caribbean influence is apparent as well as creative American dishes.

We took several pictures with a multicolored setting sun as backdrop to the waterfront setting.

Resort guests and San Diego locals alike can enjoy local craft beers, refreshing cocktails, burgers, fresh seafood and salads in *Barefoot Bar & Grill's* laid-back, waterfront setting aside a tropical waterfall, sea-life lagoon and colorful marina. Much like Florida, the attire is casual beachwear. *Barefoot Bar & Grill's* fare is made from farm fresh and organic foods grown in *San Diego*, and all dishes are created keeping sustainability top of mind.

SEE'S CANDIES CHOCOLATE SHOP

Our last stop before motoring back to *Los Angeles* and a hotel for our early next day flight back to Tampa, Florida was the *Fashion Valley Mall* and *See's Candies Chocolate Shop*.

BB was interested in picking up some gifts there for friends back at the *Hillel Academy of Tampa*, where she is business manager.

The See's Candies Chocolate Shop in San Diego sells American-made candies and chocolates where you always get a free sample and friendly customer service.

At See's Candies you can create your very own custom mixed box of chocolates and candies. The shop is famous for boxed chocolates, truffles, nuts and chews, lollipops, and sugar free candy.

San Diego *See's Candies Chocolate Shop* has been in existence for more than 90 years. *Warren Buffet* bought the shop several years ago, as he did *Dairy Queen Franchises* as well. He must have a sweet tooth or perhaps such purchases sweetened his portfolio.

*   *   *

This little travelogue commenced with a somewhat critical view of the surreal or dreamlike climate of *California*. You can see from this discussion that we found the insouciant atmosphere of the state has its value, as does a laid-back approach to *California's* seemingly insurmountable difficulties. In fact, the state manages to survive as if it were a *Walt Disney Production* of *Fantasia*, which captured the box office nearly 80 years ago when *Disney Productions* appeared to be sinking in red ink. Not to worry! That's the *California* mantra as there is something of the *Sorcerer's Apprentice* in the *California psyche*. You can see this in that ocean of cars on the highways and byways of *California* rushing away from one reality and to another.

IF I MAY BE SO BOLD AS TO ASK

A CONVERSATION WITH A READER

James R. Fisher, Jr., Ph.D.
© August 7, 2014

When you write books, *have a website and blog and fill that blog with missives that reflect what you are currently thinking, you are bound to get responses, perhaps not as many as you might expect, given some 10,000 per month read your blog, but a significant number nonetheless.*

I periodically post responses from my readers on my blog. This is an example in a Q&A format.

Reader: I'm curious, why do you write so much?

Writer: I've asked myself that same question. It might seem facetious, but it is my way of connecting first with myself and then with others.

Reader: Don't you think that is a bit narcissistic?

Writer: I suppose it is.

Reader: You don't have a problem with that?

Writer: No, do you think I should?

Reader: Duh! Yes, I do.

Writer: Can I ask you a question? Do you think it is wrong to first have a conversation with yourself before you have a conversation with others?

Before you answer, I want you to think of something, something I write about all the time, and something that you have commented on before, and that is you feel self-conscious about being a friend first with yourself before you are with others.

Well, I don't. I feel there is no way to relate to others sincerely if you are not first sincere with yourself, which means from my vantage point that I work out how I feel about a subject in a conversation with myself, and then it becomes projected as a missive, an insight, or, indeed, a book.

For example, I have been in constant conversation with myself since watching President Barak Obama's News Conference yesterday.

Reader: I know how you feel. Remember, I've been reading you for years.

You can get boring repeating the same stuff over and over again, but I suppose that's because you don't think we're listening. We are but we don't have your confidence.

Please, no lecture on confidence! But I do want to hear what you think about the president's news conference. I was working and didn't have a chance to see it. I hear he really dropped the ball, right?

Writer: Sad. After hearing the president, I feel sad. I admire him for standing there before pundits, critics, journalists, and of course the nation as well as the world, and not retreating into his cage. That's what most of us do when we are under stress, and the president clearly is under stress.

He is between a rock and a hard place, damned if he makes an emphatic declaration about this or that, and damned if he doesn't.

He is, I believe, by temperament and inclination an intellectual if not a scholar. He would have been much happier, I believe, as an academic or a novelist. He writes quite well.

Reader: Don't leave it at that. If you want to know, that is something that infuriates me about you.

You bring up these unsettling subjects, like the president's new conference, then you walk away with some irrelevancy, leaving the poor reader in the lurch having to work out for himself what you mean. I don't care about President Obama's temperament. Why do you do this?

Writer: Why do I do this? I do this because I don't have answers for you nor does anyone else. Life is all about working out what has meaning and significance to us. We are in a babysit culture in which only too many are ready to tell us what is good, bad and indifferent for us. And lazy that we have come to be, we take what they say about a subject and make it our anthem. We did this with Freud and Jung, and many others.

We have to do the heavy lifting or what we have is a *Presidential News Conference* in which the expectation for the "man in charge, the most powerful man in the world" is to release us of our impediments, to resolve our quagmire, and solve the riddle of our conundrum when only we are capable of such deeds.

No man is superman! No man ever was. But we have this myth in our heads that this one man can do for us what we best do for ourselves. He can't. The sad part of this dilemma is a man becomes elected to the *Presidency of the United States* promising, indeed, to be superman to us all.

Of course, every president since President Jimmy Carter knows the danger in truth talking to the nation. With double digit inflation and double-digit unemployment, President Carter addressed the nation from the Oval Office of the White House telling Americans they had a "crisis in confidence." He was never forgiven for that. A nation addicted to optimism doesn't want to hear that its president can see it naked.

Reader: So, what would you have the president do? What would you have us do?

Writer: Simply, start taking charge of your life and let the President and Congress take care of matters of state to which they have been elected.

Support the president in what you believe, give him credit when that is the case, and write him or your Congressman or Congresswoman about how you feel when that is not the case, but do it politely, respectfully, and sincerely.

Become an active participant in democracy, not a rotten egg thrower from the comfort of the crowd.

Don't buy into something because you think most other people buy into it in an effort to be consistent with the pack. Take a stand, have a point of view, share it with others if you like, but don't be hesitant to communicate it to people who represent you, people who are carrying out your wishes in this represented democracy.

Reader: Yeah, yeah, now you're sounding like one of your missives. I get all that. You don't have to club me to death with that – I was going to say, "with all that crap," but that would be disrespectful, wouldn't it?

Writer: It would be honest; honest I like. And do you know why?

It is not for me but for you. If you can be honest with me, chances are you will be honest with yourself. If I may, I am tired of people trying to say what they think I want to hear. I am not running a popularity contest.

In my last innings, I'm trying to experience life and people and events – not as they are framed on the media or by politicians or academia or pundits, but as they are experienced by each of us on a personal basis.

Reader: Can I change the subject? Actually, it is not so much changing the subject but bringing the subject back to what I planned to ask you originally, but as you do so well, getting me to go off on a tangent. You say that 10,000 people a month respond to your blog, is that right?

Writer: Yes, so?

Reader: Is that mainly an American audience?

Writer: What do you think?

Reader: Come on, doc, don't do that answering a question with a question. I sincerely want to know. Is that sincere enough?

Writer: My primary audience, it may surprise you, is the Ukraine, followed by the United States, then Great Britain, Western Europe, Russia and China.

To my surprise, I have only a little audience from Canada, virtually no audience from Central and South America, or Australia.

All my missives can be quickly and easily translated into the native languages of these countries, which I think facilitates the interest of those mentioned.

Reader: Ukraine? Ukraine is a bigger audience than the United States? How do you explain that?

Writer: I can't. All I can tell you is that I have great affection for the Slavic peoples.

I have had the opportunity to visit the Balkans: Serbia, Romania, Kosovo, Albania and Croatia.

I have also had an opportunity to visit the Slavic nations of the Baltic Sea such as Latvia, Lithuania and Estonia, as well as Russia.

I've never been to the Ukraine, but as an American I try to put myself in their shoes. They are a proud people under siege, a people with a proud tradition that has been constantly challenged over the centuries, and yet national pride persists and survives.

I have wondered, though, if Ukrainians had a Thomas Paine to capture the essence of their struggle as he did for the *Minute Men of the American Revolution*, how might that impact their struggle?

Remember, King George III of Great Britain was a bully like Vladimir Putin, and yet he was defeated.

The will of a people is greater than all the guns that may be menacingly camped on the border as is the case with Russian troops on the border of Eastern Ukraine.

You cannot kill the soul of a people. This is a lesson that tyrants never learn. The more tyrants attempt to crush that spirit the greater that spirit grows in a vengeance.

Writer: Please. I don't need a sermon. I get it. But quite frankly, I don't see it as our problem. I'm for the president to stand down, period, as President Eisenhower did when the French and British bombed the Suez Canal. We didn't go to war, the canal was rebuilt, and life went on.

CONCLUSION:

I thanked him for a stimulating conversation but didn't add – he'll probably read this here – that I now understood the reason the president leads from behind.

Americans are tired of wars; tired of the rhetoric of wars; tired of Americans dying in such places as Afghanistan and Iraq, and for what purpose; tired of being policeman to the world; tired of having the role of controlling the bullies of the world; tired of carrying the financial burden of the United Nations; tired of Europe including Great Britain playing both sides of the street while letting the United States foot the bill; tired of all the diplomatic mistakes after WWI and WWII; tired of playing landlord to the Middle East while countries and peoples there were Gerrymandered after both wars to the satisfaction of the Allies, but not to the satisfaction of the indigenous peoples, who are seemingly just plain tired.

Several presidents – of both political parties – put the United States and the World into this cage, and now a President of the United States in the person of Barak Obama stands before an audience in a news conference yesterday, and he has to take the heat because he's the only one in the kitchen.

My reader I don't believe is insensitive, but simply tired. He has been employed, unemployed and re-employed, making less than he formerly made, but is too tired to be bitter, too tired to worry about Ukrainians, Israelis, Palestinians, Syrians, Iraqis, Turks and Jordanians, much less the bloodshed in Africa.

It is too much!

If he weren't so tired, I would have liked to tell him that these people are tired, too, only being tired is not their greatest challenge, living for another day is.

SIGNS & SIGNPOSTS OF A

NARCISSISTIC AGE

James R. Fisher, Jr., Ph.D.
© June 12, 2016

Foolish men mistake transitory semblances for eternal fact and go astray more and more.

Thomas Carlyle (1795 – 1881), *English essayist, historian and philosopher*

When the millions applaud you, seriously ask what harm you have done; when they censure you, what good!

Caleb C. Colton (1780 – 1832), *English clergyman*

To attempt to do for others what they best do for themselves is to weaken their resolve and diminish them as persons. The same holds true of ourselves.

James R. Fisher, Jr., *Meet Your New Best Friend* (2014)

NORMALITY DEFIED!

What is the normal experience of a child of its time? From the beginning, that child is programmed to assume the collective biases, values, orientation, and history as interpreted by the times, which includes religious and intellectual orientation.

From that basis, the child takes on the veneer of the pleaser, accommodating the world that child enters. An obsession to belong with an edginess is also part of the development. The level of acceptance or rejection becomes the barometer of anxiety. The motivation to please leaves little energy to discover the person's own essence or the joy of knowing oneself. Instead of the comfort of identity and a vessel overflowing with kindness and caring, the person becomes an empty vessel that craves attention and affection. This is the reverse of the myth society perpetuated.

A content person is an enabler helping others help themselves. Conversely, a pleaser misconstrues his role and attempts to carry other people's burden, believing he will be esteemed for the caring and lack of self-regard.

Alas, it cannot be done. Instead of appreciation, dependence and the expectations enter the relationship as if a toxic contagion. The nature of life is that strength and resolve come only from enabling others to find their own way, and to carry their own baggage.

Warrick Dunn was an African American football player in the *National Football League.* Mr. Dunn created a program where he built houses for the needy, paid the construction and closing costs, and the house payment for one month. At that point, he turned the house over to its new owners who assumed the mortgage and took responsibility for its care and upkeep.

This is quintessential enabling. This is not charity. This is not flaunting one's celebrity or to see how generous I am. This is enabling where the giver takes no responsibility for the burden of others. Sadly, this is too often the exception rather than the rule.

The sensible disposition of life is to first meet our own needs before we attempt to assist others to meet theirs. The paradox is that often the generous person is needy and must seek the approval of others by appearing self-sacrificingly generous. See me? I'm a good person! But are you, or are you simply needy?

Neediness represents an elemental state of emptiness, whereas a person in the fullness of being has no need to own other people's problems. He is more likely of a mind to enable others to meet theirs.

The whole problem of a narcissistic society is to look good doing good. Narcissists believe everyone is like them in neediness, and therefore of the mind to desire what they have and are. So, in a self-aggrandizing manner, they share their wealth unaware of the damage they do. Many parents fall prey to narcissism and wonder why their children never catch hold in life or grow up.

PACKAGING DAMAGED GOODS

The other day a mother came to me about her ten-year-old son being taunted at school. "He is a big boy for his age, quite intelligent, but at the same time, not nearly as mature as his eight-year-old sister. Kids pick on him, girls tease him, and much smaller boys play pranks on him that gets him in trouble with his teachers. I don't know how many times he has come home crying. What should I do? I'm at my wits end."

Looking at the mother, obviously distraught and expecting me have a ready solution, I said, "Can I tell you a story?" Her eyes glazed over. It was clear she was in a hurry and desired only McWisdom from me.

She folded her arms across her chest doubtfully, then smiled obligingly, "If you think it will help."

The story I told her was about my first week in a new school at the age of eight. I, too, was a boy big for my age and immature. I had come home crying to my mother about a boy in my class two years older than me who was the class bully.

When it came my time to bat at recess, he took the bat out of my hands, and said "I'm batting for you." I started to cry again remembering my anger and humiliation.

My mother wrapped her arms around me and told me she would talk to my nun at school. My da hearing the conversation came over to me. "Your mother is going to do no such thing. It is not your teacher's problem. It's your problem. Now, what are you going to do about it?"

I studied this mother's distraught face to see the impact of my story.

The mother looked at me aghast, "That's it?"

"That's it."

"You expect me to go back to my son and tell him that?"

"I don't expect you to do anything. I expect you've done too much already. Don't you think it's about time he starts fighting his own battles?"

She weighed this for a time, and then in a whisper, said, "He's my baby, my first born." Then thinking about my story, asked, "What happened when you went back to school?"

I laughed. My da had told me before that bullies are cowards and have a need to dominate even when it makes no sense. He also said, when kids my age fight, they always do the rub-a-dub hitting each other in the stomach, leaving their face open for a fist. "If you get in a fight with this dude," he said, "hit him in the fricken face. I guarantee you he won't be a problem anymore."

And that's what happened. I wouldn't give up my bat the next day, and he said that we'd meet after school. We did. He did the rub-a-dub, as my da predicted, and I hit him in the nose, giving him a bloody nose. He kept yelling, "You gave me a bloody nose! See what you did?" Then right in front of all the guys, he started crying. I never had any trouble again.

GENESIS OF NARCISSISM

Since the child grows from the outside in, there is a chance that a point will be reached when he stops looking for *signs and signposts* to show him the way to his own personal growth and satisfaction. Instead, he waits for someone to tell him what to do; or he waits for a hand or hand out to lift him free of his troubles; for someone to fight his battles; to protect him from his own follies.

So often such a child finds himself bereft of courage, and axiomatically thinks it is everyone else's fault. Whenever he encounters difficulty, embarrassment, or confusion, he looks to someone else to solve his problem, someone else to blame for his predicament. Should this occur when the world is opening up to the child with all its possibilities, the adolescent self may become narcissistic at the expense of wonder and engagement. That child may never grow up.

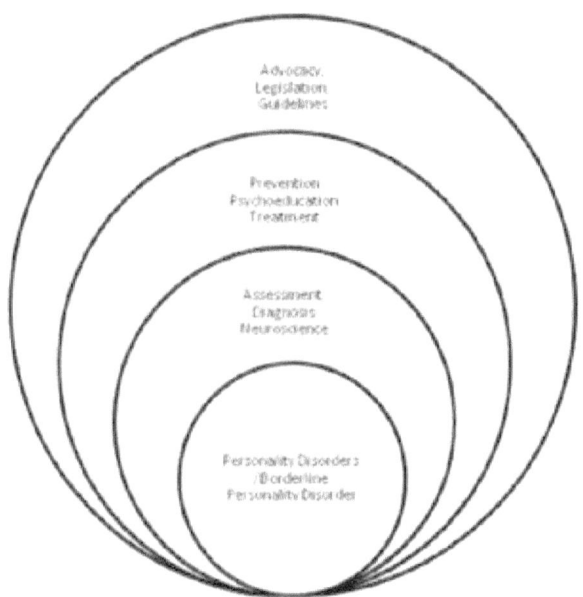

Professional caregivers can fall into this cauldron

Wonder is introspection and the key to self-knowing. The pain of confrontation with a hostile world, which is equally narcissistic, triggers this projection.

Listen to a child and you hear this reflex action as if part of the child's DNA. What stalls nascent development is the well-meaning but ill-advised intercession of a parent's assumptive ownership of their child's row with another child without understanding what is happening or why.

The parent intercedes because the parent has been there before and thinks that parent knows best. No learning is allowed! This may develop dependence in the child and a reliance on second-hand problem-solving, which could lead to a second-hand life as spectator rather than as active participant in the process. If this seems an exaggeration, look at society-at-large today.

This is not to suggest that introspection is an end itself, but rather a vehicle to self-knowing through action and reflection. German philosopher Goethe (1749-1832) advises:

Self-knowledge is best learned, not by contemplation, but action.

Experience is the best teacher, and a child is aware of experience from its earliest moments of consciousness. That said, it never occurs to a complainer that it is his duty and no one else to change his own situation; that life is about problem solving and no one can solve another person's problem. Should you think it is too early to instill this in a child, you would be wrong.

Where a person at an early age finds himself is where that person, for all intent and purposes, deserves to be. Otherwise, that person would be somewhere else. A child can be made aware of this at an early age, and once learned, it will serve that child throughout his life.

There is a teacher I know in a private school. No matter how many months pass between our visits the conversation is always the same. She insists she could make far more money in the public-school system than in the private academy in which she teaches. Now why does she not teach in a public school?

Obviously, that never occurs to her, nor does it occur to her that her complaint is a broken record. She wants more pay, better benefits, and has no interest in the fact that her little school has limited resources. This does not interest her. She doesn't see the relevance. She is a narcissistic child in an adult's body and wants satisfaction, don't tell her about limits! She is where she is because a long time ago, she quit growing up emotionally, fueling her existence with the hot air of complaint.

Introspection can be a lifelong self-awareness process governed by experience and learning, ultimately transforming into self-acceptance. Without such a mindset, the person is likely to develop self-contempt expressed in constant complaining without any action or resolution of the complaint. Life, in such cases, is reduced to a soap opera with the same episode repeated *ad infinitum*.

ADVENT OF THE PRETEND WORLD

Looking for others to solve our problems is characteristic of a flawed society that has gone from inner-self direction to narcissistic outer-other direction; from self-discipline to pervasive permissiveness; from self-awareness to self-ignorance.

With such a perspective, a person becomes a spectator to life with little sense that the motion picture in that person's head is the same old film that has been playing forever hoping desperately for a different ending.

Newspaper advertising and circulation revenues
From 1956 to 2016 (in billions of dollars)

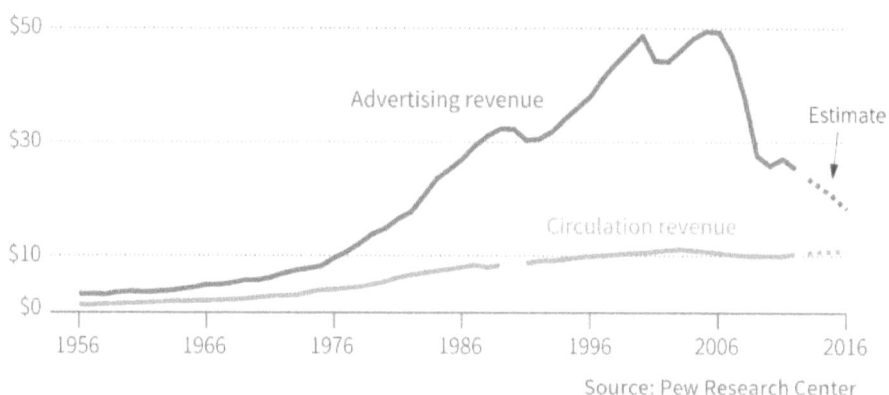

Source: Pew Research Center

Newspapers are dying!

We have become a society with a mania for super stars and celebrities to live our lives vicariously through their achievements and scandals as compensation for our own mundane inner emptiness.

Scandal rags, as all newspapers and magazines have become, were once trusted as reliable sources of information; now *The New York Times* and *Washington Post* rely on sensationalism the same as *The National Enquirer*, while 24/7 cable news has become close to disgusting for its imbecility and prurient focus. There is no embarrassment when society becomes a bottom feeder.

We saturate our waking hours with other people's experiences, people who are often living on the edge in the fiction of an increasingly pretend world. Despite this, or perhaps because of this, we live in a television or Internet fantasyland buying what we don't need or cannot afford, dreaming that we are living in that beautiful house with that fabulous automobile in our driveway that appears in constant repetitive television commercials or takes up four pages of the local daily newspaper. It is a sickness of this narcissistic therapy that social scientist Christopher Lasch claims now comes into play:

Although he may resort to therapies that promise to give meaning to life and to overcome his sense of emptiness, in his professional career the narcissist often enjoys considerable success. The management of personal impressions comes naturally to him, and his mastery of its intricacies serve him well in political and business organizations where performance now counts for less than "visibility," "momentum," and a winning record. As the "organization man" gives way to the bureaucratic "gamesman" – the "loyalty era" of American business to the age of the "executive success game" – the narcissist comes into his own. [1]

What counts today is style, panache, presence and an ability to say and do almost anything without antagonizing anyone. Personality has come to supersede performance; making an impression trumping making a difference; and pleasing others who have clout having a full-time job and the ticket to going somewhere.

The narcissist is a *"Winning-Side-Saddler"* who cues on who occupies the power and then seeks the high ground to visibly bask in that power. Lacking any notable curiosity or commitment, notwithstanding an inflated estimate of his own ability, the ploy depends on misdirection.

This finds the narcissist constantly depending on others for approval and support. He attaches himself to someone going somewhere, living a parasitic symbiotic existence. At the same time, this emotional dependence, together with his own manipulative, exploitive approach, makes relationships contrived, superficial, and unreliable.

The narcissist covers his charade with eye-catching scenarios that camouflage his intent so that the boss believes he is swimming in clover when he is walking through manure. What makes this amusing is that most *pyramid climbers* are trudging through a muddy field and not climbing a pyramid at all.

PERSAUDERS & PUPPETEERS

Swimming with sharks is the same goal of persuaders otherwise known as advertisers. Life has become an electronic billboard of desires with consumers the center of this synthetic universe. With the constant psychedelic flashing of tantalizing imagery, the only experiences that have value; the only accomplishments esteemed; the only claims to distinction are those cultivated by these persuaders. These *dream merchants* are puppeteers and the masters of a narcissistic society.

They have successfully created a superfluous, interchangeable, disposable, and inconsequential society; one that energizes the lower rather than the higher centers of being; one that mocks sincerity, spirituality, innocence, love and wonder; one that denies death and is therefore afraid of life; and one that subscribes to the formula: garbage in and garbage out.

The dominant characteristic of personality is emotion. When people go to great lengths to appear happy, healthy and wise, the words of Seneca, the first century Roman stoic philosopher come to mind:

There are no greater wretches in the world than many of those whom people in general take to be happy.

Somerset Maugham explores this folly in his novel *The Razor's Edge* (1944), where the idle rich have little more to do than fuel their hysteria with paralyzing anxiety if not on the guest list of a high-society party. To be included beatifies the narcissist with the accolade of being a "winner" with clout. Clout consists not simply of money and influence but of power, and power lies in legacy, which cannot be bought, and thus is a limited reference. Indeed, legacy has no reference outside itself.

The new ideal of success has no legacy. Performance, as Maugham points out, means, "to arrive." Success equals success. People with clout today in business, politics, sports and the entertainment world have arrived and share "visibility" and "charisma," which can only be defined as itself for it has no heritage.

The most important attribute of celebrity is to be celebrated. It has elevated Ronald Reagan from a b-movie actor to *Governor of California*, and then *President of the United States*. Again, it has led to Austrian born Arnold Schwarzenegger to become *Governor of California* with aspirations to be president, but not being native born disqualified him. It became a moot question after his scandal. [2] Schwarzenegger understood the pretend status of his adopted country and exploited its narcissism to advantage.

Narcissism is apparent when your qualifications for a job are heavily dependent on what university you have attended, not on what you bring to the job. Given this dubious indicator, it is not surprising that the quality of education is measured by the costs of that education. Consequently, families are known to make huge sacrifices to send their children to the most status-conscious universities, expecting the investment worth the cost as brand is everything in a narcissistic society. No one manages the idea of brand better than universities that cost $60,000 - $100,000 per year to attend.

Give advertisers credit. They have successfully created a collective mindset where cost is equated with quality. We have come to believe the more expensive the better anything is. And the better the university the better the chance one's child will make it to the *promised land of success* and the *comfort zone of clout*, privilege and accessibility to the people who count.

Persuaders as puppeteers selling appearance would agree with the words of American clergyman E. R. Beadle (1812-1879):

Half the work that is done in this world is to make things appear what they are not. They choose our appetites, and then punish us with them to excess.

Swiss philosopher Rousseau ((1712-1778) cautions:

Temperance and labor are the two best physicians of man; labor sharpens the appetite, and temperance prevents from indulging to excess.

We beat the idea of excess to death, only to have it become more of a monster in our presence. How else can the world know we are successful, happy and fulfilled, lest we flaunt our stuff?

It never occurs to us that we would have less enemies, experience less hostilities if we kept our excesses to ourselves. The paradox is the greater the flaunting of our self-indulgences the emptier we become; the higher we climb the more depressed we feel.

This prompted author David Awbrey to write, *Finding Hope in the Age of Melancholy* (1999). Awbrey, who suffers from depression, failed to find relief through Prozac or psychiatry. He decided to take control of his life by probing for answers on his own. He concludes that human reason and scientific enquiry, which have become the primary standards of truth, are insufficient without spiritual nourishment.

Contrast this with real estate mogul Donald Trump who rides this spiritual wasteland to celebrity. He now has his own television program – *The Apprentice* – having fun riding narcissism as television's con king with a smile. Trump evaluates fawning apprentices to applause as he declares with the catching cliché, "You're fired!" This declaration epitomizes the pathology of our times, that is, our self-estrangement marked by randomness, relativism, nihilism, marginality and cultural dislocation.

Trump's philosophy is that hard work is not enough for upward mobility. You must be more than a performer; you must be a "winner." Winning is a selling job with you as the commodity. So, what is a winner? Trump is saying that objective references, credentials, pedigree, are not enough, that making an impression overshadows achievement, personality eclipses performance, creating a brand rather than selling it trumps making a difference. Success is synonymous with publicity and the Donald is its entrepreneur turning narcissism from a disease to a cultural palliative.

*   *   *

It is difficult to escape this cage, especially when the core value of society is success and not contribution and the great betrayal is to find that wealth is not enough, for the Brahmins do not accept the nouveau rich.

Thus, cultural dislocation leads to melancholy for climbers as well as foot draggers. Betrayal is equally so for students who attend Camelot universities at great financial sacrifice to their parents, certain of acceptance only to find that they, too, do not belong. A cry of "foul" finds nobody is listening.

Yet betrayal is essentially self-betrayal for it is clear that the gullible have bought into a duplicitous system that has no room for trust. American theologian George Crabbe (1754-1832) writes:

Deceivers trifle with the best affections of our nature and violate the most sacred obligations.

Society in a cage.

American novelist Nathaniel Hawthorne (1803 – 1860) echoes these sentiments:

No man, for any considerable period, can wear one face to himself, and another to the multitude, without finally getting bewildered as to which may be true.

A narcissistic society suffers not only self-estrangement but fails to recognize the chameleon that it has become. The source of light is always outside and therefore it must always adjust to match the colors.

Apologists point out that the 21st century has accelerated, exaggerated, and hyped out of proportion what is significant. As a consequence, nothing is in balance, perspective is lost, and "what could be" is treated as "what is." Apologists explain what is not understood and often at their own detriment.

THE GREAT TRANSFORMATION

To understand this cage is to realize it has no parents. We see ourselves surrounded with everything and nothing at all. The church was once our spiritual nourishing center but is preoccupied with its own survival. Life has become a *homeless mind in search of itself* and we are its reluctant orphans.

Empty and lost, self-indulgent and self-aggrandizing, the advertising industry has come to the rescue with the narcotic of excess to ease our pain with television's 24/7 news and weather to inoculate us into a state of schizophrenia with one day differing little to the next.

We have transitioned from neighborhoods to gated communities; from mom and pop stores to conglomerates; from unsupervised playgrounds to athletics mega-sports centers; from school houses to school emporiums; from churches of worship to citadels of political intrigue; from family physicians to corporate medicine; from competitive capitalism to *corpocracy*. [3]

Old style feudalism has been transformed into Wal-Mart feudalism, which sets the table with farmers and manufacturers playing serf to Wal-Mart's demands. The world is upside down and bosses look up to professionals who are looking down at their iPhones, unconscious of anyone as they are busy tweeting and texting.

Workers have been transformed from producers to consummate consumers, working night and day to afford purchases they don't need but feel compelled to buy.

It is the new refrain to the old coal miners' song, "I owe my soul to the company store." Now, everyone is in hock to a credit card company that collects $100 billion a year in processing fees for consumer purchases.

Mothers no longer can goods and store them in their cellars as they have been convinced by advertisers that store bought goods are healthier, cheaper and better. They are not.

You can't find work in most companies now without a college education. The mania for formal education represents another control. No one is asked first about their experience, but what education they have.

Society has been transformed into a *managed society* which asserts control over every little thing. Technocrats dictate what is good and bad for us; what we should and should not value; and what we can and cannot expect from life. No one finds fault with this as everyone is too busy being robotic to wonder.

Our increasingly robotic lives are aspects of a dying culture, which has turned narcissistic for "personal growth" and "professional development," which have become a play on words. We are in a survival mode and call it reinvention. We are not happy campers; we have lost our moral compass and our way.

But that does not mean we cannot find our way back. The work ethic remains part of our genetic code, as discipline still lingers in our reptilian memory. What has not changed is our nature:

We are all self-centered.

We are born egotists, in which we come into the world believing we are the center of existence, only to find that we are not. Since our egos are fragile, we do anything to protect them which includes denying the reality of experience. This makes us difficult to deal with or influence.

We are all more interested in ourselves and what interests us than anyone else.

We are inclined to turn the conversation to what we think, feel, believe, and value away from what is being said. Failing that, we become bored, stop listening and move on.

We all want to feel important.

This is the dignity of the self and nascent need to feel ourselves worthwhile. Treat others with respect whatever their station, and respect will return to you tenfold. Be condescending and you will have a rival if not an enemy. Kindness restores balance and is therefore our greatest virtue.

We each crave the approval of others to approve of ourselves.

We find it difficult to like much less approve of ourselves, giving others the benefit of the doubt. Everyone suffers this sizable handicap despite the posturing or protest to the contrary. That is why we are grateful for simple courtesies and straightforward sincerity when being complimented or criticized.

These aspects of our nature can go a long way to enabling us to be authentic and to take charge of our life in an otherwise inauthentic world. Times may change, but people will remain essentially the same whatever the age, or whatever the peculiar circumstances of the time.

One day reading this some years hence, when narcissism has faded, you may wonder why people "back then" were so uptight and self-centered and why they enjoyed so little that was free such as the great outdoors! I look forward to that age because that will mean our societal cage has been lifted.

NOTES

[1] Christopher Lasch, *The Culture of Narcissism: American Life in An Age of Diminishing Expectations*, W. W. Norton & Co., New York, 1970, p. 44.

[2] Arnold Schwarzenegger admitted in 2011 to having an affair with his housekeeper, Mildred Baena, which produced a son. He claims he didn't know he was the father until he noticed when the boy was eight that he looked a lot like him.

[3] Corpocracy is a term I use in several of my books to indicate the nature of corporate enterprise in the complex organization, and how this approach is antithetical to personal trust and development.

VANCE PACKARD, WHERE ARE YOU WHEN WE NEED YOU?

THE GROWING INCOMPETENCE OF THE AMERICAN WORKER!

James R. Fisher, Jr., Ph.D.
© August 4, 2014

New pressures are causing ever more people to find their main satisfaction in their consumptive role rather than in their productive role. And these pressures are bringing forward such traits as pleasure-mindedness, self-indulgence, materialism, and passivity as conspicuous elements of the American character.

Vance Packard, *The Hidden Persuaders* (1966)

THE GOSPEL OF MASS CONSUMPTION

Today the average American is consuming more than twice as much as he or she did at the end of World War II. Corporate society came up with the new economic gospel of consumption, launching an army of willing psychologists as disciples to promulgate the message.

Converting Americans from a psychology of thrift to one of spendthrift proved a daunting task. *The Protestant Work Ethic*, which had so dominated the American frontier culture, was deeply ingrained in American society. Frugality and savings were cornerstones of the American way of life, which had served as a guidepost for generations of Americans determined to make a better life for their children.

For most Americans the virtue of self-sacrifice continued to hold sway over the lure of instant gratification in the marketplace.

Corporate America set out to radically change the psychology that had built the American nation with the aim to turn American workers from investors into spenders. As economist John Kenneth Galbraith says in *"The Affluent Society"* (1958), *"The new mission of business is to create the wants it seeks to satisfy."*

Advertisers, with a new role in "consumption economics," successfully made consumers feel ashamed if they were not wearing, or listening to, or using "in" products advertised on a daily basis. Brand names, once an oddity, became a permanent feature of the American economy. Many of the products were novel and required a change to the lifestyle and eating habits of consumers.

Common man and common woman were invited to emulate the rich and famous, to take on the trappings of wealth and prosperity previously reserved for the business aristocracy and social elite. "Fashion" became a watchword with companies and industries seeking to identify their products with what was in vogue and chic.

In the process, advertisers turned a nation of working people into status-conscious consumers.

A little over a decade after World War II, a nation of hardworking and frugal Americans were made over into a hedonist culture in search of ever-new avenues of instant gratification. In the process, a psychology of mass consumption was created.

As a parent, I witnessed how ridiculous this had become. Born in *The Great Depression*, a high school student in the 1950s, my mother washed and ironed my jeans that I wore to school until they were paper thin and pockmarked with embarrassing holes in the knees and elsewhere. Years later, as a parent, the style of worn jeans with holes in them became a fad with manufacturers producing such products to consumers' delight.

As economist Robert L. Heilbroner presciently observes this obsession with wealth creations, he finds *Corporate America* has replaced the dominance of the aristocracy and kings.

* * *

Over the years, I have read American sociologist Vance Packard with interest as I have watched our societal decline, often wondering if I was the only one who saw the precise connection of his social commentary with how ridiculous we have become as a society. Alas, he was an apostate against the civil religion of *Corporate America* and therefore essentially politely ignored. Virtually every aspect of American behavior to which he has addressed has surfaced.

Vance Packard died December 12, 1996 at the age of 82. In 1957, ***The Hidden Persuaders*** was published, showing how the advertising industry exploited American shoppers through subliminal stimulation with coded messages in advertisements.

He followed that with ***The Status Seekers*** (1959). This piggy backed on his previous book. It showed how advertisers and merchandisers, social and cultural programmers, exploited the American weakness for status and with an obsessive *compare and compete* mentality.

This crippling focus on status and social stratification, or "keeping up with the Jones," reveals a weakness in the American character to imitate achievers with the belief that the grass is always greener on the other side of the fence.

Hardly getting started, Packard came out with ***The Waste Makers*** (1960) in which he criticized manufacturers who purposely made products that would not last.

He called this mindset "planned obsolescence," and pointed out that the technology existed in 1960 to make automobiles last a generation. He also claimed the technology existed in which automobiles could operate up to 50 miles on a gallon of gasoline; that light bulbs could be manufactured to last decades; and that razor blades did not have to go dull so fast.

He took a quantum leap from economics to identify the growing lackadaisical trend in the American consumer to prefer the new to the used and to be psychologically exhilarated to discard and throw away rather than to preserve and maintain.

Then in 1962, when I was myself climbing the corporate ladder, he came out with ***The Pyramid Climbers.***

As I read each of his books, I had the uncanny feeling that he was writing specifically to me. So, I had to ask myself, "Am I a pyramid climber?"

"If you're trying to analyze social disintegration, you should know that Mary Vollmer here majored in social disintegration."

Charles Saxson, American cartoonist

I decided that I wasn't. Packard claimed pyramid climbing was the business of being more committed to climbing the executive ladder than doing the job you were paid to do; to be more interested in making an impression than a difference; to be bent on finding a willing mentor to assure your rapid ascendancy, while your competition fell by the wayside. *The Naked Society* (1964) followed. Much as *The Pyramid Climbers* touched my conscience, this book touched my soul.

Packard had no aspirations to be seen as a savant or soothsayer, as he made no philosophical claims to being prescient. He saw himself as a social commentator without portfolio, an observer who saw what anyone else could see if they would but open their eyes.

Remember this book came out fifty years ago, when there was already palpable evidence that new technology was a threat to our privacy. Packard was referring to computerized files, sophisticated surveillance techniques, and other intrusive technologies, which he could see were being used to influence human behavior.

The Sexual Wilderness (1968) was published in the midst of the sexual revolution, where gender identity was no longer accepted as matter of fact but had become ambiguous and ambivalent in the light of the *AIDS epidemic* and the *Gay Rights Movement*. Packard could see America had become totally self-conscious and was afraid to register an opinion that might be construed as sexist, racist, or bigoted in some manner. Academics and media stepped into this breach and shamed the majority into silence. The puppet masters of *Corporate Society* were now in charge.

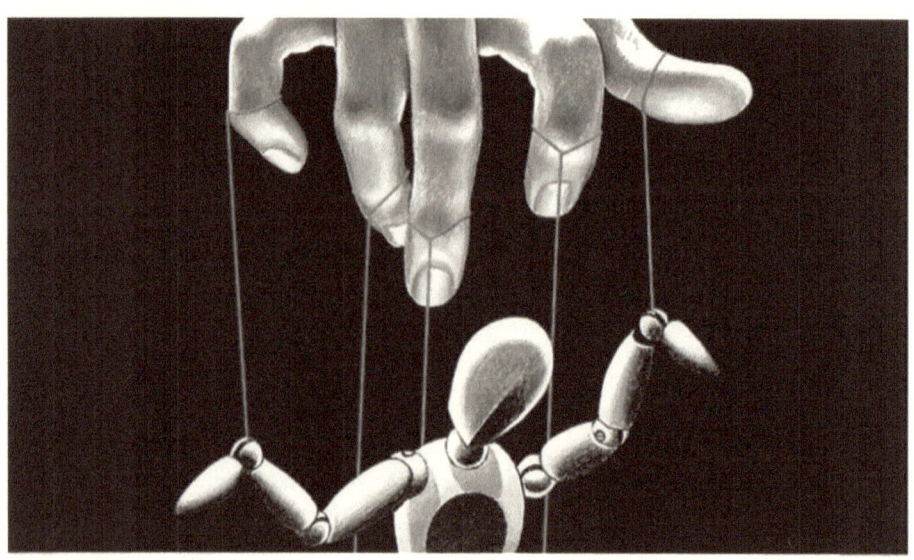

A Nation of Strangers (1972) implies that the growing presence of a *Corporate Society* was resulting in a fragmentation of communities. The book deals with the boom and bust of commercial entities: i.e., the collapse, merger or relocation of businesses; the introduction of the concepts of reengineering, redundancy and outsourcing; the forcing of families to pull up roots and relocate at the whim of corporate fathers; and the inevitable spiritual disconnect between economic advantage and spiritual need.

Packard was not done. His attention was shifted to *The People Shapers* (1977). Here he questions the ethics of the rapid use of psychological and biological testing to manipulate human behavior to find the key to the mysteries of health. This was written in the era of behaviorist B. F.

Skinner's *operant conditioning.* It was not yet the era of stem cell research or cloning, or the genetic Genome, but it did indicate a trend that Vance Packard found disturbing, and for reason.

Our Endangered Children (1983) became a concern as he could see childhood was being eclipsed by a world preoccupied with money, power, status, success, mobility, sex and immortality while the insouciance of youth and carefreeness was being bypassed as K-through-12 students now had to carry weighty book bags on their backs after school to pursue homework.

The downside of all this attention was that neither children nor parents wanted to grow up because no one wanted to grow old. Life was all about having and doing and being, leaving little time for parents to nurture their children during the impressionistic years. So, children and parents were seldom home together as parents were busy working or partying while children who got tired of the homework routine, now acting as their own parents, found new ways to get into trouble. Juvenile delinquency no longer became a crime but a lifestyle for the young.

Finally, ***The Ultra-Rich: How Much is Too Much?*** (1989) became Packard's last book. Here he did research the conventional way examining the lives and lifestyles of thirty prominent American multimillionaires. The young doc.com billionaires were on the horizon, but not yet on the radar.

It is his least refreshing book because it is so predictable whereas this was not true of his other books: *the rich want more, and the rich never have enough because someone else is always richer than they are.* Packard does manage to penetrate the myth that the rich are smarter than the average Joe, when clearly, they are not.

What makes the rich different is that they are more patient; greater risk takers; not discouraged by sometimes cataclysmic setbacks; not deterred by ethical demands as they push the envelope to its legal limits; and never have second thoughts about dissembling when it serves their purposes. As you can see, there are no surprises here.

Readers familiar with my writing will sense Packard's influence. This was also true of the Russian American sociologist Pitirim Sorokin; he an academic scholar and Packard a peripatetic researcher became author bookends for me.

*   *   *

Vance Packard came to mind today when a client shared his recent experience as an American worker. The man had a laptop that needed additional ram capacity to do his work. He went to *Best Buy* to get help. The staff member there told him he needed a certain part. He purchased the part, took it home and installed it. The part did not work.

He brought the part back and told the same staffer of his problem. He was given another part and said this should work. It didn't.

He returned with the part and was told to take credit and purchase the "correct" part on line. He said, "No, thank you. Please give me my money back," which the staffer did.

He went on line and researched the problem carefully checking every detail over and over again before he made the purchase, information he suspected the staffer at *Best Buy* should have possessed but didn't share with him if he did.

The part arrived a week later. He installed it and his ram capacity is now where he wanted it to be.

This young man wasn't through. He drives an *Audi* and has had a light fixture problem. He went to the dealership and was told the part would cost $60 but the labor would cost an additional $760 because the process was labor intensive. He told the *Audi* mechanics he didn't have that kind of money, and so he left.

Given his experience on line, he purchased the part, again after exhaustive research, with it arriving a bit later. He had to disassemble the whole light fixture of his automobile with parts all over the floor of his garage. He carefully followed the directions connecting the color-coded wires as instructed, reassembled the total apparatus and turned the lights on – they didn't work!

This young man is a learner not a knower, a person who is a student of whatever he does, and a careful student at that. He was sure he did precisely what the instructions called for, and in checking found that to be the case. What to do?

He said to himself, the only thing possible – if this is indeed the right fixture – was for him to scrap the instructions and try to figure out the connections himself. Going on that premise, he turned to what seemed most logical in tying the wires to what he believed to be the "right" connections, and "voila!" It worked!

He said to me in disbelief, "How is this possible, Dr. Fisher? How could the instructions be so wrong?"

Well, I've worked with technical writers, and found them first of all, not to be writers; and second, to be driven by deadlines and paid essentially on a piece by piece basis or in the completion of a given manual.

Pride in work has gone out the window. People are so busy collecting degrees that provide no skills; gravitating to jobs that promote winging it; failing to care one way or the other whether what they do is either customer friendly or brings about customer satisfaction. The tech writer, with deadlines, lets someone else worry about that.

"It will not occur to you," I told him, "because you have mechanical acumen and the intelligence to use that skill conscientiously that there are many like myself, with extensive university educations, that would have no other recourse then to have had to pay that $760 plus the $60 for the fixture, or the light fixture would not have been fixed."

"But, Dr. Fisher, I couldn't have afforded it."

"That is not relevant. What is relevant is that you have developed the skills to do it yourself whereas many of us have not developed such skills, and therefore are easily exploited as the Corporate System is depending on our incompetence.

"We once trusted American workmanship whatever the job, and whatever the cost to be satisfied with the work. That is no longer true, as you have discovered, and I have experienced to my sorrow."

He smiled, "I did save $760, didn't I?" Then he added, "It took me two days to get the light fixture working."

Indeed. That said, there is a growing incompetence in the American worker, and it is a cultural phenomenon touching every profession, every trades craft, every job that I can think of.

There was no point in burdening this jubilant young man with this. Suffice it to say I thought of Vance Packard and wished that he was here to take note of this further erosion in the American character and the American experience.

THE WISDOM (OR FOLLY)
OF BEING
YOUR OWN PSYCHOTHERAPIST!

James R. Fisher, Jr., Ph.D.

© March 1, 2019

"We have had the Esthetic Greek Man, the Pragmatic Roman Man, the Guilty Christian Man, the Searching Scientific man. Today's model is the believer in the Unconscious, the Self-Conscious Psychological Man."

Martin L. Gross, *The Psychological Society* (1978)

A CLOSER LOOK AT PRACTITIONERS OF PSYCHOTHERAPY AND RELATED ART FORMS

When I completed my Ph.D. course work in social, organizational and industrial psychology, a colleague of mine, a clinical psychologist, asked me to join her practice. "But I have no training as a clinician," I protested. She waved her hand dismissively, "You're a good listener. That's all it takes."

I thought that somewhat dubious until (over the years) I've learned more about psychotherapy and its practitioners.

A former professor of mine at the *University of South Florida*, now emeritus, Dr. Billy G. Gunter, developed a theory he called *"Ambient Deficiency Motivation."* Gunter claims many of us are attracted not to our strengths, but to our debilitating weaknesses when it comes to career choices.

In Anne C. Heller's biography *Ayn Rand, And the World She Made* (2009), we learn how this Russian émigré became a novelist, then a philosopher, psychologist and economist of note.

Rand wrote two compelling novels, *The Fountainhead* (1943) and *Atlas Shrugged* (1957)). In the first novel, she argued for unabashed individualism, and in the second, for the captivating wonders of capitalism. From these two works, she went on to develop a systematic philosophy known as *"Objectivism."*

Her defense of radical individualism and the virtues of egoistic capitalism won her scores of notable followers. These include: former *SEC Chairman* Christopher Cox, *Congressman* Ron Paul (the father of the current Kentucky *US Senator* with the first name, *Rand*), the *Libertarian* founder John Hospers, *The Wall Street Journal* editorial writer Stephen Moore, the economist Alan Greenspan, *Chairman of the Federal Reserve* in the Reagan administration and *Chairman of the Council of Economic Advisers* in the Ford administration, even the news commentator Chris Matthews of *MSNBC* and *CNN*, who had been chief aid to liberal *Congressman* and *Speaker of the House*, Tip O'Neil.

Ayn Rand's ideas dominated the political conversation in the 1950s through the 1970s. Born in 1905, before the *First World War* (1914-1918), she was an impressionistic youth during the *Russian Bolshevik Revolution* (1917-1918). Once in the United States at the age of twenty-five, she turned her fear and hatred of communism, and everything Russian, into art.

One critic pointed out that the engine of Rand's soul was fear not rationalism, the fundamental dictum of her *Objectivist philosophy*, which he claimed was an irrational escape from her roots. The irony is that the more she attempted to put Russia behind her, the clearer it was that she had never left. Even "Ayn Rand" was an invented name.

Beware of taking movers and shakers at face value, whatever their discipline, for lurking behind that agenda and prominence likely are aspects of Dr. Billy G. Gunter's "Ambient Deficiency Motivation."

Several prominent notables in psychotherapy and behavioral therapy come to mind who have made an imprint on our *"Psychological Society"* in this rather twisted context.

To put this in perspective, during the confusing days of the 1970s, when the Hippies and Yuppies were looking to avoid the *Selective Service Draft* and military service in the *Vietnam War*, saviors of the delicate American psyche were coming out of the woodwork.

There was "est" or *Erhard Seminar Training,* a "new age" rage to justify puerile angst and petty rebellion. It took hold on the fad conscious West Coast of the United States. Through the mid-20th century, California proved a fertile landscape for painless escape from pressing social and cultural stressors. Consistent with this ambience was the creator of "est," a man new to the locale with a new name and identity running free of personal demands left behind.

He was born *John Paul Rosenberg* (1935), but changed his name to *Werner Hans Erhard,* leaving a wife and four children behind in Ohio to give purpose and identity to hapless movie stars, celebrities, school drop outs, and the generally dissatisfied who simply felt lost. The "est" craze flourished from 1971 to 1985 and then died without fanfare.

"Erik Erikson" was born *Erik Salomonsen* (1902 – 1994) in Germany. His name was changed officially to *Erik Homburger* when his stepfather adopted him in 1911. His name would be changed again to Erik Erikson when he took a position in the United States at *Yale University*.

Erik Erikson was a tall blue-eyed man who had been raised in the Jewish faith but was said to look gentile. Anna Freud, the daughter of Sigmund Freud, who was continuing her father's work at the *Vienna Psychoanalytic Institute,* hired Erikson she said, "because he was good with children."

It would not come out for many years that Erik Erikson and Anna Freud had only high school diplomas, and no academic training whatsoever beyond that of the Institute.

This lack of academic credentials proved no handicap to Erik Erikson once in the United States with a prestigious teaching position first at *Yale,* and then subsequently at the *University of California at Berkeley.* He was accepted without credentials not only by these institutions but by many notable academics such as Margaret Mead, Gregory Bateson and Ruth Benedict.

Erikson would go on to win a *Pulitzer Prize* and *National Book Award.* Ironically, this man of multiple identities is most famous for coining the phrase *"identity crisis."*

In the December 1999 issue of *The Atlantic Monthly*, Erik Erikson's daughter, who was in crisis and felt suicidal, penned an article in this periodical in which she complained that only her mother's healing therapeutic counsel and understanding saved her as her famous father "was not available."

Perhaps more mystifying but equally fascinating is that of the Swiss psychiatrist and psychoanalyst Carl Jung (1875 – 1961). Jung is celebrated for his psychological archetypes, theories on the collective unconscious, his mystic symbolism, and his uncovering of the nature of the human psyche.

It would appear that he preferred the mystical pursuit of the human soul more than the mundane practice of psychotherapy. For example, he totally botched the treatment of the emotionally troubled Lucia Joyce, daughter of Irish novelist James Joyce (see *"Lucia Joyce, To Dance in the Wake,"* by Carol Loeb Shloss, 2003).

Others have explored Jung's mystique and strange predilections including his somewhat double life in Jeb Rubernfeld's novel, *"The Death Instinct"* (2010), and Richard Noll's *"The Jung Cult"* (1994) and *"The Aryan Christ: The Secret Life of Carl Jung"* (1997) as well as Deirdre Bair's *"Jung, A Biography"* (2003).

Famous people in the sciences as well as the arts aren't necessarily what they seem, or one might believe them to be.

Take the strange case of psychotherapist Bruno Bettelheim (1903 – 1990), known as "Dr. B," who was regarded by the public at large to be one of the world's most important psychoanalysts, a Vienna intellectual and "one of Freud's few genuine heirs to his science."

The truth, however, is that Dr. B was a lumber dealer who grandly reinvented himself with a fake set of academic credentials after emigrating to the United States in 1939. *The University of Chicago* hired him and placed him at the head of its *Orthogenic School for Emotionally Disturbed Children* which he ran for three decades. He treated these children diagnosed to be suffering from schizophrenia or autism with therapies shaped by bogus statistics generating pseudonymous case histories to enhance his security and reputation.

More incredibly, Bettelheim wrote several bestselling books including *The Uses of Enchantment* (1976) applying Freudian psychology to fairy tales and won the *1976 National Book Critics Circle Award* for *Criticism* and the *1977 National Book Award* in the *Category of Contemporary Thought*.

Suffering poor health with mounting questions about the validity of his therapeutic practices, he took his own life by suffocating himself placing his head in a plastic bag (see *"The Creation of Dr. B"* by Richard Pollack, 1997; and *"Bettelheim: A Life and a Legacy"* by Nina Sutton, 1997).

Closer to home, we have Phil McGraw who holds a doctorate in psychology, but is not a licensed clinical psychologist nor certified to practice as a clinician.

Strangely, this protects him from litigation in a way not available to practicing clinicians. He can therefore pontificate psychological and behavioral solutions to his television guests with immunity as "Dr. Phil," for his role is regarded as that of an entertainer who, incidentally, earns in the neighborhood of $80 million a year while clinicians make only a tiny fraction of that sum.

Phil McGraw's Ph.D. dissertation was *"Rheumatoid Arthritis: A Psychological Invention."* In other words, he argued that this illness is primarily psychosomatic which has much in common with his current role.

Alas, "Dr. Phil" can dispense psychological advice to his troubled guests whom he sees within the hour, sending them off with happy faces while millions of addictive viewers are anxious to "tune in again tomorrow" for more of the same. Nothing changes!

How does he get away with this? Better yet, why does he do it? The obvious answer: *"for the money!"* But perhaps closer to the truth is that "Dr. Phil" fulfills a real need.

Are people that vulnerable to the belief that a stranger on television is key to their health and happiness? You bet they are! The evidence? 80 million dollars!

During the *"Sexual Revolution"* of the 1960s and 1970s, Masters & Johnson came on the scene with their "sexual therapy." William Masters and Virginia Johnson had no training in psychotherapy or any other type of therapy. Masters was a gynecologist with an M.D. degree, while Johnson had only a high school diploma with no training in medicine much less psychotherapy. Among their claims were success with impotency, changing homosexuals into heterosexuals, and an assortment of other psychosexual hang-ups, only to have their "research" methodology questioned later and discounted for errors and false claims.

You may ask, if such professional counseling is only a self-indulgent luxury and not a necessity, what is your point?

What we all need is to have someone to talk to; someone who will tell us we are all right; that we belong; that our motives are sensible and that we don't have to apologize for our occasional mental lapses in judgment or feel guilty for our tangled sometimes ridiculous lives – in other words, we need someone to listen to us. Since most people are too busy and preoccupied in their own lives to listen, we are willing to pay for that service.

Once the neighborhood minister, priest or Imam fulfilled that function without charge, unobtrusively, confidentially and effectively, but alas, that service and that role has largely faded in our increasingly secular society.

Many readers may never have sought professional help finding solace instead with a brother or sister, a best friend, mother or father, husband or wife, colleague at work or teammate in sport, a classmate in school or a fellow parishioner at church or someone in some other social setting.

[*When I was a global executive, I traveled a lot by plane across four continents. Invariably, the person next to me would unburden his soul as if I were his confessor. More than once, the stranger said upon landing: "Thank you for all your advice. I can't thank you enough," when I hardly said a word during the entire flight, only listening. I've often thought of writing a small book about these conversations but haven't because they were given in confidence as if I were, for the moment, their priest and, indeed, their confessor.*]

We live in an obsessively compulsive *"Psychological Society"* and in a psychotherapeutic culture. Our world has been psychologized in direct proportion to our failure to be good listeners to each other, creating a culture of paid listeners practicing *pediatric therapy* throughout our active lives and during our waning days, *geriatric therapy*.

But are these times so terrible that we need all this professional attention? Psychologist Bernie Zibergeld writes:

There is not a shred of evidence that we are under more psychological stress than were our ancestors. Until recently, the masses of people suffered the daily stress of not knowing if there was going to be enough food to eat and they also had to deal with the possibility of infectious diseases, now largely conquered, that could wipe out a significant portion of the population in a few months. Nuclear weapons are new, but the threat of annihilation has been with mankind since the beginning. There is also no evidence of an increase in the incidence of serious emotional disorder since the advent of advanced industrialization. The best studies have failed to discover such a pattern of growth. To be sure, we talk more about our problems and seek help more often, but that is not the same as an increase in the number or severity of problems. The only sense in which it can be said that the number of problems has increased is that we now busily label as problems everything that limits and frustrates us.

TANGLED WEB OF OUR IMAGINED PSYCHOLOGICAL CRISIS

We are in an era when the only thing that seems to interest us is what is happening *"now!"* Historians, sociologists and anthropologists write books about the phenomenon that only they and their students seemingly read. That does not hide the fact we are in a ninety year *Post Great Depression* swoon that we seemingly are unable to overcome.

In 1930, most African American families, then known as Negroes, were with two parents in stable and relatively happy homes despite the incipient collapsing economy of the times. There was no drug culture, per se, except for isolated pockets of society occupied mainly by movie stars, musicians and other entertainers.

Children went to school and were boxed on the ears by teachers if they misbehaved. If they cheated on tests or were caught in nefarious behavior, they would be sent to the principal, disciplined and sometimes expelled. If they stole from other students or were caught in bullying tactics, they could be sent off to reform school, which in those days was the equivalent of a prison for teenagers.

The majority of America's workers were unskilled and under educated doing menial jobs working paycheck to paycheck but still finding a way to survive with family support. They had not yet assumed that the government was the employer of the last resort and expected to bail them out of their misery.

Self-reliance was part of the collective American DNA with the indigenous pride to take care of oneself and one's family. Everything changed in the early 1930s.

In 1933, President Franklin Delano Roosevelt became President of the United States. It was a time when the world was in freefall with capitalism on trial. Many leaders of the United States and Europe were intrigued with the ideas of Karl Marx and Friedrich Engels and their Communist Manifesto of 1848. This philosophy was reinterpreted by Lenin and Trotsky to lead to the Russian Bolshevik Revolution of 1917, which successfully turned Russia into a communist state.

FDR, as the president was known, virtually turned the United States effectively into a socialistic state to combat the threat of Communism and save the nation with several executive orders (giving rise to a cavalcade of presidential acts including "NRA," or the "National Recovery Act" that later was found unconstitutional by the Supreme Court) circumventing the constitutional role of the United States Congress. In the process, FDR gradually changed the nation's character, mindset and approach to its economic, political and social problems.

Obviously, this was a popular move as President Roosevelt was elected to four consecutive four-year terms, dying shortly after the fourth election.

At the same time, his actions, although well intended, stole the initiative from ordinary Americans to fend for themselves with the same self-reliant vigor that once had been characteristic of the American spirit since the colonists won independence from Great Britain in 1776.

Despite the radical change in American politics or the popularity of a sitting president, FDR's actions did not rescue the nation from the Great Depression, or the Western world from communism. World War Two did.

Still, once the die was cast, once people expected something for nothing, once the war was over, and control of their lives no longer their primary responsibility, with the heady and bizarre economic boom that followed that war, the nation lost its identity, its moral compass and its way.

Industry and government couldn't do enough for Americans, that is, as long as they surrendered control of their lives and what they did for a living. Workers handed that control over to employers, as labor unions capitulated to the demands of a growing corporate society, suing for wage concessions and benefits for this control, which were freely given during the boom years, but would lead to massive layoffs once robotics, automation and computers came into the economic mix. The same occurred in Europe in a slightly different manner.

It was a trust issue that worked as long as the United States was prosperous, fiscally solvent and stable economically. Post-World War Two gave birth to another entity, "Corporate Management."

Corporate Management was distinct from corporate oligarchs as these managers were not owners, but employees like everyone else. They came to see themselves, however, as owners and acted the part so convincingly that workers came to buy into their imagination of reality, failing to act or to protest in any effective way when these managers paid themselves 10, 20, 100 to several hundred times what the worker in the trenches made for an hour's work.

Alas, taking a thesis from the Good Book, Corporate Management successfully promulgated the idea that they were indispensable and the infallible authority of the organization.

If you think this an exaggeration, should you violate the chain-of-command to seek answers above your direct report, you entertained the possibility of being censured, demoted or fired!

When the Baby Boomer Generation, children born after 1945, came on the scene as parents the idea of parenting had already changed. Parents, were both working, married to their jobs and obsequiously cowering to the demands of their employers; thus, was born the concept of "the organization man."

Baby Boomers were forced, as a consequence, to be their own parents. Mother and fathers were either working or partying to cope riding the boom for all it was worth. Meanwhile, Baby Boomers successfully programmed themselves to have everything and anything "now!"

Planning for the future became redundant as did delayed gratification. Happiness was defined in terms of having. Baby Boomers as parents, wanting to outdo each other, gave birth to the "spoiled brat generation" and then the "Me," the "X" and the "Y" generations that followed to the present millennials and centennials.

This spawned the "Culture of Narcissism" and the whimpering self-indulgent solipsism of today's "Psychological Society."

Far from finding fulfillment or happiness, many have walked into the "Chamber of Horrors" where fear and anxiety, self-contempt and self-disgust reside, retreating instead into alcoholism, drug addiction, workaholism, promiscuity, exhibitionism, crime and suicide, or simply dropping out of school or the workforce waiting for society to come to the rescue.

Malcontents say collectively that "life sucks" and blame society for their discomfiture when they are society. It is a "catch 22" situation: failure to find purpose in life and reasons for being, whiners look to be rescued by a society that is already lost and spinning out of control.

Of course, who do these moaners blame for their plight? They blame parents, siblings, relatives, friends, classmates, teachers, coaches, the church, the school, the government, religion, God, authority figures, and the times. They are lock stepping in forward inertia rotating on a wheel and going nowhere.

They are seemingly unaware that this counter dependence, this lack of self-regard and self-initiative was seeded a long time ago in a time known as "The Great Depression."

Thanks to Sigmund Freud in his psychotherapy, and other apologists such as psychologists, ethologists and neurologists, we are not responsible for the way we are.

These apologists explain away our symptoms and instead propose a self-esteem or a "hierarchy of needs" focus; if not that, a mantra of psychosomatic explanations to assuage our discomfort. Meanwhile, sociologists explain reasons for our mood swings with a plethora of labels creating yet another escape industry.

Academic and scientific search for remedies have failed to take us off the hook of our dysfunctional propensities. Why? Because they have no answers. They too are stumbling in the dark and part of the same problem. They treat us as a species apart, statistical entities or sagittal specimens in petri dishes under the microscope, and not as flesh and blood holistic functioning human beings.

Life has become impersonal and the best indication is when someone claims to have a thousand "friends" on Facebook. If one is lucky, a person has three good and trusted friends in a lifetime.

DR. THOMAS SZASZ ENTERS THE FRAY

Psychiatrist Dr. Thomas Szasz sent shock waves through his professional community in 1961 with his book *"The Myth of Mental Illness."* The Hungarian born American doctor lived to be 92, dying in 2012, but was largely treated during his long medical career as a "gadfly," which means not to be taken seriously. While admitting there is such a thing as brain disease and brain defects, Szasz does not see mental illness as a disease. He writes:

"Disease cannot be cured by conversation. What so many doctors call mental illness is human conflict expressed in ways society cannot live with."

In his book *"Second Sin"* (1973), the *First Sin* being knowledge of good and evil, the *Second Sin* being the knowledge of clear speech, he writes:

"If a man says he is talking to God, we say he is praying. If he says God is talking to him, we say he is a schizophrenic.

Treating addiction to heroin with methadone is like treating addiction to Scotch with Bourbon.

Mental hospitals are the POW camps of our undeclared war and unarticulated civil wars.

There are two very different kinds of psychiatry, voluntary and involuntary. The difference is at least as important as the difference between psychotherapy and organic therapy. I consider all involuntary psychiatry to be punishment. The physician should be a healer not a jailer.

I object to only two things. First, I object to any and all involuntary psychiatry; to any kind of psychiatric measure that's imposed on a person against his will. Second, I object to the widespread mislabeling in psychiatry, whether it is voluntary or involuntary psychiatry, that is, calling personal problems "diseases," calling prisons "hospitals," calling conversation, "treatment."

We have already forgotten what doctors did in Nazi Germany, and we don't want to know what they did in Communist Russia. We thus persecute millions as drug addicts, homosexuals, suicide risks, all the while congratulating ourselves that we are great healers curing them of mental illness."

Elsewhere, he has written about the symbiotic relationship between psychiatry and the state:

"This is a complicated matter. As the prestige and popularity of organized religion diminished, following the Enlightenment, medicine took over many of the functions formerly performed by the churches. Physicians became the new priesthood who have played the roles of priests. They are our secular and scientific priests.

I am personally opposed to electroshock treatment. It's a barbarity. I have never used it and never would. I wouldn't dream of recommending it. If someone asked me about it, I would point out that neurologists go to great lengths trying to prevent seizures in persons who have epilepsy, because every time a person has a grand mal seizure, his brain gets damaged.

Nevertheless, psychiatrists claim that giving someone a seizure is a form of treatment. But then the history of medicine is full of instances of so-called cures that were actually harmful. You know the old saying, 'The cure is worse than the disease.' It applies to a lot of things psychiatrists do – electroshock, lobotomy, often the use of drugs, and sometimes even psychotherapy or psychoanalysis."

THE POSTMODERN HUMAN ZOO EXPOSED

Author Francis Fukuyama in *"Identity"* (2018) insists that a sense of individualism is essential to the well-being of us as persons, along with a sense of recognition, appreciation, and sense of worth.

But the irony is that *identity*, which is an internal monitoring device and the engine to our motivation has been nullified by our overwhelming preoccupation with being *"other-directed"* rather than *"self-directed,"* imitating, emulating, comparing and competing with those we esteem, while we become increasingly self-estranged to the point that we don't know ourselves very well if at all.

This finds us anxious if not terrified to be alone only with ourselves, or to find ourselves temporarily in a climate of silence with a total absence of noise.

In such a situation, we are apt to be close to panic with a feeling of being neglected and excluded from the company of others. Why? Being left alone, unoccupied and unstimulated, cut off from the outside world if only for a short time is for many tantamount to being abandoned.

Alas! The wonder of iPhones and other electronic devices have come to the rescue. Steve Jobs and Steve Wozniak, Apple, Inc. inventors, couldn't have chosen a more propitious time although they were actually trying to create electronic video games for those addicted to this form of escape. Now, escapism has become the *modus operandi* and cultural pacifier of society. The evidence?

Persons below the poverty line, who lack the wherewithal to conduct healthy lives, not only are likely to have cell phones, but their children as young as five or six as well. How is that possible? Necessity is the mother of motivation.

Electronic manufacturers and advertisers know this well. These electronics have become the 21st century's ultimate pacifier with society showing little need or intent to grow up much less take charge. These devices are the new opium of the masses, an approvable escape into wonderland.

Not only Western society, but societies across the globe have caught the fever, which is a flight from the *reality of imagination* into *the imagination of reality*. Dr. Thomas Szasz's *"Second Sin"* message still rings relevant.

Physicians, psychiatrists and psychotherapists know that patients today cannot stand discomfort, pain, failure, success, struggle, loneliness, depression, anxiety, or exclusion, so they designate stressors of life as "diseases," and propose pharmaceuticals and "talking cures" as remedies.

People don't get better for all this attention but have become more dependent on these pacifiers. It has resulted in the society we have today.

Electronics have become necessities as well as *"toys of the mind"* and the new "social media" religion. Manufacturers of these devices treat what is legal with the same broad brush as what is ethical. Not surprisingly, manufacturers are constantly in litigation or caught in some scandal.

Facebook, alone, has nearly two billion participants who give new meaning to passive aggression and approach avoidance behavior. *Twitter* adds the bizarre to it with its voiceless contributors and surrogate newsmakers. Then they are the faceless hackers and unprincipled troublemakers who have too much time on their hands.

[*As this was being written, Tampa Florida's Police Department was investigating how Tampa's Mayor Bob Buckhorn's Twitter account had been hacked posting racist tweets and pornographic messages. Among the tweets was one threatening the City of Tampa staff, Tampa International Airport and the Tampa Veteran Administration offices (February 21, 2019).*]

It may change in the future when participants grow up and take control of this new medium. Meanwhile, the chatter is mainly white noise with many users spreading veiled threats, hatred and evil.

On another front, we still arrest and prosecute drug dealers when the biggest drug dealer, the pharmaceutical industry and the medical profession, receive essentially a free pass or a slap on the wrists for dispensing mind-altering prescriptions in a rather cavalier fashion.

Meanwhile, people in the limelight, many career politicians or lobbyists play to the social media and the cable and network television audience to promulgate polarizing policies or to make divisive pronouncements. Is it any wonder that gridlock has taken hold of the *United States Congress* or that this is the *"Age of the Absurd"*?

FALLACY OF PSYCHOTHERAPY RESEARCH – THE PLACEBO EFFECT

There are nearly 110,000 psychotherapists in the United States today with nearly 60 million Americans in regular psychotherapy. Since Americans spend so much for this treatment, it should not be surprising that the majority claim the therapy beneficial.

This is however misleading. The therapy movement has been driving traditional values to the curb for decades while successfully forwarding its own postmodernism therapeutic worldview.

That said, people don't talk much about Sigmund Freud today, but the *"Father of Psychoanalysis"* remains a real presence as this therapy fills the void left by the decline of religion.

Yet, given this development, how effective is psychotherapy?

Studies comparing behavioral therapy and psychoanalytical therapy have proved interesting. Conducted by highly experienced therapists, roughly 90 percent of the behavioral therapy clients and 80 percent of the psychotherapy clients show improvement on a scale of overall adjustment. This looks impressive until you compare these results with the *control group* which consistently shows an 80 percent improvement on a scale of overall adjustment (*"The Shrinking of America,"* p. 125).

The *control group,* incidentally, involves people who don't receive the therapy but who have similar problems to those receiving the treatment.

Study after study conducted in this manner fails to demonstrate statistical significance with the *control group.* A procedure (in this case a therapeutic treatment) in which the results cannot be attributed to the properties of the placebo itself must be due to the patient's belief in the therapy as an effective treatment. The positive results are therefore considered *"the placebo effect."*

Consequently, when it comes to the efficacy of therapeutic therapy, there is vast disagreement on what can be construed as beneficial. Too often therapists believe changing behavior rather than gaining an understanding of the client as a person is more important than what is happening and why.

You flunked out of school; were fired from your job; you can't hang on to gainful employment; your wife (husband) has left you; your teeth are falling out, but you can't stop smoking; your friends won't hang out with you anymore; your children are driving you crazy; your husband won't work; your wife is never home; nobody listens to you; you have an eating, spending, gambling, or other secret disorder you can't talk about; you're dying inside but nobody cares.

Exhausted, at wits end, with nothing making any sense to you anymore, you rush into therapy, pay a stranger with credentials to find what is wrong with you in the belief that therapy is the answer to your dilemma when what you receive in treatment is a new vocabulary to master as to what is wrong with you and why.

Dr. Thomas Szasz would say, loosen up, you're just experiencing the normal conflicts of life. Your best therapist is a friend who knows and understands the person that you are.

That person, however, cannot solve your quandary. Only you can do that. But by talking to this friend, whom you trust, that deep-down terrible pain causing you such heartache may gradually surface as Dr. Szasz suggests.

Once no longer remote or buried in your psyche, disturbances are far less intimidating. This is an introduction to yourself as a person. You have confronted your disturbances and are ready to deal with them and get on with your life.

[A person of whom I had not seen or thought about since my youth, dropped by out of the blue. He told me he flunked out of college in his freshman year as an eighteen year old, then went into the US Army, came out of it and labored as a construction worker for a few years, took some junior college courses, then asked his university if he could return now that he had found purpose in life. The registrar of his university was impressed with his candor

and allowed him to re-register. Now in his late twenties, he went on to become a scholar, claiming to have received only two "B's" on his way through his master's and doctorate studies in plant physiology to earn his Ph.D. Once out of the university, he became a professor writing a textbook and doing scientific work. It was obvious he delighted in looking back and sharing his productive life with me these many years later.]

German philosopher Arthur Schopenhauer (1788 – 1860) points out that when you reach an advanced age and look back over your lifetime, it can seem to have had a consistent order and plan, as though composed by some novelist. Events that when they occurred had seemed accidental and of little moment turn out to have been indispensable factors in the composition of a consistent plot. So, who composed the plot? Schopenhauer suggests that just as your dreams are composed by an aspect of yourself of which your consciousness is unaware, so, too, your whole life is composed by the will within.

Nothing in life is written in concrete. Nothing is final or absolute in the ups and downs, successes and failures, peaks and valleys of an ordinary life. Why? Because this is but the rhythm of life. When you talk with a friend, and the friend listens, your problems surface to be more easily defined and prioritized with clarity. Over time, that clarity improves as conversation takes on form and develops substance. Eventually, if sincere and mature, you will choose to act in your own best interest.

Not only will your situation improve, but you will be more of a mind to listen to someone else who needs help to climb over the obstacles holding him or her back, obstacles now no longer treated as if the grandest of mountains.

Psychologist Carl Rogers has been ahead of this charge. His *"client-centered"* therapy was a reaction against analysis while the aim of his therapy was not to solve a client's particular problem but to assist the individual to grow and mature.

Among other things, this means that the person in pain must come to understand that he is the cause rather than the effect of his experience. Once the cause is clear the effect can ultimately be dispatched, not immediately, but with due diligence.

Meanwhile, this is not an attempt to convert the masses who believe in behavioral and psychotherapy. On the contrary, it expresses the benefits I have enjoyed in my long life from friends listening to me and therefore helping me to liberate myself from the ties that bind. That said, there appears little unity among therapists. Carl Rogers notes:

Therapists are not in agreement as to their goals or aims . . . They are not in agreement as to what constitutes a successful outcome of their work. They cannot agree as to what constitutes a failure. It seems as though the field is completely chaotic and divided.

So, while the wisdom of being your own psychotherapist may be a road less traveled, it could be the road that leads back to you becoming your own best friend.

A FINAL WORD ON THE FATHER OF PSYCHOANALYSIS

Psychoanalysis begins and ends with Sigmund Freud through many interpreters in psychotherapy. In our restlessness for answers, we are vulnerable to ideas from thinkers who are apt to present their own personal dilemma or psychological needs as those likely to be ours as well. It has happened throughout history with thinkers and philosophers, and it happened with Freud in the late 19th and early 20th century with the Western world being especially receptive to psychoanalysis and subsequently psychotherapy.

Professor Louis Breger writes in *"A Dream of Undying Fame"* (2009):

Freud's neglect of the importance of society was another deficiency in his thinking. Because of his need for a universal theory, he had almost nothing to say about cultural or social differences; everyone in the world was driven by the same motives and beset by the same conflicts. At the core of this neglect was his theory of human instincts as non- or antisocial, his view that we are, from the beginning of life, driven by self-centered pleasure. The instinct theory missed what has since been amply proven to be the powerful motive of attachment, the intrinsic need for social bonds. . . The baleful effects of shaping psychoanalysis as a cult-like movement or cause grew out of Freud's need to be a great man; it was the basis of all of the other problems with his theories and approaches to therapy (pp. 116-117).

A TUTORIAL OF IDEAS

YOU ARE THE WORLD!

THE KEY TO THE FUTURE IS IN YOUR HANDS!

James R. Fisher, Jr., Ph.D.
© March 3, 2014

The premise of *CONFIDENT SELLING* is that you are the world, and if you know how to look and learn, then the door is there, and the key is in your hand. Nobody can give you that key, or open that door but you.

A second premise is that we are all selling something. Therefore, we are all sellers. If selling is your profession, and you have what it takes, but haven't reached your true potential, then this book is for you.

CONFIDENT SELLING is designed to help you help yourself by developing the confidence that will bring you success to continuing success.

CONFIDENT SELLING
SECOND EDITION

Dr. James R. Fisher, Jr.

By opening that door with that key, you become all that you can become, self-confident, self-reliant, and self-directed. You are ready to make the biggest sale of your life, belief in yourself.

CONFIDENCE AS IT MAY MATERIALIZE

James R. Fisher, Jr., Ph.D.
© December 20, 2009

People often write and ask me how I got started into writing. The short answer is that I've always been writing ever since a boy. The long answer is more complicated.

My first book was written while on assignment in *South Africa* for *Nalco Chemical Company*. It was called, *"Sales Training & Technical Development"* (1968), and was written for field engineers and salesmen in South Africa who lacked such a guide. I still hold the copyright.

When I returned to the states in 1969, having retired while only in my thirties, I thought nothing would be easier than to become a writer. I acquired a national agent on the strength of some short fiction I had written, but he was unable to place my work.

Then I contacted the *William Morris Literary Agency* in New York City, explained my interest, and got a blistering reply claiming never to have had such a cockamamie entreaty from somebody in the flush of life making an impressive income, but wanting to give it all up for the uncertainty of being a writer. While the writing samples I sent were considered promising, they lacked commercial appeal.

Was I discouraged? No. Disappointed? Yes. If writing had been a job, I suppose I would have been discouraged, but writing for me was a vocation consistent with psychologist James Hillman's *"The Soul's Code"* (1996). As he points out, a vocation is a journey not an end. A vocation understands disappointments are part of the process.

So, I sat down in 1970 and turned out a manuscript in six weeks, called it *"Let's Take the Worry Out of Selling,"* which was based in part on what I had written for the men in the field in *South Africa*.

The manuscript was sent off to *Prentice-Hall, Inc.* without protocol. Within a month, it was accepted for publication without editing, and published as *Confident Selling* in September 1970 with a 1971 copyright. It sold roughly 100,000 copies and became a national bestseller with more than 20 printings.

Confident Selling was also printed in a monthly series in a national magazine, offered in shorter form in airline magazines, and was considered for an audiocassette and video version.

The latter is mentioned because the 11 o'clock television news anchor for Tampa's ABC affiliate wanted to form a consortium around *Confident Selling* to reach a wider audience. I told him *Prentice-Hall* held the copyright. P-H's demands proved excessive, so the project was dropped. I have never surrendered my copyright since. Trust me, an author has no rights of his own material once he gives up his copyright. (Incidentally, I do own the copyright to this book now and have since April 30, 1990.)

Some of you wonder why I call the corporation "corpocracy," or why I am so hard on the corporation. It is visceral as my writings are based on my own empirical experience. For example, I would not have received royalties for the serialized version of the *Confident Selling* had I not seen my book on the cover of that national magazine in a kiosk.

THE CHALLENGE

If you're a sales person who's got what it takes to be *The Best*, but you haven't proved yourself yet, or you have proved yourself, but you're finding it rough maintaining the tempo, here's a dynamic new confidence builder that helps you *Leap* over the final hurdle *From Success to Continued Success!* This book, as your own private counselor, will show you *Why You Should Be Confident. Here's the Door to Opportunity* – with *You Holding the Only Key* to the biggest sale of your life, *Belief in Yourself!*

THE DESCRIPTION

Confident Selling is a breakthrough book in that it looks at the selling situation from the perspective of the seller, which it claims is the main obstacle in the selling situation. The assumptions the seller makes about the buyer, the buyer's interest in and ability to buy, are predicated too often on faulty information, information derived from the failure of the seller to sell him or herself on the cost benefit to the buyer to purchase the product or service.

The book insists that selling is not a matter of intimidation or a matter of finessing the buyer into a mood to purchase the product or service being offered. On the contrary, *Confident Selling* is about gauging the buyer's need and ability to form a partnership with you the seller. *This requires the seller to think not as a seller but as the buyer, as the one that is to purchase the product or service and the consequences of that transaction.*

Confident Selling argues that every endeavor in life is one between a seller and a buyer whether the seller is in an actual selling situation as a sales person, or is a doctor, lawyer, accountant, consultant, administrator, priest, minister, rabbi, nun, teacher, factory worker, independent contractor or an employee of a public or private agency.

Selling is the noblest of all professions as it involves everyone in everything on a daily basis.

This theme was elaborated in the *Pulitzer Prize* nominated book, *Confident Selling for the 90s* (1992). It was a breakthrough book in that it viewed the selling problem the reverse of how it is traditionally viewed or a partnership rather than an adversarial relationship between buyer and seller.

DEVLIN

DOWNTOWN CHICAGO LOOP – Friday, June 13, 1969

The tall blond young American walked with the cocky self-assurance of an athlete. Dressed in a deep blue Hickey Freeman vested pinstripe suit, white shirt with monogram cufflinks, burgundy tie with a Phi Beta Kappa clasp, his highly polished Florsheim shoes clicking like happy feet as he strolled down Chicago's Michigan Avenue.

His head moved like a periscope with flat eyes above the early evening crowd. Everyone was in a hurry going nowhere. The crowd was unaware of him, but he was conscious of it. He ran his hand through his short military clipped hair and over his chiseled features. He could pass for a Nordic European except for the scornful assurance of an American.

The wind off Lake Michigan forced his head down into his chest. He cut his way through the midtown shoppers as he once did through the line for Crescent High as a fullback. He avoided eye contact, as if someone might recognize him. Why? He didn't know. Was it because people believed he could see through them? It was nonsense, but it worked for him. His long quick strides were a force of habit as he had no special place to go.

Earlier in the day, he was standing by the door of the El waiting to step off at the loop, when two young toughs came down the aisle rolling their shoulders menacingly. He felt his body tense, a delicious sensation coursed through him, his steel blue eyes taking measure of the lads like bionic lasers.

"You got a problem, pretty boy?" one asked. He waited for the slightest hint of aggression. The tough's accent was from the projects on the lower south side, where his da had been born in the Irish ghetto. They were dressed like clones of some wannabe gang, baseball caps on backward, Chicago Cubs' jackets, cigarettes dangling from thin lips, baggy jeans, US Army surplus boots, acne complexions, bad teeth, soldiers without a cause. They passed giving him a wide berth.

If that was intimidation, he smiled, it beat putting them in the hospital. They were too young to understand rage. You have to suffer real pain, real loss to have a fire in your belly. Theirs was an imitation brand.

His intensity inward, his amused expression masking his outward malevolence. Why should he be surprised? He lived an accidental life, here today gone tomorrow. The young toughs hadn't a clue. The fact they act tough to control their fear differed little with his dressing up to control his. He doubted seriously if they had ever been east of Evanston.

He had worked everywhere, seen everything, but was he not equally anxious? They hid their angst in bravado; he hid his in a well-tailored suit. Life is up for grabs and nothing works out as you expect. Most people stay close to home, do nothing, go nowhere, just fester like boils, then explode and die. Others like him, do everything, go everywhere, and die just the same. You would think doers would be happier, but they aren't. He's proof. We're here a little while to fool around and then die. Happiness is a myth. The toughs seem to sense this. Perhaps that is their real beef.

* * *

Life was a puzzle to Seamus "Dirk" Devlin. Its perplexities found him wandering the streets wherever he was. Tonight, it found him at the door of old St. Patrick's Catholic Church off Michigan Avenue and Randolph Street. He pushed open the large wooden door of the vestibule immediately smelling the incense and age of the place. His hope was to find some quiet to placate his demons who had been riled up earlier in the day by the company brass. Like spiteful children, they took pleasure in firing colleagues unable to fathom a colleague firing the company as he had done.

The Friday Novena was just ending with people lining up to go to confession. He made his way to the center aisle, genuflected making the *Sign of the Cross*. Except for those going to confession the church quickly emptied. He moved down the aisle looking at the bas-relief statues of the *Stations of the Cross* on the side walls of the clerestory with secondary altars framing the main nave with the Blessed Virgin Mary's on the left and St. Joseph's on the right flanking the main altar. He glanced back at the line of confessors at the confessional, wondering if any were as lost as he was.

Devlin lit a candle at the foot of the statue of the Blessed Virgin Mary, knelt down at the white marble altar rail and made a wish instead of saying a prayer, as this was his first visit to the church, then remained there until the last person left the confessional.

Before the priest could leave the confessional, he rushed to the confessor's door, inhaling the scented rosemary wood, knelt on the cushioned kneeler, breathing hard waiting for the priest to slide the lattice window open, separating the priest from the confessor, feeling a bit frantic and winded after escaping the world that controlled him only to enter the world that owned him.

The priest mumbled his greeting in a few automatic Latin words, then paused for the confessor to fill the void. Devlin cleared his throat, then in a distinct stentorian voice said, "Bless me Father for I am bored. I am sorry for this and all my past boredom. It has been about a week since my last Confession."

"Pardon me, my son? What did you say?"

"I said, 'I am bored', Father," his voice rising to a shrill.

"You don't need to shout, my son. Do you understand this is a confessional and that I'm a Catholic priest?"

"Yes, Father."

"Are you a Catholic?"

"Yes, Father, of the worst kind, Irish Roman Catholic."

Silence.

"It has been a week since my last Confession."

"You've already said that, my son, but I don't understand."

"Father, you mean you've never heard a person confess to being bored to death; that life is meaningless, empty; and that that person feels utterly useless, robotic, disengaged?"

"Well, yes, I suppose I have. But what are your sins, my son?"

"What are my sins?" Devlin laughed nervously. "Pardon me for that, Father, but first of all, I am not your son, and secondly, you are not my father; you are my confessor, my priest."

"Yes. I hear anger in your voice."

"It is not anger, Father, it is boredom! My sins, Father, are that of being bored. I feel powerless to go forward or to be able to do anything about it."

"Why are you bored?"

Devlin sighed. "Why am I bored? Well, now that is a story."

"Well, this is not the place to tell stories, my son, you should know that. This is the place to expiate your guilt, confess your sins, and ask for absolution."

"Those are good but meaningless words, Father, especially *expiation* and *absolution*. You're going to expiate my boredom and grant me absolution?"

Before the priest could answer, he continued. "May I be candid?" Devlin didn't wait for a reply.

"I'm weary, just turned 31, what you might call an educated man with a degree in chemical engineering, a master's in industrial chemistry, earning $60,000 this past year not counting perks and privileges and paying no American income taxes." He took a deep breath surprised at his candor but muddled on. "I have everything and nothing at all. I am reduced to a dichotomy."

"You earn what?"

"$60,000, and as I said, and paid no taxes. I am what you call an ex-patriot doing my bidding for an American company abroad."

"Are you speaking in American dollars?"

"Indeed I am. If it were in Kruger Rand, it would be R84,000."

"You must be very successful."

"Not anymore. I've retired."

"You've retired? But you said you were only 31."

"Yes."

Silence. "What is your explanation for this?"

"Absolute, unequivocal, unmitigated boredom."

Silence.

Devlin filled the void. "That is why I'm here, Father."

Pause. "You mentioned the Kruger Rand. You work in South Africa?"

"Worked, Father, past tense. I no longer work there. Yes, the Rand is the monetary currency equivalent to 1.4 American dollars."

"I see. I still do not see what sins are troubling you, my son."

"Cannot boredom be a sin, Father? I am drowning in boredom. I am unable to shake it, I have no idea what the next chapter of my life will be."

Father Anthony Dressler sighed deeply. It had been a long day: two masses in the morning, light breakfast, off to Cook County Hospital for sick call, no lunch, quick drink at O'Hara's on Halsted with a priest friend from St. Mark's, back to St. Patrick's for dinner with Monsignor Donovan, Novena at 7 p.m., then confessions, knowing he still had to say his Office. He craved a cigarette and three-fingers of scotch. How to get rid of this impertinent young man? The seven deadly sins came to mind. He took a deep breath, and asked, "Have you committed adultery, my son?"

"Have I committed adultery?" Devlin laughed heartily causing his confessor to involuntarily wince.

"Oh, yes, Father, adultery and I are old friends."

"But that's a mortal sin, my son."

"Yes, indeed, it is."

"Have you committed adultery recently?"

"Indeed, I have."

"Are you sorry for that sin?"

"Well, yes and no."

"You cannot be ambivalent about mortal sin, my son, surely you know that."

"I'm ambivalent about everything, Father, which is the reason I'm here if that is at all helpful."

The priest crossed himself to hide his exasperation. "Do you have a family?"

"Yes, Father, a wife and four children."

"Can't you see where you've compromised them?"

"Yes."

"Are you sorry?"

"Yes and no."

"I don't understand, my son."

"Yes, Father, I'm sorry for the pain I've caused my children. They are innocent in this affair, but no, I'm not sorry for the pain I've caused my wife. You see I have no sense of guilt or remorse, only anxiety and boredom."

"This is a most unusual Confession."

"Well, it's a most unusual situation. I just came back from South Africa and . . ."

"You've already told me that."

Devlin ignored the interruption. "I was imagining while I was waiting for you, what if *apartheid* was practiced here in Chicago; what if Mayor Richard Daley was its architect. What would the policy of Cardinal John Cody of the Archdiocese of Chicago be towards this racial betrayal? Would the good Cardinal fight it? Or would the diocese collapse to the whim of the mayor's authority and be a puppet to the government? That is the case of the Roman Catholic Church of South Africa: blind, deaf and dumb to the basic freedoms denied the Bantu peoples."

"That is a libelous view, my son, I think on reflection you would see that. The church is puppet to no one except the Mystical Body of Christ and Holy Mother Church."

The silence was like a heavy syrup suffocating the breathing on both sides of the confessional. After nearly a minute, the priest said, "Well?"

"Father, it may sound dubious," Devlin uttered in a somewhat more conciliatory voice, not wanting the priest to bolt, "but my pastor in South Africa, a missionary from Ireland, was as much a tool of the Afrikaner Government's *apartheid policy* as any man could be."

"Don't you think that's a bit harsh?"

"I only wish that it were. I kept a notebook of the number of times I attempted to have a conversation with my pastor about this practice without success. I was rebuked, ignored, cut off at the pass by an assistant priest, and finally threatened with deportation."

"Perhaps that could be traced to your ill-mannered hostility."

"Not at first, Father, but yes, that is a fair assumption. I became increasingly angry the more I witnessed abuses to the Bantu peoples. I needed to talk to someone; attempted the subject in confession only to have my pastor shut the window on me without granting me absolution, can you believe that?

"Corporate people such as I have a vested interest in *apartheid*. I thought my pastor the exception. I was wrong. I think it hostile when people are murdered and nothing is done about it; when land is taken without redress to its owners; when families are split up as a matter of State and not the will of the people; when people are forced to live in the most deplorable conditions; when the 20 percent white minority have the vote, and the 80 percent black majority do not; when the rule of law and order stops at color. Yes, I think hostility is an accurate assessment of my angst."

"This is all very interesting, my son, but of course subjective, possibly irrational. It is what you assume to be the case, am I correct?"

"Father, my gardener was murdered on my estate. When I attempted to find out why and by whom, the police treated the matter as if a dog had been killed. He was my friend, a good man, an honorable man, and he was twenty-seven-years-old. That is concrete, not speculative. When events keep crashing against your values, your frustration blunted by disgust, what other purchase can there be?

"Was the murder the cause of your depression?"

"Father, now you're being patronizing."

"I don't mean to be, but I sense you're feeling helpless."

Devlin gave a deep sigh, "You have no idea."

"I'm listening." Father saw fire in the eyes of the young man through the lattice curtain that separated them. He had seen it before. He forgot about his cigarette and drink.

"My anchors" Devlin made a sweep of the confessional with his hands in its narrow confines, "have been my company, country, government and church, and they now are all gone. They have been swept out to sea. I have been treading water, Father, in a foreign land buttressed by disturbing news about the United States from secondary sources, and I'm drowning. Do you understand what I'm saying? America is coming apart at the seams. Not just me. Meanwhile, South Africa is lock stepping to *apartheid* that I see every day. It leaves me disconnected. I have had no other option than to sink into boredom."

"You're a most disturbed young man."

"I think that is an accurate if patronizing assessment. Yes, I am disturbed, but from my perspective, with reason. But words hide resolve, Father. I know. I am good with words.

"If I'm disturbed, Father, and I think I am, what does that make of my rational ordering society to which I have returned? If I'm disturbed, what does that say about Roman Catholicism and Christian morality? No one is more Christian than Afrikaners. If I'm disturbed, what does that say about my country, which appears at war with itself? Am I to take it I'm disturbed and everything else is under control? I find that ironic. Pathetic."

"If you insist."

"Father, I'm not trying to win debating points. Can't you see the basis of my boredom?"

"Again, if you insist."

"I do, Father, for everything has lapsed into contradiction: everything real is not acknowledged as such, while everything that is not real is celebrated as real."

The priest smiled, but not unkindly. "So, now you're a psychologist."

"No. Nor am I a philosopher, Father. This has been my experience in a pivotal year for me, but it seems a pivotal year for my country as well. If I live a long life, I'm certain I will look back on this as a defining moment."

He laughed self-consciously wondering if the priest was still listening. He could feel him breathing.

"If I'm having a nervous breakdown, Father, it seems so is my country. 1968 was a traumatic year for us both. Our country's leadership is in shambles; our infrastructure is in chaos; our institutions a mockery of ineptitude; our value systems as porous as a sieve. I have no anchor, Father, nor apparently does my country. We are both seemingly detached from reality. We wander off into space or explore the ocean's depths; we make fancy new things, but our crumbling spirit is ignored which is the engine of everything.

"You mentioned psychology and philosophy. We have them both in spades, but what good are they? These disciplines play word games only to blight our spirits. Obviously, I'm disturbed. Why wouldn't I be, having seen what I've seen, done what I've done? Am I wearing the mask of sanity in an insane world, or insanity's mask in a sane one? Father, which is it?"

The priest furrowed his brow, cupped his hands under his chin and bowed his head in prayer. Was this why I became a priest, or was it to escape this? This young man is disturbed, quite so, but what he says, had I not thought it as well? For the first time, the priest felt some empathy for the young man. Confused? Angry? Yes, but what to do?

The priest said finally, "It is clear you are in pain, my son, however, I wonder if this is the place to continue this."

"Father, I am the last one in this church. I am the last one having my confession heard. I have traveled more than 12,000 miles in the last 36 hours. I've been drilled all day by a bunch of pompous asses who sit on mahogany row mesmerized by numbers oblivious to the real world. They have no idea what I am about. Each time I see them, I marvel. They never change; they stay the same; they miss the changes; and wonder why the future is always such a surprise to them. I would like you to indulge me a bit longer. I'd like to tell you a story. Then perhaps you can advise me whether it is I or my world that is mad."

"A story?"

"Yes, it is a story about sins of omission and commission; about the multinational corporation and how it views indigenous peoples as disposable symbols of profit and loss; about a church more interested in its survival than its mission; about a time obsessed with the products of the mind at the expense of those of the heart; about not being able to truly love a woman or hate a man. It's about the present panic of now; about the greatest sin of all, which is waste; and about not being able to live a useful life. In the absence of love in a universe of hate and betrayal, everything is reduced to the common denominator of boredom."

"Is it a true story?"

"I only wish it wasn't."

"Then, my son, please continue." Devlin does.

Note
This is the introduction to *Devlin, A Psychological Novel,* available at Amazon.com, Kindle Library

A TUTORIAL OF IDEAS

THE ASCENT OF THE WORKING WOMAN

James R. Fisher, Jr., Ph.D.
© January 11, 2018

ABOUT "THE ASCENT OF THE WORKING WOMAN"

German philosopher and jurist Hermann Kantorowicz (1877 – 1940) consider ideas as weapons. He writes, *"There is an important distinction between thoughts and ideas. Men possess thoughts. Ideas possess men."* French novelist Victor Hugo (1802 – 1885) is even more provocative insisting, *"Men have sight, and women have insight."*

"The Ascent of the Working Woman" is a journey of ideas that tracks such sentiments. If you sense that something is amiss, but can't put your finger on it, Dr. Fisher will guide you through the trivia that passes for

knowledge to show mythical gender and cultural clashes that consume so much of our attention. They no longer have purchase for the working woman as men move out of the shadow of the dying *Sensate Culture* of our magnificent past into a new *Ideational Culture* of a creative tomorrow.

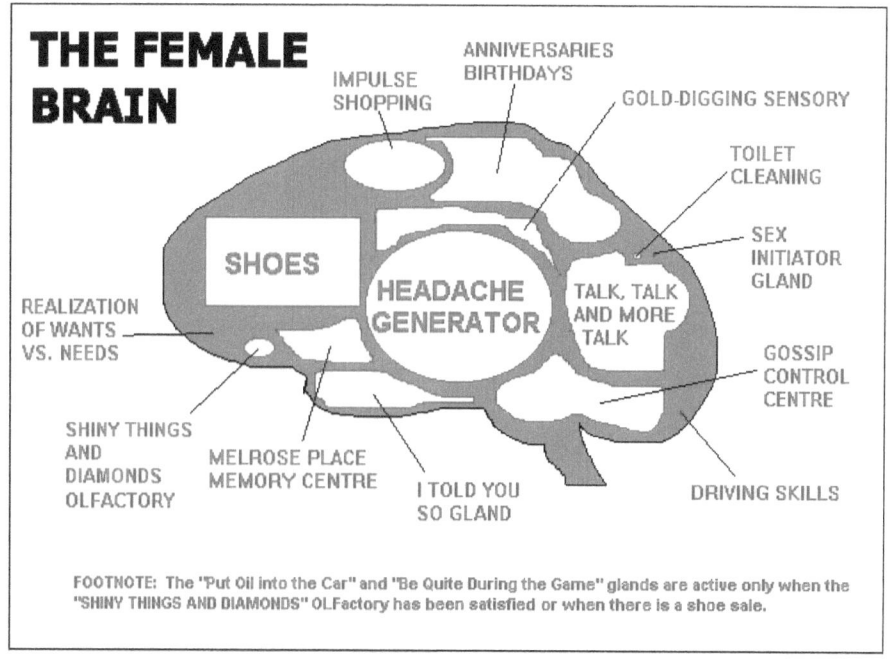

THE FEMALE BRAIN

- IMPULSE SHOPPING
- ANNIVERSARIES BIRTHDAYS
- GOLD-DIGGING SENSORY
- TOILET CLEANING
- SEX INITIATOR GLAND
- SHOES
- HEADACHE GENERATOR
- TALK, TALK AND MORE TALK
- REALIZATION OF WANTS VS. NEEDS
- GOSSIP CONTROL CENTRE
- SHINY THINGS AND DIAMONDS OLFACTORY
- MELROSE PLACE MEMORY CENTRE
- I TOLD YOU SO GLAND
- DRIVING SKILLS

FOOTNOTE: The "Put Oil into the Car" and "Be Quite During the Game" glands are active only when the "SHINY THINGS AND DIAMONDS" OLFactory has been satisfied or when there is a shoe sale.

Popular *Male Brain* misperception of the *Female Brain*

Over the past seventy years, or since WWII, while familiar impediments to the working woman have been disappearing, new ideas relating to women have taken root. These ideas form the basis of *"The Ascent of the Working Woman!"*

Principally, women have risen to the fore, manifesting new prominence in what this author calls, *"The Feminine Paradigm"* with its accent on "right brain" thinking, complementing the *Masculine Paradigm* of "left brain" thinking—subsuming the collective *mindset* of the brain to all spheres in the problem solving.

Regarding the eminent cultural shift, according to the theories of sociologist Pitirim Sorokin (1889 – 1968), we are at the end of a 600-year dying *Sensate Culture* into a transformational period to a glorious 600-year *Ideational Culture* of the creative tomorrow.

Author Fisher urges us to embrace this new day that is now upon us. He challenges us to discard our cherished assumptions about present day work and life, and to embrace a new solidarity as men and women immersed in a common and equal partnership move out of the shadows of obsessional materialism and self-conscious sexism into the dawn of a creative and spiritual tomorrow where instrumental and terminal values blend into a common pursuit toward economic, social and emotional well-being.

21ST CENTURY REALITY CHECK - THE NEW/OLD PLAGUE

While literally everything has changed, conditions for the working professional, that vaunted *knowledge worker*, have not. In shameful fashion, workplace professionals are assigned, evaluated, categorized and promoted by means of criteria intended for a time long past with protocols that have little to do with their potential, ethics or, most incredibly, their actual job requirements.

Inexplicably, the "modern" workplace is managed, motivated, mobilized and manipulated to conform to an outdated workplace model; a model characterized by *position power,* hierarchies, and chain-of-command ritualistic practices with rules and regulations tied to nostalgia, contributing little to the bottom line; actually, quite the contrary.

In part, we can blame this on the unrelenting explosion in technology, which has accelerated since *The Worker, Alone* was published in 1995. This tsunami of technology has resulted in spiraling costs to employers and constant stress and accelerating demands to employees. Call it an emotional as well as an economic crisis.

If the obvious purpose of a company is "what it does," and "what it does" is simply cosmetic housekeeping, not aligned to changing corporate challenges, then it becomes a serious problem, and it has.

Meanwhile, against this backdrop of coping with new technology, the corporate "system" engages tenaciously in *business as usual* practices with implacable infallible authority, despite setback after setback. It operates as a *knowing* rather than a *learning* institution, disregarding valuable lessons.

Rx: For a Healthier Workplace

How then do we reawaken and revitalize a profoundly unconscious workplace?

It's easy to point fingers at management, but that does not address the real issue. Nor does it deal with the larger problem of a devotion to the *status quo*. Workers are content to wait for someone to take charge and lift them out of their malaise while managers reprove workers for their reluctance to exercise initiative. Ironically, professional workers wait and hope for someone to lead when it is, they alone, who possess the necessary tools and acumen. They wait, timidly, for the vested powers to finally come to their senses, when those interests have far too much invested in the current *status quo* to gamble on change.

Meaningful change will come about only when workers, aided by managers, summon the courage to bring about change from within. There is neither an upside to hope nor a downside to courage. But make no mistake, courage is both the engine of survival and the means to prevail.

Change as a natural occurrence has its own impetus but lacks conscious direction. It is aimless and unreliable. Change is a random variable in the work environment and thus of secondary concern. Change of the deliberate sort is *needed change* which comes within the individual. It comes from having a center, a central governor, and a manifestly reliable behavioral construct.

There are pitfalls to avoid, however. Needed change takes more than a change in attitude, more than good intentions, more than catchy slogans, more than a positive work climate, or a generous confection of incentives. Necessary change requires a radical change in mindset accompanied by a structural change in the way workers and managers execute their roles and conduct their relationship vis-à-vis each other. Stated simply, it takes hard work. Favorable impressions may result, but they are not the goal.

Essential change now calls for professional workers to go against the grain, to oppose the status quo. It is time professional workers take charge!

How We Got Here

The corporate luxury of passively believing that "doing everything one can for workers, and in return expecting workers to be motivated to do everything they can for the company" is an extravagance companies can no longer afford. It's a strategy that has proven counterproductive to the extreme.

Entitlements and perks were expected to increase worker creativity and productivity. Instead, these confections have resulted in *counter dependence* and *learned helplessness*. When the connection between contribution and compensation was scuttled, workers became isolated from the reality of the company's challenges in terms of the relentless demands of the competitive marketplace.

Instead of this essential linkage between performance and demand, workers became reliant on the comforts delivered by management. It led to professional complacency and counter dependence on the company for workers' total well-being.

Workers brought their bodies to work and left their minds at home. Captive to this chronic disorder, many companies now struggle to remain solvent and to compete in a global economy. As a consequence, the trend has been for companies to rely on manpower outsourcing or the use of temporary workers rather than to address the problem of corporate apathy and worker complacency.

Contrary to what orthodoxy insists, harmony is not the glue that holds a company on task. *Managed conflict does*. Unfortunately, employees have been conditioned to shy away from confrontation, to avoid conflict, to recruit safe hires, to shun risk taking, and therefore to miss the advantages of self-directed engaged workers.

More than a half-century of this programming has resulted in the workforce that we have today; one largely reactive to crises rather taking the initiative to avoid them. Now, when creativity is required, workers are unable or unwilling to respond. It's simply not part of their collective DNA. For far too long, companies promoted security while being willing to give workers everything except control of their work. Lethargy, and passivity have been the bitter products of this oversight.

When workers operate as renters instead of owners and stakeholders, contribution consists of safely following protocols, not creative collaboration between workers and managers.

Dumping the Trash

Envisioning a new reality, workers and managers can be equal partners, but not until we see the following changes:

Performance Appraisal Systems (PAS) phased out.

Perfunctory PAS is an elitist management practice that does nothing except reinforce *position power.* The new relationship between workers and managers is organic, fluid and interdependent. Workers pursue goals consistent with company directives, while managers provide clarity and context.

Personal reward and recognition programs for professionals (i.e., cash and prizes) eliminated.

Incentives have proven to encourage bad behavior and to demotivate and divide knowledge workers, inhibiting cooperation and fostering wasteful internal competition. Workers prefer ownership of what they do provided they are given the tools to do the job, and the liberty (control) to perform the task in their own inimitable style, measured against parameters understood and agreed upon. The work is the reward for professionals.

Departmental and functional group competition suspended as overall organizational performance is emphasized.

Creating discrete business units or departmental functions to compete against each other stymies creativity and leads to imitation at the expense of the overarching mission of corporate enterprise.

Although counterintuitive, it is nonetheless true that when each function or department in a complex system is performing as well as it can, the overall system is not. Conversely, when these departments or functions focus on one shared objective, the organization succeeds beyond expectations. It is the nature of synergy. Cease and desist with micromanagement.

Over control creates reactionary   workers. When failures occur, it is "not my problem!" Workers wait for management to solve the problem, when only they have the faculties to do so.

Micromanagement weakens workers resolve creating a vacuum in which chaos thrives. Crisis management follows, a perpetual cycle in which management solves problems it creates, while workers take pleasure in the charade, failing to see they are also its victims. On the other hand, when workers are given ownership of what they do, they quickly resolve each issue as it arises, not waiting for management to intervene. In this work climate, chronic problems are addressed at the source.

Cease to see management as distinct from professional workers.

Managers are atavistic and management, as we know it, is anachronistic, an outmoded technology. No longer are eighty (80) percent of the workforce unskilled blue-collar workers, and twenty (20) percent management and administrative support. Now, less than twenty percent of workers are unskilled while eighty percent are professionally trained.

Management today is essentially everybody. Therefore, workers need to have a sense of this new role and accountability. Stated another way, this new work climate cannot be partitioned. Quality, for example, is not only a quality department function in human resources, engineering, and production, administration, sales and marketing. Quality is a matter of concern for everyone. Quality is a ubiquitous mindset as all functions are interdependent, part of one organic whole.

Refrain from faddism.

There was a time when companies were "searching" for excellence, imitating successful companies to the nth detail. Many of these companies in the end failed. Emulation was often at the expense of disregarding companies' indisputable uniqueness.

Each company is as unique from another company as individuals are unique from each other. Each company has a distinctive history, value and belief system, infrastructure and relational heritage, along with proprietary highs and lows, and matchless secrets.

A corporation's (internal) aspirations are manifested in its (external) propensities. As fixated as people may be, this is more the case with companies. They run on the momentum that has brought them to this time, place and space. Mergers often end poorly because they fail to acknowledge this inherent characteristic of individual companies.

The seeds for rejuvenation are never "out there!" The better wisdom for an enterprise is to create the new out of the ashes of the old. This exploits the collective mindset. The reticent majority often reveals answers concerning survival. Too frequently in panic mode, these voices are dismissed as unimportant and therefore ignored. Instead, grandiose schemes and quick fixes are entertained.

These quick fixes range from "hot house" training programs to cutting edge technologies to tantalizing shortcuts supposed to ensure instantaneous course corrections and cure decade's old faux pas.

Stopgap measures usually carry the seductive scent of cosmetic change, while merely postponing the inevitable. Change for change's sake is no change at all.

Finally, Professional Women Taking Charge

Twenty years ago, it was "crunch time" for workers as professionals. This was essentially ignored, as they were too busy complaining to seize the initiative. Now they inhabit a dysfunctional system that they inherited, a system they did not create, but have not improved.

A new crop of professional millennials is coming into the system with their heads down as well. They have invested heavily in education with a disappointing return on that investment, as good paying jobs prove difficult to find.

Once these professionals have a job, there is little sense of security as the train wrecks of conglomerates are heard in the distance. They are as angry at "the system" as were their elders, failing to realize they are now the system.

Nothing changes at work until male and female professionals change. Games of trendy themes like empowerment continue because they're enticing, safe and risk free to those in power. It is now up to workers to put this house in order. Neither house cleaning nor finger pointing will do. Professionals must get off the dime and boldly take charge of their work, which is the path to taking charge of their life.

WHEN MEN WON'T WORK &
THE WOMEN WHO CARRY THEM!

James R. Fisher, Jr., Ph.D.
© May 19, 2011

A generation ago, when the *Feminist Movement* was in full stride, women came to view life through the feminist prism. They campaigned for an *Office of Gender Equity*, insisting there was a gender bias favoring men, especially with regard to education. What now seems like ancient history, in 1970, it was then observed:

- While boys get higher scores in mathematics, girls get higher scores in reading and writing;
- Boys in eighth grade are 50 percent more likely to repeat a grade, while boys in high school constitute 68 percent of the special education population;
- 67 percent of female high school graduates go on to college, compared to 58 percent of male high school graduates.
- Women were only 41 percent of all college graduates.

Regarding graduate education, in 1970:

- Women receive 40 percent of all master's degrees;
- Two thirds of all master's degree candidates and more than half of all master's degree holders today are women;
- Women earned only 6 percent of all first professional degrees; by 1991 that figure had increased to 39 percent, and now hovers around 50 percent;
- Only 14 percent of all doctoral degrees went to women; by 1991 that figure was up to 39 percent, while today it is pressing 50 percent.
- The medical degree earned by women between 1970 and 1991 jumped from 8 percent to 36 percent. By 1993, 42 percent of first-year medical students were women; today more than half of all medical students are women.
- In 1970, 5 percent of women earned law degrees; by 1991, that figure was up to 40 percent, and today is around 50 percent;

- In 1970, women earned 1 percent of dental degrees compared with 32 percent in 1991, and today more than half first-year dental students are women, and more than 40 percent have earned dental degrees;
- Women today earn the majority of doctoral degrees in pharmacy and veterinary medicine.

The gender imbalance is even more pronounced for African American and Hispanic women. In 1990, fully 62 percent of all bachelor's degrees to African Americans went to women, while 55 percent of Hispanic students receiving bachelor's degrees were women. In 1990, the white student imbalance was 53 percent to 47 percent in favor of women. It is even more pronounced today.

BACKGROUND

On April 4, 2011, I wrote an article in longhand on my observations on men who refused to work and the women who support them. I wrote it while waiting for my daughter at the eye clinic where she was operated on for a detached retina.

On May 11, 2011, *New York Times* columnist wrote an article on the very same subject, not speaking from empirical data but economic statistics. David Brooks insisted that energy define us, and that we are becoming less energetic insofar as American males are concerned.

In 1954, 96 percent of American men between the ages of 25 and 54 were actively engaged in some kind of regular work. Today, that number has slipped to 80 percent, whereas women, once only allowed to enter the workforce in small numbers in menial tasks have steadily increased in the last half-century.

According to the *Organization for Economic Cooperation and Development*, the United States now lags behind all other G-7 nations in prime age men in the workforce. David Brooks quips,

"More American men lack the emotional and professional skills they would need to contribute."

Most startlingly, however, according to the *Bureau of Labor Statistics*, 35 percent of those males are without high school diplomas whereas only 10 percent of college degreed men are out of work.

Brooks becomes something of an apologist for the structural changes in the economy, which although relevant, fail to get inside the fact that there are more idle men walking the streets of the *United States* anytime since the *Great Depression*. Brooks sees the problem in terms of economics when it seems clear it has been a natural progression since the *Feminist Movement* as many American males feel emasculated by the soaring prominence of women in the workforce.

James Burke and Robert Ornstein presented a conceptual framework for such perturbations in *The Axemaker's Gift: A Double-Edged History of Human Culture* (1995). They argued that with each *cultural change* something is gained at the expense of something lost, never to be experienced again. Half the world's population is women. Yet, prior to WWII, they had been given secondary and subjugated roles. It was evident ten-years after WWII that society wanted to put the genie back in the bottle as displayed in *Good Housekeeping Monthly* (May 13, 1955):

The Good Wife's guide:

- *Has dinner ready, plans ahead, even the night before to have a delicious meal on time for her husband's return. This is a way of letting him know that you have been thinking of him and are concerned about his needs.*
- *Prepare yourself. Take 15 minutes to rest so you'll be refreshed when he comes home. Touch up your make up, put a ribbon in your hair and be fresh looking.*
- *Be a little gay and a little more interesting for him.*
- *Clear away the clutter. Make one last trip around the house before he arrives.*
- *Gather up schoolbooks, toys and papers and run a dust cloth over the furniture.*
- *Over the cooler months of the year light a fire for him to unwind by.*
- *Prepare the children. See that they are clean, are not noisy, and eliminate all noise from vacuum cleaners to dryers.*
- *Be happy to see him.*

- *Greet him with a warm smile and show sincerity in your desire to please him.*
- *Listen to him. You may have dozens of important things to tell him, but this is not the moment. Remember, his topics of interest are more important than yours.*
- *Make the evening his. Never complain if he comes home late, or goes out to dinner, or other places of entertainment without you. Try to understand his stress.*
- *Your goal is to make your home a place of peace, order and tranquility.*
- *Don't greet him with complaints and problems.*
- *Don't complain if he's late or stays out all night.*
- *Make him comfortable. Have a cool or warm drink ready for him.*
- *Arrange his pillows and offer to take his shoes off.*
- *Don't ask him about his actions or question his judgments or integrity.*
- *A good wife always knows her place.*

The retinue of this fading fantasy is evident in 20 percent of American men ages 25 to 54 who aren't working, or if working, not doing what they were trained to do. I know:

- An attorney with several degrees including a doctor in jurisprudence refuses to practice law, or when he does, gives away his services to friends, while his family suffers mightily for the indulgence, forcing his wife to work as a freelance model driving fifty, sixty or more miles for auditions while still being mother, housekeeper, and taxi service for her husband and children.
- A father of two who sits at home strumming his guitar when he is able bodied except for the carpal tunnel syndrome, a disorder from overworking the hands performing the repetitive task of strumming the guitar all day.
- A number of college graduates who have given up the effort to find work while living with and off wives or girlfriends.
- Women who work at the expense of time with their children when husbands make a good living but feel the wife should be working bringing in money, too, forgetting that being a homemaker is a full-time, non-paying job as wife, mother, baby watcher and primary nurturer of the children.

- Of a couple that has four preteen children in which the husband is a high school graduate and the wife a college graduate. She is a dedicated mother feeling she cannot afford to take on a full-time teaching position, but substitutes and cleans houses to make ends meet, while her husband refuses to leave a job that, at best, is only part-time employment and brings in little income.

Women described here are treated in the manner of this 1955 *Good Housekeeping* guide although none of them were yet born. They subscribe to the 1955 dictum, "a good wife knows her place."

THE WALTER MITTY SYNDROME

Humorous James Thurber wrote a short story in 1939, *"The Secret Life of Walter Mitty,"* which touched the collective American psyche denoting the ineffectual male who spends his time in heroic daydreams paying little attention to the real world.

Many of the men described above fit into the *Walter Mitty Syndrome* as they live in the "what if" world:

- Had I gotten the breaks I would have made something of myself.
- Had I been born into a better situated family I would be better off now.
- Had I gotten the breaks writing a song I might have had a career.
- Had I married the right woman I would not have been dragged down to this.
- Had I not had children I would not have had to struggle.
- Had I gone into the military or the government I'd be retired by now with a good pension.

Men who don't work are great daydreamers, which is consistent with Thurber's short story. Walter Mitty would spend his day in a deep state of daydreaming imagining himself a fighter pilot during WWII, a world-class doctor, always someone far removed from what he was doing.

It was why in that eye clinic waiting for my daughter that I wrote this missive, which follows.

WHEN MEN WON'T WORK & THE WOMEN WHO SUPPORT THEM

People in the 1970's watched their families disintegrate as women increasingly carried the economic and emotional load.

Since then, women not only do most of the work, but they are a taxi service for the demands of their mate. They carry their children to and fro, go to the grocery store, and dry cleaners for their husbands, and suffer the aggravations as well as the joys of their children.

They are the silent partners in the marital relationship, and never in the know, until their husbands need a signature on a second or third mortgage. Husbands make deals and then tell their wives after the fact. It would never occur to them to ask for counsel and input from their wives. They are always in the know, and often to the family's ruin.

Husbands' scheme, daydream, and find no need to consult their wives for ideas on the matter, thinking they have the superior minds and information.

The nostalgia for the way it was hangs on. Men are involved. Their women are treated as maids, housekeepers, nannies, chefs, dishwashers, launderers and supervisors of their children, keeping order and avoiding chaos with little allocated down time.

This situation is independent of socio-economic status, education, or social standing. Families with the advantage of affluence, education, cultural enhancement, travel and social engagement are just as likely to have this male attribution.

The only time attention is brought to this matter is when women are coming apart, in failing health, and are forced to slow down or stop this demanding schedule. Women persevere, for the most part, in the most trying circumstances.

PRIDE ON THE LINE

Cultural bias would imply that I am addressing the dregs of society. Not true. Men who won't work can be physicians in their forties who won't practice medicine; attorneys who won't practice law; and carpenters who won't apply their craft; and yes, poorly educated men who have lost their safe jobs in automobile factories, chemical processing plants, oil refineries, or other previously safe jobs for the unskilled and undereducated. These workers refuse to suffer the embarrassment of going back to night school or junior college to learn twenty-first century skills.

These men could be teachers who are no longer up to engaging students who challenge their methods and authority; engineers unwilling to adjust to the digital demands of new engineering; managers who refuse to adapt to the shift in power from authority to knowledge now possessed by the professional workforce.

These men are caught in a time warp in which their authority once was infallible, whether they were doctors, teachers, engineers, or managers. They relied on no one having the gumption to challenge their views. That has all changed now. Yet, they continue to bask in nostalgic pride finding excuses for why they have had no other choice than to give up and give out.

Men across society at every socio-economic level have been dropping off and dropping out of the workforce because it has changed, and they cannot or will not change.

They read self-help books, attend self-help workshops or seminars, daydream, write music, strum guitars, or do anything to avoid looking for work. They are Walter Mittys looking for the quick score, the perfect franchise, standing on acres of diamonds looking for answers in all the wrong places.

Others eat and drink themselves to a state of permanent inertia depleting their energy to the point that they couldn't look for work if their lives depended on it, retreating into some kind of real or psychosomatic illness.

Still others spend the little money they have gambling, following their favorite professional sport teams, or supporting a girlfriend.

Men born after the Good Housekeeping 1955 guide for the "good wife" are the spoiled brats of our culture and made so by mothers and fathers, siblings, girlfriends and boyfriends who make excuses for their profligate behavior. In a paradoxical way, mothers continue to enslave their daughters and liberate their sons from responsibility.

Yet, these same women that are nursemaids to their husbands and children, taxi service and maid service to the family, housekeeper and sergeant at arms in maintaining order, are often ridiculed rather than appreciated. Men often resent when these women use their limited free time to go back to school to better themselves when they are not so inclined.

THE DOUBLE-EDGED SWORD, OR WHAT HAS BEEN LOST

The generation of the Great Depression entered maturity in the 1950s and survived because they were small in number with unlimited opportunity in a post-World War II climate. They had been schooled in scarcity and learned to live with little. When they came to maturity, they failed to teach these same lessons to their children. Not only were parents guilty of this, but also teachers, the religious, managers, and leaders. An insouciant society developed without guidance or direction, and therefore without wisdom.

The irony is that children of the Great Depression had more freedom, more creative license as it was a climate of the survival of the fittest, an ambience conducive to developing leadership, personal identity and integrity as nothing was written in concrete but energized by self-regard in the natural flow of things.

The generation of the 1950's, essentially pre-television era, lived within their means, didn't buy expensive houses, or drive fancy cars; nor did they dress or attempt to mimic the rich and famous, but lived within themselves, and they prospered.

The societal train went off the track in the 1960's as parents denied children the pain of struggle that had made them, and instead pampered their young to the extent that they made school a war zone.

Sons of WWII veterans burned their draft cards; refused to serve their country; created chaos on college campuses; or retreated to Haight Asbury Park in San Francisco California to maintain a psychedelic high in a hedonistic lifestyle in defiance of the culture that spawned them. The generation that felt sexually repressed looked for liberation in free love, but instead gave birth to the "United States of Anxiety," and the burgeoning psychotherapy industry that is still with us.

THE POWER OF DENIAL

People who came to maturity in the 1950's, now parents, were not prepared for a world that had caught up with the United States economically and technologically.

1950 style parents were drunk with success and had little time for child rearing. Their offspring were allowed to be their own parents as birth parents were seldom home. Children invented their own play, but the world of 1960 was a very different world than the 1930's, something parents refused to acknowledge. It was a much more dangerous place.

At the same time, the inchoate power shift to women was underway. Men were being pushed aside in leadership, scholarship and professional acumen, as women climbed to eventually become the majority in college, whatever the ethnicity or profession. Women have not allowed the fact that they make only 75 percent as much as men for the same work to slow them down.

Women, once biased for being baby factories, are working their way up the corporate pyramid to the boardrooms and into the highest offices of government.

RIGHT BRAIN, LEFT BRAIN

In this digital age, we are finding the right brain, the so-called "feminine brain" is a powerful and necessary complement to the left-brain, the so-called "masculine brain."

The key to the problem solving is not only aggressive action, but also an appropriate response to chronic problems. Likewise, the key to economic health is not only the competitive verve, but also the spirit of cooperation.

Although rational cognitive thinking is still important, intuition and the use of the affect have come into new prominence (see David Brook's "The Social Animal," 2011), as the personal is an important counterpart to the cerebral in the successful discharge of business. In that same vein, analysis need not lead to paralysis if suitable attention is given to synthesis.

No one has been more energetic in exposing the limits to pure Socratic thinking, or linear logic than Edward de Bono in such books as "Lateral Thinking" (1977) and "Parallel Thinking" (1994).

LEFT BRAIN	RIGHT BRAIN
Masculine	Feminine
Demanding	Contracting
Aggressive	Responsive
Competitive	Cooperative
Rational and Cognitive	Intuitive and Affective
Analytical	Synthesizing
Concrete Orientation	Conceptual Orientation

Women are inclined to problem solve conditionally when dealing with contradictory situations, which are common to experience today.

Aware of their biological clock, delayed gratification is programmed into their psyches as well as genes. The necessary investment of time, patience and care are familiar territory. Stated another way, women preserve the race by pruning the good earth. They have their feet solidly on the ground while men prefer to soar to avoid the detritus and normal obstacles of everyday life.

The decline and fall of men have been accelerated by women as mothers, sisters, girlfriends, wives and teachers, who make excuses in perpetuity for men when they won't work, won't study, won't get off their behinds and do something useful. Women instead attempt to support and carry their men as if they were still dependent children suspended in terminal adolescence at the age of twenty, thirty, forty, fifty, or older.

Women have complicated the picture of carrying men who refuse to work by taking physical, mental, and emotional abuse from these same men as if they deserved it. If the situation were reversed, chances are the men would walk out on their women, something that seldom happens with instinctual women.

WHAT CAN BE DONE WITH MEN WHO WON'T WORK?

The short answer is for women to tell their men to get off their behinds and look for work or get out.

Better to understand the spinelessness of such men, and from this understanding find a way to tap their diminished capacity by directing their interest to some kind of employment.

Everyone has interests. Few men follow their bliss but instead chase the buck doing what pays the most or something that has very little risk. Women have been locked into this prison for centuries and continue to thrive despite repressed bitterness.

Men are not made of such firm stuff. Interest may be kindled by having men volunteer at school, church or in a community project, or some favored activity such as music, sports, or some other venue. In this age, men could find a way of making a living at home surfing the Internet.

Another possibility would be to cut off giving them money for beer and cigarettes, tickets to sporting events or other incidentals without them doing something specifically for the money. They could be cleaning the house, painting, doing the grocery shopping, going to the cleaners, doing the laundry, taking the kids to and from school, and to youth events.

The shoe is on the other foot with men who won't work and the women who support them, as the person who has the coin, has the power.

These men often keep their women out of the loop as to how they spend their money. Now, they can experience a little of their own medicine.

Here is the rub. I've talked to countless women who don't have a clue as to how their husbands spent the family income; never understand why they have had to sign papers without prior conversations on their husband's investments; never know why they have to co-sign for a second or third mortgage on their home; are never asked beforehand if they would like to go to this or that event, assumed they have no voice in the matter and therefore are obliged to go to satisfy their husband without question or protest.

Now, these men who won't work and are not bringing in the bacon have wives who incredibly still feel obliged to get permission from these men to do this or that with their hard earned money, something they never experienced when their men were making the majority of the coin.

Moreover, women are reluctant to take legal action against deadbeat husbands and fathers, blaming themselves for the anxiety in the family. Deadbeat dads are good at assuming the offense against their wives and mothers of their children who obligingly assume the defense.

Eventually, given the stress and strain of carrying these men, given it is unlikely the situation will change, these women have to decide if it would be better for the family without these men, or would it be worse?

I have known families who have gone through more than one generation of deadbeat men, men who would work only for premium wages or not at all; men who were alcoholics and abused their wives and children physically and psychologically; and women who were willing to accept such treatment because they knew no other.

In the last quarter century, the plush jobs in the automotive and steel industry have evaporated. Generation after generation of workers with high school diplomas or less were conditioned to make $50,000 to $75,000 a year in unskilled jobs, and to retire with pensions of $40,000 with full medical benefits. The boilerplate for this workforce still exists but the jobs are essentially gone.

Then there are men who soared during the booming 1990s, and have suffered major setbacks, finding themselves in deep financial trouble, unable to cope much less work. They need help but they are unwilling to seek it. Many are well educated in law, medicine, engineering and education. They are the walking wounded that are part of this problem and need help not criticism.

The world of the Big Easy, be it Detroit or Gary or Seattle, or Chicago, or New Orleans is gone. We are a declining nation in a world that has not only caught up with us but is passing us.

We cannot complain our way back to prominence or deny the reality. I've known engineers making near six-figure incomes who were made redundant when high tech companies downsized dramatically. Some started new businesses using their skills, many waited for the downturn to end, and of course they are still waiting. I know of one engineer who was given a quarter million-dollar separation package from IBM, and went through it in two years, and has never had a stable income since. I would like to think this an isolated case, but I don't think so.

Men who won't work are not a mirage. I am confident everyone reading this has someone in their family who fits this profile. We are aghast that unemployment hovers around 9 percent, when I think it is closer to 18 percent, when you take in part-time workers, and workers working far below their skill levels, if working at all.

One day soon there will be an eruption of attention to this issue, and the focus will be on economic dimensions of the problem, when the problem, then as now, is basically a behavioral and psychological one.

These are not bad men who won't work. These are men who need help. I'm not sure we have the societal tools to do the job. The psychological and psychiatric professions create mainly explanatory models that develop interesting vocabularies to explain personal and social problems but have little impact on changing behavior or ameliorating our economic and social maladies.

For wont of being misunderstood, I would suggest it is mainly a spiritual issue retreating into biological and mathematical paradigms to explain our lethargy when it is our sick soul that is the culprit. We have lost our will to prevail.

Alas, we are not happy campers. We have lost our moral compass, and the ideals of our forefathers, and thus our way. We need help to crawl out of this deep ditch of despair, knowing that the answers to this dilemma are not "out there" but inside us waiting to be explored.

A COMMON CRY

A woman writes: I divorced my first husband after a year of marriage, and realized he was not working more than he was while I was working steadily. My next husband and soul mate worked until an accident affected his health, but he still contributed by doing the shopping, housework, cooking, lawn work, and car maintenance. Now, my daughter is married to one of these guys who will not work outside or inside the home and what he calls babysitting is minimal care. How can these men look in the mirror and not be overcome with guilt?

Unfortunately, it is quite apparent that they can and do without qualms.

Another perceptive reader writes:

Many people think the simple solution is to throw the deadbeat out, but they fail to realize that the courts now protect the deadbeat husbands. Lazy unemployed husbands are rewarded with alimony, half of the hardworking wife's IRA or 401(k), as well as any investments, home equity or savings. So much for the women's lib movement of the 1960s. As with everything, there are always unintended consequences.

Not being an attorney, I would advise the long-suffering woman who has such a deadbeat husband to not show her hand, or make any threats, but to quickly get in touch with a reliable lawyer to protect her interests as best she can.

As suggested in an earlier missive, I would suggest you become your own therapist by seeking out your best friend, someone you trust and with whom you can have a candid exchange of confidences to work out a winning strategy for yourself.

A FINAL WORD

Over the years, I've been asked to publish a little book with what readers consider some of my more thought-provoking missives along with meaningful excerpts from my books, claiming they simply don't have the time to read many books. "Give us a sense of what you're trying to say." Well, this is an attempt to fulfill that request. Let me know what you think by e-mail: thedeltagrpfl@cs.com

LIST OF PUBLISHED WORKS

Confident Selling

Work Without Managers: A View from the Trenches

Confident Selling for the 90s

The Worker, Alone! Going Against the Grain

The Taboo Against Being Your Own Best Friend

Six Silent Killers: Management's Greatest Challenge

Corporate Sin: Leaderless Leaders & Dissonant Workers

In the Shadow of the Courthouse: A Memoir of the 1940s Written as a Novel

A Look Back to See Ahead: Our Chronic Culture Viewed from the 1970s

Purposeful Selling for the 21st Century: It Starts with Creative Confidence

The Ascent of the Working Woman

Meet Your New Best Friend

Time Out for Sanity: Blueprint for Dealing with an Anxious Age

Confidence in Subtext: Keys to Life

Who Put You in the Cage?

A Way of Thinking about Things: Essays of Dr. Fisher on Social Psychology

The Velvet Glove & Iron Fist

Confident Thinking: A Silver Bullet for an Unconscious Age

Ten Creative Stages to Confident Thinking

The Short Inscrutable Life & Terrible Fate of the Domesticated Lion, Zimba!

Self-Confidence: You deserve to be Self-Confident!

Devlin: A Psychological Novel

Near Journey's End: Can Planet Earth Survive Self-Indulgent America?

The Postmodern Worker Exposed – Unmasking an Under-Achieving Workforce

ABOUT THE AUTHOR

Social psychologist James R. Fisher, Jr., Ph.D., sees himself as a peripatetic philosopher intrigued with the eclectic imagery of his time, which he reports on dutifully in terms of his own empirical experience in this genre through a score of books.